WITHDRAWN
HARVARD LIBRARY
WITHDRAWN

Philosophers in Depth

Series Editors: **Stephen Boulter** and **Constantine Sandis**

Philosophers in Depth is a series of themed edited collections focusing on particular aspects of the thought of major figures from the history of philosophy. The volumes showcase a combination of newly commissioned and previously published work with the aim of deepening our understanding of the topics covered. Each book stands alone, but taken together the series will amount to a vast collection of critical essays covering the history of philosophy, exploring issues that are central to the ideas of individual philosophers. This project was launched with the financial support of the Institute for Historical and Cultural Research at Oxford Brookes University, for which we are very grateful.

Constantine Sandis and Stephen Boulter
Oxford

Titles include:

Alison Denham (*editor*)
PLATO ON ART AND BEAUTY

Philip Goff (*editor*)
SPINOZA ON MONISM

Leonard Kahn (*editor*)
MILL ON JUSTICE

Arto Laitinen and Constantine Sandis (*editors*)
HEGEL ON ACTION

Katherine Morris (*editor*)
SARTRE ON THE BODY

Charles R. Pigden (*editor*)
HUME ON MOTIVATION AND VIRTUE

Sabine Roeser
REID ON ETHICS

Henrik Rydenfelt and Sami Pihlström (*editors*)
WILLIAM JAMES ON RELIGION

Daniel Whiting (*editor*)
THE LATER WITTGENSTEIN ON LANGUAGE

Forthcoming titles:

Pierre Destree (*editor*)
ARISTOTLE ON AESTHETICS

David Dolby (*editor*)
RYLE ON MIND AND LANGUAGE

Edward Feser (*editor*)
ARISTOTLE ON METHOD AND METAPHYSICS

Philosophers in Depth
Series Standing Order ISBN 978–0–230–55411–5 Hardback
978–0–230–55412–2 Paperback
(*outside North America only*)

You can receive future titles in this series as they are published by placing a standing order. Please contact your bookseller or, in case of difficulty, write to us at the address below with your name and address, the title of the series and the ISBN quoted above.

Customer Services Department, Macmillan Distribution Ltd, Houndmills, Basingstoke, Hampshire RG21 6XS, England

Also by Henrik Rydenfelt

PRAGMATISM, SCIENCE AND NATURALISM (*co-editor*)

IDEAS IN ACTION (*co-editor*)

PRAGMATIST PERSPECTIVES (*co-editor with Sami Pihlström*)

Also by Sami Pihlström

NATURALIZING THE TRANSCENDENTAL

PRAGMATIC MORAL REALISM

"THE TRAIL OF THE HUMAN SERPENT IS OVER EVERYTHING": Jamesian Perspectives on Mind, World, and Religion

PRAGMATIST METAPHYSICS

TRANSCENDENTAL GUILT

PRAGMATIC PLURALISM AND THE PROBLEM OF GOD

CONTINUUM COMPANION TO PRAGMATISM (*editor*)

William James on Religion

Edited by

Henrik Rydenfelt and Sami Pihlström
University of Helsinki, Finland

Selection, introduction and editorial matter © Henrik Rydenfelt and
Sami Pihlström 2013
Chapters © Individual authors 2013

All rights reserved. No reproduction, copy or transmission of this
publication may be made without written permission.

No portion of this publication may be reproduced, copied or transmitted
save with written permission or in accordance with the provisions of the
Copyright, Designs and Patents Act 1988, or under the terms of any licence
permitting limited copying issued by the Copyright Licensing Agency,
Saffron House, 6–10 Kirby Street, London EC1N 8TS.

Any person who does any unauthorized act in relation to this publication
may be liable to criminal prosecution and civil claims for damages.

The authors have asserted their rights to be identified as the authors of this work
in accordance with the Copyright, Designs and Patents Act 1988.

First published 2013 by
PALGRAVE MACMILLAN

Palgrave Macmillan in the UK is an imprint of Macmillan Publishers Limited,
registered in England, company number 785998, of Houndmills, Basingstoke,
Hampshire RG21 6XS.

Palgrave Macmillan in the US is a division of St Martin's Press LLC,
175 Fifth Avenue, New York, NY 10010.

Palgrave Macmillan is the global academic imprint of the above companies
and has companies and representatives throughout the world.

Palgrave® and Macmillan® are registered trademarks in the United States,
the United Kingdom, Europe and other countries.

ISBN 978–0–230–34976–6

This book is printed on paper suitable for recycling and made from fully
managed and sustained forest sources. Logging, pulping and manufacturing
processes are expected to conform to the environmental regulations of the
country of origin.

A catalogue record for this book is available from the British Library.

A catalog record for this book is available from the Library of Congress.

Typeset by MPS Limited, Chennai, India.

Contents

Acknowledgements   vi

Notes on Contributors   vii

Introduction   1
Sami Pihlström and Henrik Rydenfelt

Part I

1   Religion and Pragmatism from
'The Will to Believe' to *Pragmatism*   15
Wayne Proudfoot

2   Anti-Dogmatism as a Defense of Religious Belief   30
Charlene Haddock Seigfried

3   The Varieties and the Cognitive Value
of Religious Experiences   56
Niek Brunsveld

4   Pragmatic Realism and Pluralism in Philosophy
of Religion   78
Sami Pihlström

Part II

5   'The Ethics of Belief' Reconsidered   111
Susan Haack

6   Sensitive Truths and Sceptical Doubt   128
Henrik Rydenfelt

7   Reconceptualizing Evidentialism and the Evidentialist
Critique of Religion   145
Dirk-Martin Grube

8   Possibility and Permission? Intellectual Character,
Inquiry, and the Ethics of Belief   165
Guy Axtell

Index   199

Acknowledgements

This book project was originally launched as a result of one of the many workshops and/or conferences that the editors have co-organized both together and with several collaborators over the past five years in all the five Nordic countries with the Nordic Pragmatism Network (http://www.nordprag.org). The workshop on pragmatism and the ethics of belief took place at the University of Jyväskylä, Finland, in December 2008. Several of the papers included in the volume were presented in their original versions at that meeting. However, some new ones were invited as well. Two essays, those by Susan Haack and Wayne Proudfoot, have also been published previously: Haack's '"The Ethics of Belief" Reconsidered' first appeared in *The Philosophy of R. M. Chisholm*, eds. P. A. Schilpp and L. E. Hahn (La Salle, IL: Open Court, 1997), copyright by Open Court, while Proudfoot's 'William James on Religion and Pragmatism' appeared in *Sats: North European Journal of Philosophy*, vol. 10, no. 2 (2010), copyright by Walter de Gruyter, Berlin (although his contribution is based on his talk in Jyväskylä in 2008.) We would like to express our sincere gratitude to the copyright holders for the kind permissions to reprint, with minor editorial changes, these two essays here. We are grateful to Dr. Constantine Sandis, the series editor of *Philosophers in Depth*, as well as the editors at Palgrave Macmillan, especially Melanie Blair, for their help and patience. We should like to thank Mr. Taavi Sundell, one of the Research Assistants of the Helsinki Collegium for Advanced Studies, for his valuable assistance in the completion of the manuscript. We also duly acknowledge the financial support from NOS-HS and NordForsk that the Nordic Pragmatism Network has enjoyed in 2008–2012; this Nordic funding has made this book as well as many other recent pragmatism-related projects possible.

Notes on Contributors

Guy Axtell is Assistant Professor in Philosophy and Religious Studies at Radford University, Virginia, USA, where he also serves as Critical Thinking Coordinator for Radford University's general education sequence. He is author of 'Teaching James' "The Will to Believe"' (2001, Teaching Philosophy) and numerous other recent articles in epistemology, metaphysics, and philosophy of religion; he is often found blogging at JanusBlog, the site he founded for news and discussion about all aspects of contemporary virtue theory (www.janusblog.squarespace.com).

Niek Brunsveld received his PhD in Philosophy of Religion and Ethics from Utrecht University's Faculty of Humanities in December 2012, where he was Junior Faculty in 2008–2012. He was Fulbright Visiting Researcher at Harvard University's Faculty of Divinity in 2010/2011. His paper on 'Putnam on truth (again). Conceptual truth in religion and morality, and the risk of relativism' received the Hilary Putnam International Young Scholars Essay Prize in 2011.

Dirk-Martin Grube is Professor of Philosophy of Religion at the University of Utrecht, the Netherlands. His main publications include the monograph *Ostern als Paradigmenwechsel* (2012) and the co-edited volume *Religions Challenged by Contingency* (2008).

Susan Haack is Distinguished Professor in the Humanities, Cooper Senior Scholar in Arts and Sciences, Professor of Philosophy and Professor of Law, University of Miami. Her work includes *Philosophy of Logics, Deviant Logic, Fuzzy Logic, Evidence and Inquiry, Manifesto of a Passionate Moderate, Defending Science—Within Reason, Pragmatism, Old and New, Putting Philosophy to Work*, and around 200 articles. Her work has been translated into 13 languages, and she has lectured around the world. Haack is one of the tiny handful of living philosophers included in Peter J. King, *100 Philosophers: The Life and Work of the World's Greatest Thinkers*.

Sami Pihlström has since 2006 been Professor of Practical Philosophy at the University of Jyväskylä, Finland, and since 2009 the Director of the Helsinki Collegium for Advanced Studies. He has published widely on pragmatism, the problem of realism, philosophy of religion, and transcendental philosophy. His books include *Pragmatist Metaphysics* (2009) and *Pragmatic Pluralism and the Problem of God* (2013).

Wayne Proudfoot is Professor of Religion in the Department of Religion at Columbia University. He is the author of *Religious Experience* (1985), of articles on Peirce and James, and is working on religion and naturalism in American pragmatism.

Henrik Rydenfelt is Researcher in Theoretical Philosophy at the University of Helsinki. His recent publications are concentrated on a pragmatist approach to normativity, addressing key questions in epistemology, meta-ethics, ethical theory and social philosophy. Rydenfelt is the coordinator of the Nordic Pragmatism Network, assistant review editor of the *Transactions of the Charles S. Peirce Society*, associate editor of *Pragmatism Today*, editor of *Nordic Studies in Pragmatism*, and a member of the editorial board of the *European Journal of Pragmatism and American Philosophy*.

Charlene Haddock Seigfried is Purdue University Professor Emeritus of Philosophy. Key publications include *William James's Radical Reconstruction of Philosophy* (1990) and *Pragmatism and Feminism* (1996). She edited *Feminist Interpretations of John Dewey* (2002) and wrote introductions to *Addams, Democracy and Social Ethics* and *The Long Road of Woman's Memory*. Her awards include the Joseph L. Blau prize for her paper on Jane Addams's pragmatist influence on John Dewey and the Herbert W. Schneider Award for distinguished contributions to American Philosophy.

Introduction

Sami Pihlström and Henrik Rydenfelt (Editors)

The essays collected in this volume seek to provide an up-to-date and comprehensive account of William James' philosophy of religion. The volume is divided into two parts. The first part discusses James' pragmatism and his philosophy of religion at a relatively general level, while the second one focuses on his best-known idea in this field, the 'will to believe' argument. Some of the essays are primarily historical, aiming at a careful scholarly interpretation of certain aspects of James' philosophy of religion (in relation to his ideas in related fields, such as general metaphysics and epistemology, as well as ethics); others focus on a more systematic application of James' views to key topics in this area of philosophy, including the issue of realism and the ethics of belief.

This introduction will first offer a brief picture of James' philosophical life and works (section 1) and then consider his importance for the philosophy of religion, both historically and regarding the contemporary state of the art in this field (section 2). James' famous, or notorious, will to believe argument will be considered in section 3, while section 4 will very briefly summarize the main ideas of the articles included in this volume.

Our present volume will, we hope, provide a balanced overview of James' philosophy of religion by contextualizing it both in his general pragmatist thought and the current situation in the philosophy of religion. The book is intended both for James scholars and for non-specialists, including students, who are seriously interested in the philosophy of religion and want to get an overview of what this classical figure thought about religious faith and experience. However, the contributions are not introductory but are also intended as crucial reference material for specialists on the philosophy of religion today. Accordingly, while several books on James have been published over the past few decades (see the brief 'Further Reading' section below), there is, as far as we know, no single book that would serve the same purpose as this volume. *William James on Religion* can, we may hope, be used as a text-book and/or further reading material in courses on modern philosophy of religion, pragmatism, and related topics.

1 James' Life and Works: A Brief Sketch

William James (1842–1910), one of the most original and influential American philosophers and psychologists, was among the founders of the philosophical tradition of *pragmatism*, emphasizing the intimate connection between philosophical (and generally intellectual) theory and reflection, on the one side, and human action and practices of life, on the other. Trained as a medical scientist but also deeply interested in art, James turned first to psychology and then increasingly to philosophy, as well as to what would today be called religious studies, making lasting contributions to all these academic fields—without ever really keeping them apart. As a distinguished Harvard professor, James was one of the leading intellectuals of his time, well known both in the United States and in Europe, although his philosophical status is somewhat debated, especially in comparison to the other co-founder of pragmatism, Charles S. Peirce, whose lectures and writings in the 1870s, in particular, crucially influenced James' emerging conception of the 'pragmatic principle'.

James' psychological work (culminating in his magnum opus, *The Principles of Psychology*, 1890) played a decisive role in the development of scientific psychology in the late nineteenth century. His explorations of the psychological and philosophical dimensions of religious experience (as presented in *The Varieties of Religious Experience*, 1902) have gained recognition across disciplinary boundaries. James was an original thinker with an unusually broad scope, ranging from psychology and philosophy to religious studies and even psychical research. In his core pragmatist writings, such as the lectures published as the volume *Pragmatism: A New Name for Some Old Ways of Thinking* (1907) and the articles collected in *The Meaning of Truth* (1909), including responses to critics of *Pragmatism*, James defended the key ideas of pragmatism: the pragmatic method, the ensuing pragmatist conception of truth, his religiously motivated notions of pluralism and meliorism, and the view that the world—whatever there is—ultimately depends on, or is in some sense structured by, our practical interests and purposive (habits of) action. His late philosophical writings from those same years, appearing in his last published book, *A Pluralistic Universe* (1909), the unfinished introduction to philosophy, *Some Problems of Philosophy* (1911), and the posthumously published collection of articles, *Essays in Radical Empiricism* (1912), defend a rather non-systematic set of views supplementing the core idea of pragmatism, namely, the 'radically empiricist' doctrine of 'pure experience' and a pluralistic conception of reality (or even, as he called it, 'piecemeal panpsychism') designed to overcome the monistic idealists' as well as the causal determinists' 'block universe'.

It is extremely important to note that James' reasons for defending freedom, novelty, and chance were not only metaphysical and epistemological but also profoundly ethical. Although James wrote little directly on ethics, scholars have also increasingly recognized that a (if not the) central current of his work is ethical. The 1891 essay, 'The Moral Philosopher and the Moral Life' (included in James' 1897 volume, *The Will to Believe and Other Essays in Popular Philosophy*), is his only article explicitly concentrated on ethics; yet, ethical considerations are built into his pragmatism, especially its leading idea that our concepts, theories, and world-view should be examined in terms of their potential practical relevance. If one argues that ethics is the core of James' thought, one must recognize that it is available in no single place in his corpus, in no book specifically on ethics; it is, rather, to be found everywhere in what he wrote, at least implicitly. For James, ethical questions, in turn, were always connected with religious ones, and his ethical discussions cannot be separated from his defenses of a religious pluralism as pragmatically the most viable world-view.

James' key philosophical principle, the *pragmatic method*, was for him not only a 'method of making our ideas clear', as it primarily was for his friend Peirce (who had formulated the principle already in the early 1870s, though James was the first to use the term 'pragmatism' in print in 1898), but also, arguably, of making our ideas *ethically* clear—of tracing out the conceivable ethical and more generally world-view-related (or *weltanschaulich*) implications of our philosophical (and other) concepts and conceptions, even the most abstractly theoretical ones. Ethics is, perhaps, in this sense the true center of James' pragmatism. The ultimate purpose of his pragmatic method is to 'distill' the ethical kernel of—apparently nonethical—metaphysical issues and ideas by means of pragmatic reflection that is itself deeply moral. This ethical element is inseparable from James' work on religion in his considerations of the metaphysical questions relating to the existence or reality of the divine, his investigations into the relevance of religious experiences, and his defense, in the 'ethics of belief', of a believing attitude towards the religious hypothesis.

2 James and the Philosophy of Religion

Why is James important for (contemporary) philosophy of religion? An answer to this question must be sought by briefly considering what is going on in this field today, and how this situation has historically developed. Clearly, James is not the only pragmatist whose views may be fruitful in the current situation in the philosophy of religion. Charles S. Peirce's and John Dewey's ideas—as well as those of numerous other early pragmatists—have turned out to be promising in this regard as well. Neopragmatists like Richard Rorty and Hilary Putnam are also increasingly discussed within this field. James' contribution, however, is especially relevant in that it cuts through and in many ways surpasses most of the central debates and divisions in the contemporary discussion.

It is relatively easy to observe that contemporary philosophy of religion is characterized by deep disagreements about the very nature and methods of the field. These debates do not just arise from the *theism vs. atheism* dispute about the existence of God or from the currently popular *science vs. religion* controversy. The positions known as *evidentialism* and *fideism* offer different meta-level views on the justifiability of religious faith and on its relation to science and reason: while evidentialism urges that religious beliefs, basically like scientific ones, require justification in terms of general, religiously neutral criteria of rationality, fideism draws a sharp distinction between faith and reason, advancing faith in the absence of evidence.

In addition to this primarily epistemological debate, a metaphysical and semantic dispute concerns the nature of religious reality and our ability to linguistically refer to it (*if* there is such a reality). *Realists*, affirming the existence of a mind-, concept-, language-, and discourse-independent world, maintain that human language can be used to refer to such a reality and that truth is a matter of correspondence between linguistic items and the (generally) non-linguistic elements of the world that 'make true' our truths. *Antirealists*, in contrast, understand the nature of religious language—and language in general—in terms of its use within practices or forms of life, rather than any referential or representational relations.

The major traditions in Western analytic philosophy of religion have been evidentialist and realist, and the standard arguments for and against theism and atheism are mostly discussed in a context presupposing both realism and evidentialism. In the twentieth century, however, philosophers inspired by Ludwig Wittgenstein were increasingly drawn toward fideist and antirealist views. Wittgensteinians as well as some 'postmodern' (or, as some authors prefer to put it, 'post-onto-theological') philosophers and theologians (e.g. Gianni Vattimo) have argued that realist approaches fundamentally mischaracterize the distinctive ways in which religious belief differs from, say, scientific theory-construction.

The field is, then, divided into deeply opposed camps that often speak beside each other rather than speaking to each other. While the debates just mentioned are concerned with the nature of religious beliefs and statements from the perspective of what is often called theoretical philosophy (metaphysics, epistemology, philosophy of language, etc.), there are no less serious disputes in so-called practical philosophy (ethics and political philosophy). The relation between religion and morality (and politics) is both increasingly important and highly unclear today. It remains particularly unclear what the place of religious values in the good life—individual or social—might be, and how this issue ought to be discussed in largely secularized yet multicultural societies promoting religious tolerance.

Richard Rorty's proposal to treat religion as a private affair disconnected from public use of reason, related to his suggestion that traditional philosophical issues should be redescribed as issues in cultural politics (i.e. issues about whether, and how, to use certain 'vocabularies'), is a recent attempt to approach these topics by moving beyond mainstream analytic philosophy of religion. However, long before Rorty's radical neopragmatism, classical pragmatists like James sought to mediate between rival extremes in various areas of philosophy—and the philosophy of religion is no exception.

A new look at James and religion will show that a truly pragmatist approach in the philosophy of religion need not, and arguably should not, be Rortyan—for it can be, and has been, plausibly demonstrated that Rorty's version of pragmatism gives up normative criteria for adequately evaluating religious, or any, discourse. But it should also evince that a healthy understanding of religious thought presupposes a pragmatist and practice-oriented standpoint, which, in James' case, is also inherently *pluralistic*. There is no single, absolute, overarching perspective from which religious issues ought to be viewed but a plurality of relevant philosophical standpoints, reflecting the plurality of our practices of life, such practices that may arise from the kind of individual religious experiences James examined in the *Varieties* but which do not exclude the social and communal role of religion.

The above-described problems of realism vs. antirealism and evidentialism vs. fideism, among others, receive new interpretations when seen from a pragmatically pluralist perspective, which views religion as a human practice (or, better, as a set of practices) with certain inherent aims and goals, responding to specific human needs and interests, and serving vital and ineliminable human values. This by no means precludes rational criticism of religious ways of thinking; on the contrary, such criticism itself is served by an enhanced understanding of the ways in which religion functions in our practices—or *is* a family of practices. Pragmatist philosophy of religion, including James', is obviously committed to the *normative* task of the philosophy of religion, seeking to critically evaluate, and not just to explain and understand, religious beliefs and practices. The dialogue between science and religion, in particular, vitally needs a comprehensive and tolerant account of both scientific and religious practices and their diverging conceptions of rationality and intellectual (as well as ethical) responsibility. Pragmatism—in our view, particularly Jamesian pragmatism—promises to advance such understanding, offering us pluralism and tolerance without succumbing to uncritical relativism, according to which 'anything goes' in philosophical, theological, and religious matters.

In particular, a new look at James and religion, such as the one offered by the present volume, should re-emphasize that a healthy understanding of religious thought presupposes a genuinely practice-oriented standpoint. For pragmatists, there is no single, absolute, overarching perspective from which religious issues ought to be viewed but a plurality of relevant philosophical approaches, reflecting the plurality of our practices of life—as well. In contrast to this pragmatist standpoint that remains irreducibly *pluralistic*, the mainstream positions in the philosophy of religion are *monistic*, privileging some particular essentialist conception of the true nature of religious language, belief, experience, etc. A possible exception is Wittgensteinian philosophy of religion, with its focus on the plurality of language-games; yet, this tradition has its own dogmatic features, too.

In many cases, the Jamesian pragmatist can, avoiding dogmatisms of all kinds, steer a critical middle course between various extremes opposed to each other. Therefore, the best and most plausible (as well as ethically most sustainable) ideas inherent in both realism and antirealism, as well as evidentialism and fideism, can be critically integrated in Jamesian pragmatist philosophy of religion. James may, then, offer us a richer and more nuanced picture of religion and of its relation to science and other intellectual endeavors than either leading analytic evidentialists like Richard Swinburne, reformed epistemologists like Alvin Plantinga, or fideists like D. Z. Phillips—not to mention anti-philosophical, scientistically oriented militant atheists like Richard Dawkins. These considerations are among the reasons why it is important, especially in the both philosophically and more generally culturally confusing situation we live in, to take another look at what kind of resources William James might offer for understanding religion.

3 The Will—or the Right—to Believe

Another reason for James' relevance in philosophy of religion is his position as a staple of reference in that field for over a century. Even though James published extensively on religion and dedicated one of his main works—*The Varieties*—to the topic, his lasting influence is to a greater extent due to the essay 'The Will to Believe'. In this piece, James famously argues that the decision between a doubting and a believing attitude towards some hypotheses or claims—including what James calls the *religious hypothesis*—may and must be made on 'passional' rather than 'intellectual' grounds, formulating his main conclusion as the claim that 'Our passional nature not only lawfully may, but must, decide an option between propositions, whenever it is a genuine option that cannot by its nature be decided on intellectual grounds [...]'. First presented as a public lecture in 1896 and published in *The Will to Believe and Other Essays in Popular Philosophy* in 1897 (as well as anthologized countless times), this essay has been argued to be not only the most influential individual article in the philosophy of religion ever published but also the most widely read essay ever written by an American philosopher.

James' essay has not always been equally widely respected, however. Beginning from its first publication, it has been met by highly contentious debate, including fierce criticism by contemporaries such as Bertrand Russell. Even today, there is no consensus about the exact nature and merits of the 'will to believe' argument, and the controversy surrounding its correct interpretation as well as its success continues to occupy pages in philosophical journals, textbooks, and popular magazines. One central debate concerns the exact nature of James' (intended) conclusion. Its crudest interpretations view James as abandoning, in some cases, the scientific quest for truth in favor of an anti-intellectualist resignation to wishful thinking, while others have pointed out that his conclusion pertains only to cases where 'intellectual' (viz., scientific or empirical) evidence is unavailable. Another issue in this debate concerns whether James suggested, contrary to our usual understanding of the nature of belief, that we can believe 'at will' or whether he more narrowly defended the already existing (religious) belief of those in his audience to whom such belief remains a 'live' option, in line with his later remark that he should have titled his piece 'The Right to Believe' instead. James' interpreters are also divided on whether James' conclusion allows for individualistic decisions on 'passional grounds', potentially leading to differing and indeed contradictory beliefs being entertained as products of the 'will to believe' strategy, or whether we should jointly make similar passional decisions.

More differences in opinion concern James' argument itself. Is James recommending religious belief, instead of doubt, as a useful belief in a manner resembling Pascal's famous wager—the argument that the possible, eternal benefits of belief in God outweigh the discomfort faced by the believer during the course of his life? Or is James' argument rather intended to rest on ethical or moral grounds, as its position as a central classic in the (even at this time rather underdeveloped) discussion on the ethics of belief suggests? Or, as a third option, is the argument epistemic or epistemological in nature, and aiming to show a set of duties and rights we have as (scientific) inquirers?

Yet other issues concern the premises and preliminaries of the 'will to believe' argument. Due to his suggestion that truths are somehow sensitive to our initial belief, James has been read as proposing that our beliefs can 'create' facts, or make themselves true in some manner—a suggestion which threatens to collapse James' view into subjectivist forms of idealism and relativism. This view has been contested by others who have argued that the discussion of 'The Will to Believe' concentrates on the attainability of evidence, which James, in this reading, argues will in certain cases require a passional, believing attitude towards a hypothesis. Further complications are presented by the dependence of James' argument on the core pragmatist idea that our beliefs are habits of action and that a higher clarity as to their meaning is to be discovered by a consideration of how they would lead us to act. By the pragmatist maxim, which James reflects on in a footnote to 'The Will to Believe', religious belief and its alternatives, including agnostic doubt and atheistic disbelief, must (at least in some circumstances) result in differing courses of conduct; otherwise the whole debate between these options is one of words merely. But it has turned out difficult to spell out the real practical differences between the actions of the believer and the doubter; and indeed, this issue of the true, pragmatic meaning of religious belief appears to be one which James attempts to come to terms with throughout his later writings. The complexity of James' 'will to believe' argument as well as its complicated reception motivates the decision to dedicate half of the pieces in this volume to this topic. Aside its continuing relevance in contemporary debates in the philosophy of religion, such as those concerning the connection between religious belief and (scientific) evidence, any serious study of the topic of the ethics of belief must take James' proposal into account. Moreover, despite its possible faults, James' argument continues to be an inspiration to novel applications and redevelopments of the 'will to believe' strategy and its analogies in different fields of philosophical inquiry.

4 The Contents and Structure of this Volume

The essays included in the present volume approach the above-discussed themes of James' philosophy of religion—and thereby, inevitably, James' philosophy more generally—from a number of different perspectives.

Part I of the book is opened by Wayne Proudfoot's relatively general discussion of James' pragmatism in the philosophy of religion, tracing the development of James' understanding of what he took to be the central religious question and his reinterpretation of Peirce's pragmatic criterion of meaning (Chapter 1). In Chapter 2, Charlene Haddock Seigfried emphasizes the profoundly anti-dogmatic character of James' pragmatic experimentalism. Chapter 3, by Niek Brunsveld, focuses on James' *Varieties* and the key issue concerning the (possible) veridicality of religious experience—a theme that is shown to be relevant to contemporary pragmatism-inspired philosophy of religion (e.g., Putnam's) as well. The first part is concluded by Sami Pihlström's examination of realism and pluralism in James' pragmatist philosophy, proposing a broadly Kantian account of James' conception of the 'construction' of reality within human practices and perspectives and connecting the issue of pluralism with James' notion of the 'sick soul' (Chapter 4).

The essays in Part II more specifically deal with James' ethics of belief and the controversial 'will to believe' argument. In Chapter 5, Susan Haack returns to the dispute between James and W. K. Clifford and reconsiders the relation between epistemic and moral appraisal of our beliefs, formulating an alternative to what she finds Clifford's 'morally over-demanding' and James' 'intellectually over-permissive' positions. Chapter 6, by Henrik Rydenfelt, offers a systematic reading and criticism of the 'will to believe' argument and then reconnects James' argument with the presuppositions of the pragmatist (especially Peircean) account of inquiry. In Chapter 7, Dirk-Martin Grube reconstructs the will to believe argument as a contribution to decision theory rather than to the inquiry into 'the realm of truth', and explores the consequences of doing so. Finally, Guy Axtell provides, in Chapter 8, a thoroughgoing reinterpretation and reconstruction of the 'will to believe' in relation to the concept of 'intellectual character'.

5 Further Reading

No volume on a classical figure of philosophy, let alone a multidisciplinary figure such as James, can claim to be exhaustive. We duly recognize the unavoidable lacunae in the picture of James' philosophy of religion this book offers. Thus, we feel that it is our duty to refer the reader to a number of other publications on James, listed and briefly described below.

Yet, while there are several volumes available on James' thought, including his philosophy of religion, none of the books known to us approaches James' philosophy of religion in the way this one does. Other collections of articles on James are either broader, covering his philosophy generally (e.g., *The Cambridge Companion to William James*, edited by Ruth Anna Putnam, Cambridge University Press, 1997), or more selectively specialize in some special aspects of his philosophy of religion (e.g., *William James and the Science of Religions*, edited by Wayne Proudfoot, Columbia University Press, 2004). In addition, several monographs on James' philosophy of religion have been published (e.g., Eugene Fontinell, *God, Self, and Immortality in William James's Philosophy*, Fordham University Press, 1981; David Lamberth, *William James and the Metaphysics of Experience*, Cambridge University Press, 1999; and more recently Michael Slater, *William James on Ethics and Faith*, Cambridge University Press, 2009); some commentators have also focused on the 'will to believe' argument in book-length studies (e.g., Robert J. O'Connell, *William James on the Courage to Believe*, Fordham University Press, 1984). Sami Pihlström's *'The Trail of the Human Serpent Is over Everything': Jamesian Perspectives on Mind, World, and Religion* (University Press of America, 2008) is a previous work by one of the co-editors of this volume; it is, however, primarily an attempt to apply some Jamesian insights into the philosophy of religion (as well as ethics and metaphysics) today instead of a historical scholarly treatise of James' thought as such; the same can be said about Pihlström's new volume, *Pragmatic Pluralism and the Problem of God* (Fordham University Press, 2013), in which James also plays a major role.

These and many other relevant books offer a number of further discussions of James' philosophy in general and his views on religion in particular. In any event, the present volume obviously differs from the monographs available on this topic by presenting a plurality of independent perspectives on James' views on religion. It is our sincere hope that this book will be read as a definite set of up-to-date interpretations of James on a topic of vital human significance and that it will also attract the interest of scholars for whom James is a new acquaintance.

Part I

1
Religion and Pragmatism from 'The Will to Believe' to *Pragmatism*

Wayne Proudfoot

1 The Will to Believe

William James' essay, 'The Will to Believe', has been read in many different ways. James describes the article as a 'defense of our right to adopt a believing attitude in religious matters, in spite of the fact that our merely logical intellect may not have been coerced'.[1] His criticism seems to be directed chiefly at William Clifford's claim that 'It is wrong, always, everywhere, and for anyone, to believe anything upon insufficient evidence.'[2] But this is not so clear. We might expect that in cases in which the evidence is insufficient, or in James' terms 'our logical intellect has not been coerced', Clifford's principle would call for withholding assent. But James tries to set up the issue in such a way as to preclude this possibility.

He begins by writing not of whether to adopt a particular hypothesis, but of options, that is to say, choices between two hypotheses, and restricts his focus to what he calls genuine options. A genuine option, for James, is one in which both hypotheses are live ones, the opportunity at stake is momentous, and the choice is forced. The fact that the choice is forced means that there is no place on which to stand that is outside the two alternatives. So the difference with Clifford cannot be over whether or not one should withhold assent, or remain agnostic, when the evidence is insufficient. James has already built into the description of the cases that he will consider a stipulation that the choice is forced. To withhold assent is actually to choose. He thinks that there is a practical and momentous difference between a life informed by religious belief and one without it, that therefore the choice is forced, and that the evidence is insufficient to settle the matter one way or another. For Clifford, of course, the burden of proof is on the person who adopts the religious hypothesis, and the default condition is to reject it in the absence of convincing evidence. James has replaced Clifford's asymmetric description with one in which both logic and evidence are insufficient to determine a choice between two live hypotheses.

After stipulating what he means by a genuine option, James turns to look at what he calls the 'actual psychology of human opinion'. He notes that it seems impossible to decide to believe something. If I am engaged in inquiry about a particular topic, it seems both impossible and illegitimate to try to settle the question by just deciding. Charles Peirce had addressed this question in his essay 'The Fixation of Belief', in which the first and least effective way of resolving a problem and eliminating doubt that he considers is what he calls the method of tenacity, to just will to hold on to a particular belief come what may.[3] As Peirce points out, this is very difficult to achieve and usually does not satisfy the inquirer.

James is not concerned with this kind of willing, but with something much broader. What has made certain hypotheses dead for us, he says, and unavailable for belief, is for the most part a previous action of our willing nature. By 'willing nature', he writes,

> I do not mean only such deliberate volitions as may have set up habits of belief that we cannot now escape from—I mean all such factors of belief as fear and hope, prejudice and passion, imitation and partisanship, the circumpressure of our caste and set. As a matter of fact we find ourselves believing, we hardly know how or why.[4]

James' topic in the article is not solely, and not chiefly, explicit acts of volition, but the ways in which believing and change of belief are shaped, in part, by interests, by something other than logic and evidence. As he writes after introducing Clifford's jeremiad against believing on insufficient evidence: 'if anyone should ... assume that intellectual insight is what remains when wish and will and sentiment have taken wing, or that pure reason is what settles our opinions, he would fly ... directly in the teeth of the facts'.[5]

An important point in James' essay is his identification of empiricism with fallibilism, or what we might call anti-foundationalism. We can know something, but we can never know with certainty that we know it. No concrete test of what is really true has ever been agreed upon. Different philosophers have proposed different criteria, but none of these criteria is infallible. As empiricists, he says, we give up the doctrine of objective certitude, but we don't give up the quest or hope of truth itself. Pragmatists, James writes, represent the empiricist attitude in a more radical and less objectionable form.[6]

James' thesis then reads:

> Our passional nature not only lawfully may but must decide an option between propositions, whenever it is a genuine option that cannot by its nature be decided on intellectual grounds; for to say, under such circumstances, 'Do not decide but leave the question open,' is itself a passional decision—just like deciding yes or no—and is attended with the same risk of losing the truth.[7]

The main point of this thesis is a descriptive one: not that our willing nature *may* tip the balance in such instances, but that it *must*; that is to say, it always does. So the essay is not so much a proposal that we decide these matters as it is a claim that our interests are always at work in fixing belief. Given that our interests, or willing nature, play this role, James wants his readers to acknowledge that, to make those interests explicit, and in some cases to self-consciously endorse one or another of them. Later in the essay he adopts the rhetoric of persuasion to encourage the reader to ask what she can do with a particular belief and then to actively side with that interest, when the issue is one that cannot be decided on intellectual grounds.

When James arrives at the point in the essay where he identifies what he takes to be the religious hypothesis, it seems frustratingly vague and empty. He writes:

> Science says things are; morality says some things are better than other things; and religion says essentially two things. First, she says that the best things are the more eternal things, the overlapping things, the things in the universe that throw the last stone, so to speak, and say the final word. Perfection is eternal ... is the first affirmation of religion ... The second affirmation of religion is that we are better off now if we believe her first affirmation to be true.[8]

To unpack the meaning of this cryptic summary we need to look briefly at the development of James' conception of religion.

The volume *The Will to Believe* was published in 1897 and dedicated 'To my old friend Charles Sanders Peirce, to whose philosophic comradeship in old times and to whose writings in more recent years I owe more incitement and help than I can express or repay.' The first six essays in that volume, those most relevant for the philosophy of religion, are the product of twenty years of reflection on the fact that interests shape belief and on the extent to which that might be epistemically acceptable. In 'The Fixation of Belief', published in 1877, Peirce had argued that genuine inquiry is elicited by doubt, had described several ways of satisfying that doubt, and had concluded that 'it is necessary that a method should be found by which our beliefs may be caused by nothing human, but by some external permanency—by something upon which our thinking has no effect'.[9] In articles beginning with 'The sentiment of rationality' in 1879, James argues that it is neither possible nor desirable to find a method by which our beliefs are caused by something on which our thinking has no effect. Our non-intellectual nature does influence our convictions, and that is a normal factor in our making up our minds.

In three articles published in the early 1880s James sets out what he takes to be the religious question. 'The radical question of life', he says, is 'whether, at bottom, this be a moral or unmoral universe'.[10] It is the question of materialism. Despite the comments of some of his critics to the contrary, James was interested, both as a philosopher and as a person, in the truth of the matter. Clearly it is underdetermined by the evidence and his interests motivate the inquiry. In these articles James considers how we might fix belief on such an issue. He reflects on the criteria by which we decide that one belief is more rational than another.

In 'Rationality, Activity, and Faith' (1882), James writes that 'of two conceptions equally fit to satisfy the logical demand, one may awaken the active impulses or satisfy other aesthetic demands far better than the other. This one will be accounted the more rational conception and it will deservedly prevail.'[11] This statement, like its analogues in 'The Will to Believe', is first descriptive ('It will prevail') and then normative ('It deserves to prevail'). What are those demands? James proposes two: (1) it must define expectancy in a way that fits with future consequences, and (2) it must define the future congruously with our spontaneous powers. The first means that it must not be refuted by future experience. The second is more elusive, but is central to James' conception of religion. The future, and in fact the universe of which we are a part, must be characterized in a way that is congruous with, or continuous with, our moral life, where 'moral' is not narrowly defined but means our interests and our powers. Idealism is to be preferred over materialism, James says, because it makes the universe more intimate, more continuous with us and with our values. When he tries to set out the lineaments of his metaphysics in his final book, *A Pluralistic Universe*, he proposes that intimacy be used as a criterion for an adequate metaphysics. Here, in this early essay, he writes: 'A nameless *Unheimlichkeit* comes over us at the thought of there being nothing eternal in our final purposes, in the objects of those loves and aspirations which are our deepest energies ... We demand in (the universe) a *character* for which our emotions and active propensities shall be a match.'[12]

Approaching the same topic in a different way in 'The Dilemma of Determinism', James writes, descriptively, that we work to cast the world into a more rational shape than we have found it, and, prescriptively, that he is 'as willing to try conceptions of moral, as of mechanical or logical necessity'.[13] We employ logical and scientific concepts to make sense of the world and there is no reason to think that we don't, or shouldn't, try to make moral sense of it as well. His argument in this article is that determinism, which he takes to be a 'block universe' devoid of freedom or novelty, makes a mockery of our moral perceptions and judgments, especially the judgment that some actions and events are bad and that the universe would be better off without them.

Reflecting on the need to define the universe congruously with our spontaneous powers, James thinks that only a conception of reality defined in a way similar to the way God is described in traditional theism is both rational and possible for the mind.[14] While idealism is more intimate than materialism, mysticism and the idea of the rational absolute go too far. They amount to a kind of gnosticism, of which he thinks that Hegel's philosophy is the most recent variety. Theism lies between gnosticism and agnosticism and accords most fully with the mind's interests.

Peirce also held that there is a natural fit between the mind and the cosmos. His later metaphysics reflects this and his 'Neglected argument for the reality of God' rests on it.[15] But it wasn't an open question for Peirce and therefore not a central topic for inquiry, as it was for James. James expressed what he took to be a universal need for this kind of fit and looked constantly for confirmation or legitimation of belief in it. The question of whether or not this is a moral universe is not meaningless, he wrote, because contrary answers lead to contrary behavior. The religious hypothesis could not be verified in a single lifetime, but a person could act on it and see whether or not it harmonized with experience. 'If this *be* a moral universe,' he wrote, 'all acts I make on that assumption will fit with the phenomena, and ... the more I live, the more satisfactory the consensus will grow.[16] If (it is) not, experience will produce even more impediments.' This wasn't solely a speculative matter for James. 'If this (life) is not a real fight,' he writes, 'it is only play-acting. But it *feels* like a real fight.'[17]

James thought that confirmation need not come only from individual experience, but from historical evidence as well. In the preface to *The Will to Believe* he writes:

> If religious hypotheses about the universe be in order at all, then the active faiths of individuals in them, freely expressing themselves in life, are the experimental tests by which they are verified, and the only means by which their truth or falsehood can be wrought out. The truest scientific hypothesis is that which as we say, 'works' best; and it can be no otherwise with religious hypotheses. Religious history proves that one hypothesis after another has worked ill, has crumbled at contact with a widening knowledge of the world, and has lapsed from the minds of men. Some articles of faith, however, have maintained themselves through every vicissitude, and possess even more vitality today than ever before: it is for the 'science of religions' to tell us just which hypotheses these are. Meanwhile the freest competition of the various faiths with one another, and their openest application to life by their several champions, are the most favorable conditions under which the survival of the fittest can proceed.[18]

The scientist ought not to worry about this, James says, because those faiths that best stand the test of time will adopt her hypotheses and incorporate them into their own. James' language here echoes not only Darwin, but also John Stuart Mill's argument in *On Liberty* for freedom of opinion and experiments in living.

2 Pragmatism and *Varieties*

In *The Varieties of Religious Experience* James proposes that philosophy of religion transform itself from theology to a critical science of religions. Such a science would begin with spontaneous religious constructions as well as doctrine, eliminate those beliefs that conflict with natural science, and arrive at some conceptions and hypotheses that are possible, testing them and trying to distinguish what is to be taken literally from symbolic expressions. It would be a critical reconstruction that depended for its original material on facts of personal experience.

In 1898 James traveled to Berkeley to deliver a lecture entitled 'Philosophical Conceptions and Practical Results', which was the first public use of the term 'pragmatism' as the name for a philosophical method.[19] There he introduced the pragmatic criterion of meaning, giving full credit to Peirce and applying this criterion to the concept of God. This lecture was also, as he wrote to his son, a rehearsal for the Gifford Lectures he was to give in Edinburgh, which became *Varieties*. Much of the lecture is included verbatim in *Varieties* and most of the rest of it in the book *Pragmatism*. David Lamberth argues that James' pragmatism is unimportant for understanding *Varieties*, which grows out of his independent work on radical empiricism.[20] Lamberth offers an excellent reading of *Varieties* and calls attention to some important supplementary material, but it is misleading to suggest, as he does, that the book is only marginally related to James' pragmatism.

James introduces the principle of pragmatism in the Berkeley lecture by paraphrasing accurately from Peirce's 'How to Make Our Ideas Clear'. The same thought may be expressed in different words, Peirce writes, but if the words suggest no different conduct, they contribute nothing new to the meaning of the thought. In order 'to develop a thought's meaning we need only determine what conduct it is fitted to produce; that conduct is for us its sole significance'.[21] 'Consider what effects,' Peirce wrote, 'which might conceivably have practical bearings, we conceive the object of our conception to have. Then, our conception of these effects is our whole conception of the object.'[22] Peirce illustrates this criterion by examining the concept 'hard', in the sense in which we say that a diamond is hard. We can elucidate its meaning, Peirce says, by noting that a diamond cannot be scratched by most objects. 'Hard' means 'not easily scratched'.

Peirce wrote 'How to Make Our Ideas Clear' for a series he called *Illustrations in the Logic of Science*, and his model here is the clarification of scientific terms and hypotheses by designing and conducting experiments. To elucidate a thought we need only determine what conduct it is fitted to produce. We can use a diamond to cut glass or to scratch most metals, but we cannot expect to scratch it easily.

James comments at this point that he would like to interpret Peirce's principle more broadly, and his reinterpretation is in fact a revision. He removes it from the logic of experiment to that of descriptive phenomenology:

> I should prefer for our purposes this evening to express Peirce's principle by saying that the effective meaning of any philosophic proposition can always be brought down to some particular consequence, in our future practical experience, whether active or passive; the point lying in the fact that the experience must be particular, (rather) than in the fact that it must be active.[23]

James has broadened the principle and has changed it considerably. In Peirce's diamond example, the meaning of 'hard' tells us what to expect, what reactions to prepare, if we act with or on the object. We can't expect to scratch it. This is what Peirce takes to be required for the clarification of scientific concepts. James is interested in the difference made to our future experience but not in the logic of the concept. The effect could be something that we take ourselves to experience rather than the result of some active intervention on our part.[24] (James' focus on particular experience is also a sign of what Peirce referred to as James' nominalism. In the diamond example, Peirce is interested in the general case, in what 'hard' means. James looks rather toward particular experiences.)

Applying his revision of Peirce's criterion to the term 'God', James asks what is at stake in the debate between theism and materialism. Continuing the reflection from his earlier essays, James says that theism and materialism point to completely different practical consequences, to opposite outlooks on future experience. The notion of God, he writes,

> guarantees an ideal order that shall be permanently preserved. A world with a God in it to say the last word, may indeed burn up or freeze, but we then think of him as still mindful of the old ideals and sure to bring them elsewhere to fruition; so that, where he is, tragedy is only provisional and partial, and shipwreck and dissolution not the absolutely final things. This need of an eternal moral order is one of the deepest needs of our breast. Materialism means simply the denial that the moral order is eternal, and the cutting off of ultimate hopes; theism means the affirmation of an eternal moral order and the letting loose of hope.[25]

It is clear, James says, that this is a genuine issue and not some empty metaphysical debate, but abstract theological ideas and systems do often seem empty. The place to look for what is at stake in religion is not religious doctrine, but concrete religious experiences in the lives of ordinary people. As examples, James lists 'conversations with the unseen, voices and visions, responses to prayer, changes of heart, deliverances from fear, inflowings of help, assurances of support, whenever certain persons set their own internal attitude in certain appropriate ways'.[26] What the word 'God' means, he says, is just those passive and active experiences. Theological doctrines are secondary effects on these direct experiences of the spiritual life. In both this characterization and in *Varieties* James' understanding of what difference religion makes is highly influenced by what seemed most salient in late nineteenth century American religious life, Protestant revivalism, and various forms of spiritualism.

The project of a science of religions as pursued in *Varieties* rests on an examination of personal experiences described from the first person point of view. James writes in the book that 'feeling is the deeper source of religion, and that philosophic and theological formulas are secondary products, like translations of a text into another tongue'.[27] He defines religion as 'the feelings, acts, and experiences of individual men in their solitude, so far as they apprehend themselves to stand in relation to whatever they may consider the divine'.[28] In his proposal for a science of religions he says that people always define the divine in ways that harmonize with their temporary intellectual preoccupations, but philosophy ought to be able to eliminate the local and accidental from these definitions. As a result, even though James' quotations are sometimes extensive, he doesn't attend to the details of what a particular person considers the divine and how he takes himself to stand in relation to it.

James writes at the outset of *Varieties* that his descriptive account of religious experience has filled the whole book and that the philosophy has had to be postponed until later. But, in fact, philosophical distinctions and judgments are at work throughout the book and are often made explicit. After introductory methodological comments in the first three chapters, James structures the book around a classification of his often quite vivid first person narrative accounts.

One of James' methodological remarks is especially important. He says that in recent books on logic a distinction is made between two orders of inquiry.[29] The first is an inquiry into what something is, including its constitution, origin, and history; the second is an inquiry into its value. They proceed, he says, from diverse intellectual preoccupations and one cannot be deduced from the other. These two judgments, the first of which he calls existential and the second spiritual, must be made separately. The allusion to recent books on logic is to Peirce's point in 'The Fixation of Belief' that the epistemic value of a hypothesis is to be judged not by its origin, but by how well it works. A physicist who has been working on a problem might come upon a hypothesis or formula that she finds promising. The value of that hypothesis will depend on how well it works when she plugs it into the appropriate equations or designs an experiment to test the hypothesis. How the formula or hypothesis came to her is irrelevant, whether it came in a dream, from poring over her notes, or by association from something seemingly unrelated. What matters is how it works for the task at hand.

James takes this to be a descriptive point as well as a normative one. Despite what people claim, he says, they don't judge the significance or value of a hypothesis or an experience by its origin, whether they are appealing to the Bible or Aristotle or some other source for authority. In fact, when Luther goes back to the New Testament, for example, he is quite selective about what he takes from there. He takes those things that will be of value and use to him. The criteria we employ when judging experiences, James says, are three: (1) immediate luminousness, that is, the authority it seems to convey, (2) philosophical reasonableness, and (3) moral helpfulness.[30] The first is often unreliable and usually gives way, upon reflection, to the other two.

These remarks shed some light on the problems with James' examination of experiential reports. James defines religion as the feelings, acts, and experiences of individuals so far as they apprehend themselves to stand in relation to whatever they may consider the divine. This means that a religious experience is identified under a description, and that that description includes reference to the way the person who has the experience understands himself or herself to stand in relation to what he or she considers the divine. But James does not take his own definition sufficiently seriously. The first of his two chapters on conversion is devoted chiefly to a description of the experience of the convert and the second to explanations of that experience. He speculates that sudden conversions might be explained by activity that goes on subliminally in the subconscious mind, and that invasive experiences from that region abruptly interrupt the primary consciousness. After making that suggestion, he writes: 'I don't see why Methodists need object to such a view.'[31] 'You may remember', he writes,

> how (in my first lecture) I argued against the notion that the worth of a thing can be decided by its origin. Our spiritual judgment, I said, our opinion of the significance and value of a human event or condition, must be decided on empirical grounds exclusively. If the *fruits for life* of the state of conversion are good, we ought to idealize it and venerate it, even though it be a piece of natural psychology; if not, we ought to make short work with it, no matter what supernatural being may have infused it.[32]

For a person who has a sudden conversion experience, a belief about the cause of the experience is itself a part of the experience. A convert at a revival experiences what happened to her as the work of the Holy Spirit. Were she to become convinced that it could be exhaustively explained by crowd psychology, or by some other natural explanation, it would no longer be the same experience. James seems to recognize this in his definition, but he forgets it when he says that he doesn't see any reason why a convert would object to such a view. A belief about the cause of the experience, in this case the belief that it cannot be completely explained by natural causes, is itself constitutive of the experience.

James' sharp separation of judgments about what an experience is and how it is to be explained, on one hand, and judgments about its value or significance on the other, may have blinded him to the fact that for the one who undergoes the experience a judgment about its proper explanation might figure into, or be assumed in, a judgment about its significance. Ordinary perceptual judgments are of this sort. If I discover that what I took to be a sighting of a tree up ahead was the result of a certain kind of reflection or refraction of light through the fog, I will change my judgment about whether or not there is a tree in that spot. Similarly, for some of the subjects whose reports James quotes, learning that what they had taken to be the action of the Holy Spirit on their hearts could be convincingly explained by natural psychological and social causes might diminish the importance of the experience. By arguing that causal explanations and judgments of value are completely independent, James misses this point.

In an essay published in 1905 John Dewey criticizes appeal to immediate experience in a way that raises questions about James' extensive use in *Varieties* of first person narratives. He cites as an example a person's being frightened by a strange noise. After investigation, she realizes that the source of the noise is the wind tapping the shade against the window. Reality is now changed, reorganized. Her fright, as a reaction to the sudden noise, turns out to be useless or even detrimental. It is, he says, a maladaptation. Then he adds: 'pretty much all of experience is of this sort ..., and the empiricist is false to his principle if he does not duly note this fact'.[33] Immediate experience, what something is experienced as, is only what something seems to be. It is not knowledge until it has been tested, subjected to inquiry, explained and thus understood.

James selects his examples because they are vivid and because they are experienced by their subjects as religious. Any one of them could be similar to the frightening noise in Dewey's example. Further testing and inquiry might yield other causes that would give rise to a new explanation, reinterpretation, and thus a changed reality. The religious explanations, and thus the religious experiences, might be transient stages in the inquiries into the causes of each of these examples. James assembles and classifies them, observes that all attest to something

More beyond and continuous with what he calls the higher parts of the self, and adds his overbelief that though this may be partially explained by appeal to the subconscious it is not exhausted by that kind of natural explanation. Dewey's point is that experience only tells us what something is experienced as, that is to say, what it is taken to be. To focus on the fact that these experiences seem to their subjects to be religious, may arrest inquiry rather than serving it.

In the postscript to *Varieties* James criticizes those whom he calls universal supernaturalists, transcendental idealists like his colleague Josiah Royce and others who affirm an absolute mind beyond the world of natural causes, but hold that it is indiscernible and that its existence would not make any difference in what we could observe and do. James thought that this was too facile. Such a claim is meaningless if it doesn't make some kind of experienceable difference. While *Varieties* was directed chiefly against naturalism, offering examples of experiences that seemed to suggest something beyond the natural realm, James' 1907 lectures on *Pragmatism* were directed chiefly at Royce and the idealists. Early in the lectures James distinguishes between two types of philosophy of religion, transcendental idealism and traditional theism. The pragmatic criterion, he says, requires us to ask 'What difference would it practically make to any one if this notion rather than that notion be true?' Not what difference would it make if we were to believe this hypothesis rather than that, but what difference it would make if it were true. James agrees with the idealists that truth is correspondence with reality, but wants to transform the empty and static notion of correspondence into some kind of active commerce between particular thoughts and experiences. The rationalist philosophy of absolute mind, he thinks, doesn't allow for any such commerce. 'It is no *explanation* of our concrete universe, it is another thing altogether, a substitute for it, a remedy, a way of escape.'[34]

James repeats in *Pragmatism* the passage from the Berkeley lecture in which he says that the practical meaning of the concept of God is a guarantee of an ideal order that shall be permanently preserved. 'Materialism', he writes, 'means simply the denial that the moral order is eternal, and the cutting off of ultimate hopes; spiritualism means the affirmation of an eternal moral order and the letting loose of hope.'[35] At the end of *Varieties* he had concluded that such a guarantee may not be possible and may not be necessary for religion. In the final chapter of *Pragmatism* James elaborates on this point. He has argued that pragmatic reflection on the issue of one and many shows that while we unify our world in our knowing the idea of an already existent unity in an absolute knower is empty. Both our knowing and our moral experience of the world are best accounted for by pluralism. There is in the world as much unity as we can find or can make, but we should not begin by assuming it. James says that this pluralistic view fits better with pragmatism. Perfection is not guaranteed, but is contingent on actual agents doing their best. The pragmatist is willing to accept this moralistic religion, without a guarantee and with real losses. Evil is not *aufgehoben*. It is up to us to bring about the moral order. But, James adds, 'I firmly disbelieve, myself, that our human experience is the highest form of experience extent in the universe ... We may well believe, on proofs that religious experience affords, that higher powers exist and are at work to save the world on ideal lines similar to our own.'[36]

In his review of *Pragmatism* Dewey argues that when James applies the pragmatic principle to determine the meaning of the term 'God' and of the debate between theism and materialism, he assumes that that meaning is already fixed ahead of time.[37] James proceeds as a teacher who is trying to elucidate the meaning of a certain concept rather than as a philosopher who is trying actively to determine the meaning in a way that might possibly transform it. This, Dewey says, is quite different from Peirce's procedure. To use one of Peirce's examples, the meaning of the term 'force' is determined by asking what consequences we can expect if we act on an object in a certain way. That is not an elucidation of traditional meanings of the term 'force', but it is a clearly defined meaning that has served useful for modern physics.

James writes: 'The whole function of philosophy ought to be to find out what definite difference it will make to you and me, at definite instances of our life, if this world-formula or that world-formula be the true one.'[38] Dewey responds that this is not the whole function of philosophy. The pragmatist should first determine the meaning of the world-formula, not just accept it as given and then try to elucidate its meaning. After concluding that the concept of God means a 'guarantee of an ideal order that shall be permanently preserved', James had written in the same paragraph: 'Here then, in these different emotional and practical appeals, in these adjustments of our concrete attitudes of hope and expectation, and all the delicate consequences which these differences entail, lie the real meanings of materialism and spiritualism.'[39] Dewey argues that James takes the latter specification of its consequences to illumine and to justify the traditional use of the term 'God' when the pragmatist ought not just accept that traditional use but transform it so that it refers directly to something like the adjustments of our concrete attitudes of hope and expectation.

For James, Matthew Arnold's conception of God as 'an eternal power, not ourselves, that makes for righteousness', a description to which James alludes at several points, is a live option. The religious question for him, from the outset, is whether or not there is such an order, whether this is a moral or unmoral universe. It is a pressing question for James. He eventually relinquishes his requirement that such a God would guarantee that an ideal order be permanently preserved, but he still believes 'that higher powers exist and are at work to save the world on ideal lines similar to our own'. For Dewey that is no longer a live option. Dewey takes this to be James' failure to pursue the pragmatic method thoroughly. But Dewey is already well on the way toward a naturalism from which it seems clear that the idea of 'God' defined as an antecedently existing source of moral order is of no practical use and therefore is in need of radical transformation. That shift, from the search for a 'power, not ourselves, that makes for righteousness' to a belief that any moral order in the world is one that we ourselves make using the resources of the natural world, is not solely the result of applying the pragmatic method to religious concepts and questions, but of larger changes in their conceptions of the world.

Notes

1. W. James (1979) *The Will to Believe and Other Essays in Popular Philosophy* (Cambridge, MA: Harvard University Press), p. 13.
2. Ibid., p. 18.
3. C. S. Peirce (1992) 'The Fixation of Belief' in *The Essential Peirce*, Vol. 1 (1867–1893), eds. N. Houser and C. Kloesel (Bloomington: Indiana University Press), pp. 109–23.
4. James, *The Will to Believe*, p. 18.
5. Ibid.
6. Ibid., p. 27.
7. Ibid., p. 20.
8. Ibid., pp. 29–30.
9. Peirce, *The Essential Peirce*, I, p. 120.
10. James, *The Will to Believe*, p. 84.
11. Ibid., p. 66. 'The Rationality of Faith' was published in *Princeton Review*, 2 (1882), pp. 58–86, and was subsequently incorporated into 'The Sentiment of Rationality' in *The Will to Believe*.
12. James, *The Will to Believe*, p. 71.
13. Ibid., p. 115.
14. Ibid., p. 93.
15. C. S. Peirce (1998) 'A Neglected Argument for the Reality of God' in *The Essential Peirce*, Vol. 2, ed. Peirce Edition Project (Bloomington and Indianapolis: Indiana University Press), pp. 434–50.

16. James, *The Will to Believe*, p. 86.
17. Ibid., p. 55.
18. Ibid., p. 8.
19. W. James (1978) 'Philosophical Conceptions and Practical Results' in *Pragmatism* (Cambridge, MA: Harvard University Press), pp. 255–70.
20. D. Lamberth (1999) *William James and the Metaphysics of Experience* (Cambridge: Cambridge University Press).
21. James, *Pragmatism*, p. 259.
22. Peirce, *The Essential Peirce*, Vol. 1, p. 132.
23. James, *Pragmatism*, p. 259.
24. James' focus on particular experience is also a sign of what Peirce referred to as James' nominalism. In the diamond example Peirce is interested in what 'hard' means in the general case. James looks rather toward particular experiences.
25. James, *Pragmatism*, p. 264.
26. Ibid., p. 266.
27. W. James (1985) *The Varieties of Religious Experience* (Cambridge, MA: Harvard University Press), p. 341.
28. Ibid., p. 34.
29. James, *Varieties*, p. 13.
30. Ibid., p. 23.
31. Methodism was the largest Protestant denomination in the United States in the nineteenth century and was the locus of many of the revivals.
32. James, *Varieties*, p. 193.
33. J. Dewey (1998) 'The Postulate of Immediate Empiricism' in *The Essential Dewey*, Vol. 1, eds. L. Hickman and T. Alexander (Bloomington and Indianapolis: Indiana University Press), p. 117.
34. James, *Pragmatism*, p. 18.
35. Ibid., p. 55.
36. Ibid., pp. 143–5.
37. J. Dewey, 'What Pragmatism Means by Practical' in *The Essential Dewey*, Vol. 1, pp. 377–86.
38. James, *Pragmatism*, p. 30.
39. Ibid., p. 55.

2
Anti-Dogmatism as a Defense of Religious Belief

Charlene Haddock Seigfried

William James asserts that philosophy and science will only have something positive to contribute to determining the objective truth of religious claims when they cease to be dogmatic and become experimental. In this chapter, I focus on how James' anti-dogmatic approach affects his defense of religious belief and psychical research. I conclude that in his efforts to undermine the dogmatic rejection of the very possibility of genuine religious phenomena by positivistic scientists and naturalist non-believers, James appeals to the pragmatic experimental method but is unable to produce convincing evidence. His version of pragmatic anti-dogmatism is then contrasted with John Dewey's.

After explaining why William James was opposed to dogmatism and what he argued for in its stead, I will be focusing on how his anti-dogmatic approach affects his philosophy of religious experience and his defense of psychical research. According to Robert A. McDermott, James dismisses the dogmatism of both scientific skepticism, on the one hand, and religious belief, on the other, and offers instead a defense of religious and psychic modes of perception.[1] James uses the same scientific or radically empiricist methods in both his psychic and religious research; namely, searching for concrete facts through a wide range of experiences and formulating them as testable hypotheses.

While such evidence is still being gathered, analyzed, and tested, James contends that it would be mere dogmatism for psychologists to prematurely dismiss such possible additions to the range of experiences they investigate.[2] Since he conceived of *The Varieties of Religious Experience* as being his contribution to developing a science of religious experience which had important philosophic repercussions, I will use the evidence provided by some contemporary researchers in the area of psychic or para-normal phenomena to test the cogency of James' anti-dogmatic pragmatic method as a useful means of mediating disputes over religious phenomena.[3] By now, such evidence can no longer be considered premature.

1 Dogmatism Versus Experimentalism

In a familiar passage from *Pragmatism*, William James compares the pragmatic method to a corridor in a hotel.[4] Innumerable rooms open off from it, variously occupied by atheists, religious believers, chemists, metaphysicians, and anti-metaphysicians. The only thing they have in common is the corridor: that is, a practical way of getting into or out of their rooms. The attitude or orientation they all share is a willingness to judge beliefs by their usefulness for purposes deemed worthwhile. Switching metaphors, James denies that theories are transcripts of reality, asserting instead that they are man-made languages giving a report of nature from some perspective or other. The point being stressed is that languages, unlike truth claims, tolerate many choices of expressions and many dialects. Both the hotel metaphor and the language metaphor illustrate James' claim that pragmatism 'has no dogmas, and no doctrines save its method'.[5]

James is quite proud of this aspect of pragmatism, which he takes to be its central strength, and repeats it often. He says even more emphatically that pragmatism is well suited to mediating disputes and reconciling opponents because it 'has in fact no prejudices whatever, no obstructive dogmas, no rigid canons of what shall count as proof'.[6] *Prima facie* such a claim would be hard to defend, but it is somewhat mitigated if attention is paid to two modifiers James adds in this formulation of his anti-dogmatism. Is he perhaps saying—not that pragmatism has no dogmas—but only no dogmas sufficient to obstruct inquiry, and that it does have canons of what shall count as proof, only that they are not rigid ones because not restricted to certain forms of evidence, such as that produced in laboratories or by use of statistical analysis? Even if we accept this weaker sense of being non-dogmatic, though, it is clear that James himself does not; he is keen to distance himself from dogmatism of any sort. He is also at pains to demonstrate that pragmatism is committed to no beliefs whatever, so certainly to no beliefs held dogmatically, but instead is only 'an attitude of orientation'.[7] He instructs us to judge beliefs solely by looking for the consequences they lead to.

Since pragmatism is often summarily dismissed as a worthwhile philosophy on the grounds that it is a method merely, a position that aligns it with positivism's value-free stance, how can James' claims be reconciled with a more responsible, value-oriented approach? How can it even be reconciled with James' own claims to be combating positivism by explicitly defending the absolute dignity of the human person and the centrality of values to every way of organizing experience, not excluding scientific procedure? One way has been to distinguish between pragmatism as merely a method and the theory of radical empiricism as a defense of a particular world-view or metaphysics. But this defense cannot be sustained because, as I have argued elsewhere, James equates the two, distinguishing them only as expressing different emphases, and he even uses the same definition for both.[8] He says that pragmatism starts from the same postulate as the principle of pure experience; namely, that '[e]verything real must be experienceable somewhere, and every kind of thing experienced must somewhere be real'.[9] As a pragmatist method for determining the truth, the emphasis is on workableness, not correspondence with objects, and as a doctrine of radical empiricism that limits discussion to what is or can be experienced, the emphasis is on the fact that the relations among things *can* be directly experienced.[10]

James' explanation for why pragmatism is a method without metaphysical or other biases is that it will accept any premises as long as they can be shown to have practical consequences. Nothing is ruled out beforehand. But 'practical' is not a vernacular term for James. It has specific meaning within his philosophical perspective: 'the practically real world for each one of us, the effective world of the individual, is the compound world, the physical facts and emotional values in indistinguishable combination'.[11] In this context, he means that the 'only test of probable truth is what works best in the way of leading us, what fits every part of life best and combines with the collectivity of experience's demands, nothing being omitted'.[12] Of all possible consequences, only the best solutions for the ends desired should be selected, and these ends in turn must be answerable to the widest demands of experience. The 'leadings' we seek as we navigate our way through experience must be worthwhile as well as efficacious.

Even taking James at his word that experience has such resources, is it enough to keep working at a solution until every interest is accommodated, every relevant aspect of experience accounted for? Will acceptable values result from this process and unacceptable ones be rejected? On the other hand, is such a criterion even possible? How can we know that a particular belief fits every part of life at all, let alone fits them the best? How can we know that nothing in experience has been omitted? James uncharacteristically uses the absolute term 'the best' twice, rather than his more usual comparative term of what is 'better' given the circumstances and the ends-in-view. Is it significant or merely a rhetorical flourish that he uses as his test of probable truth (note the 'probable'!) what works *best* and what fits *best*? Are there on pragmatist grounds any approach to the best except through comparisons of what is better? And since truth is always truth for us, who is it best for? He seems to be saying that whatever leads all of us to our ends in every aspect of life is best. But can we start out from the global mass of people, which encompasses a diversity of premises, beliefs, values, ways of life, and experiences, and agree on a path that fits all our demands without dogmatically, surreptitiously, sneaking in someone's, or some sub-set of, beliefs and values as more worthwhile?

It seems that we cannot. In *The Meaning of Truth* James says that '[t]he only *real* guarantee we have against licentious thinking is the circumpressure of experience itself, which gets us sick of concrete errors'.[13] To the criticism that the 'humanist will always have a greater liberty to play fast and loose with truth than will your believer in an independent realm of reality that makes the standard rigid', James appeals to 'empirical methods of inquiry in concrete affairs. To consider hypotheses is surely always better than to dogmatize *ins blaue hinein*.'[14] In this sense, dogmatic belief is rigid because it claims a secure hold on reality. If one already has the truth, there is no need to entertain mere hypotheses. This hold on reality is independent of experience, however, derived as it is from some extrinsic source of enlightenment, whether rationally independent or religiously transcendent. The dispute is over conflicting beliefs about how reality is apprehended—directly through insight or revelation, or indirectly through empirical experimentation guided by interests. Even assuming that reality is always reality-for-us and that rationalists must therefore have some experience on which to base their beliefs, it is nonetheless the case that

> [w]hen absolutists reject humanism because they feel it to be untrue, that means that the whole habit of their mental needs is wedded already to a different view of reality. . . . Their own subjective apperceiving mass is what speaks here in the name of eternal natures and bids them reject our humanism—as they apprehend it.[15]

Humanists do not experience reality the same way, as James points out in identifying himself with them: 'Just so with us humanists, when we condemn all noble, clean-cut, fixed, eternal, rational, temple-like systems of philosophy.'[16] Such coolly rational systems conflict with our own experiences, which disclose 'the *dramatic temperament* of nature'.[17] It is not that humanists reject objectivity and the independence of truth as the rationalists claim, but they find it in the surprises and uncertainties more characteristic of forays into a wilderness than in the 'neater and cleaner intellectual abodes' artificially erected by dogmatic rationalists.

James assures us that 'the concrete truth *for us* will always be that way of thinking in which our various experiences most profitably combine'.[18] But he also explains how, as unique individuals, we will have different experiences according to different temperaments, leading to different beliefs as well as to different actions. He even formulated what I call a pragmatic hermeneutic principle to convey the dynamic character of the way that beliefs function experientially to yield a sense of the truth:

> We plunge forward into the field of fresh experience with the beliefs our ancestors and we have made already; these determine what we notice; what we notice determines what we do; what we do again determines what we experience; so from one thing to another, altho [*sic*] the stubborn fact remains that there *is* a sensible flux, what is *true of it* seems from first to last to be largely a matter of our own creation.[19]

As Dewey will later phrase it, experience has its own resources for sifting and testing beliefs: experience is experimental. But if the truth is subjectively apprehended as the most useful way of organizing my own particular experiences, and the world, like language, tolerates many forms of expressions, then we are still left with irreconcilable world-views seemingly immune to arbitration on rational *or* experiential grounds.

James insists that new opinions or experiences have to cohere with the stock of old opinions an individual already has.[20] When some new experience strains or challenges our beliefs, we try to save as much of our old beliefs as we can. But if even 'the most violent revolutions in an individual's beliefs leave most of his old order standing', and if this 'older stock of truths' is a settled religious view strongly held, then it is unlikely that any experimental outcome will be sufficiently persuasive to overturn it. In fact, James asserts that loyalty to older truths is not only the first principle that guides us in our determination of truth, it is often the only principle, 'for by far the most usual way of handling phenomena so novel that they would make for a serious rearrangement of our preconceptions is to ignore them altogether, or to abuse those who bear witness to them'.[21] The verb, 'abuse', is telling, given the long history of religious strife and intolerance.

Despite this coercive force of preconceptions, James also exclaims over 'how plastic even the oldest truths nevertheless really are', as shown by the reinterpretations of old truths in light of new evidence. Except for James' posing the imagined possibility of his unexpectedly exhibiting such erratic behavior on stage as to cause his audience to reassess his sanity, all the examples he gives of the malleable character of even long-held truths are taken from the sciences. In contrast to this scientific willingness to transform old beliefs in light of new evidence which challenges them, rationalism rejects the claimed plasticity involved in determining what satisfies old and new beliefs. Rationalists exalt the objective truth of an absolute reality and denigrate the pragmatist view of truth as accommodating any number of definite working-values in experience. They are implacably opposed to views of the pragmatist model of the 'go-between function' of truths continuously made and re-made, and prefer instead a universe 'so much purer, clearer, nobler' than 'the rich thicket of reality' offered by the pragmatists.[22]

James' intention is to show that even truths 'petrified in men's regard by sheer antiquity', 'purely objective truth, truth in whose establishment the function of giving human satisfaction in marrying previous parts of experience with newer parts played no role whatsoever, is nowhere to be found'. This is because the reason anything is thought to be true is precisely 'because it performs this very marriage-function'.[23] However convincing this explanation of how even absolute truths have been continually reinterpreted over time as new needs and interests have emerged and new situations have succeeded old ones, the point I want to make is also one James recognizes; namely, that it is the way those holding ancient truths understand them—as absolute and unchanging rather than subject to revision—that separates the dogmatist from the experimentalist. But it is this very attitude that calls into question James' prematurely optimistic hope 'that pragmatism may be a happy harmonizer of empiricist ways of thinking, with the more religious demands of human beings'.[24] If religious demands are as implacable as those of the rationalist, it seems impossible, or at least extremely unlikely, that they could be reconciled with the pragmatist point of view. As long as the religious absolutist holds onto his or her beliefs unconditionally, the pragmatic method has to omit this attitude from the collectivity of experience's demands.

Dogmatism and experimentalism are irreconcilable as attitudes, but are they mutually incompatible in all respects? Only by adopting the concrete point of view and putting the pragmatic method to work within the stream of experience does it become possible to begin considering what the pragmatist response should be to dogmatists other than sheer rejection. As James says, 'it is evident that something happens when you pass from the abstract to the concrete, that complicates the situation'.[25] When considered 'less as a solution than as a program for more work, and more particularly as an indication of the ways in which existing realities may be *changed*', we may begin to find some way beyond the impasse.

2 'The Moral Philosopher and the Moral Life'

In *The Varieties of Religious Experience* James is uninterested in the particular religious meaning or theological metaphysics of the religious and mystical experiences he relates. This is because pragmatic meaning, as we have seen, consists entirely in what acting on any given belief predictably leads to. Even the question of God's existence lies in the way such an existence affects ours: 'Not God but life, more life, a larger, richer, more satisfying life, is, in the last analysis, the end of religion.'[26] It is not God's metaphysical but his moral attributes that signify anything.[27] The nature of moral conduct is therefore central to James' critical science of religions, as is obvious in the way he explains moral philosophy, to which I will now turn.

Despite all of James' lectures and appeals to the 'common man', the gentleman whose tastes are the most developed, or—on a more charitable reading disregarding the gendered nature of his remarks—to each person's own experience as the ultimate arbiter of beliefs, James twice draws a sharp distinction between the philosopher as a professional and everyone else.[28] Once, he also makes the distinction in regard to knowledge and truth. Because of the overriding need to put oneself into a satisfactory relationship with the ends sought in life, the ordinary person's most urgent concern is to be right, even for the wrong reasons. By contrast, the philosopher must obtain a license—a warrant—for his (or her) beliefs.[29] Another time, in regard to morality, James contrasts the right of each person to embody and fight for those values they hold most dear with the moral philosopher's duty to arbitrate among conflicting views. This is similar to the role he accords the impartial scientist of religions, who would sift out a common body of doctrine from the many differences found among pantheists, theists, mystics, and other supernaturalists.[30] Is the manner of this mediation different in the moral realm than in the realm of reality as apprehended by knowledge? For it is surely the case that James' purpose in holding religious experiences up to scrutiny is to find a warrant for what he already believes or at least deeply desires.[31]

James wants to undermine the dogmatic rejection of the very possibility of genuine religious phenomena by positivistic scientists and naturalist non-believers, but he himself does not enter the arena as a neutral observer, but as an interested party. Do not such interests predispose him to finding evidence for his position and ignoring or underplaying counter-evidence? After all, he believes that sensations supply only hints, which 'we extend by imagination or add to by analogy'.[32] His personal overbeliefs are already full of unseen forces or presences whom he imagines reaching out to assist us from beyond the fringes of our everyday sensibilities. He explains our failure to be aware of their presence by analogy with animals, like dogs, being unaware of the human content of the books in any library they might happen to be in. I am not arguing that these overbeliefs are dogmatically held by James; after all, he continually tries to find experiential collaboration for them, but neither will they be rejected for the lack of any such evidence.

James announces his intentions in the first line of 'The Moral Philosopher and the Moral Life' when he proclaims that its purpose 'is to show that there is no such thing possible as an ethical philosophy dogmatically made up in advance'.[33] Not only do we continually contribute to reworking our ethical beliefs, but the final truth of any ethical position, like any proposition of physics, can only be known at the end of time, when all our experiences have been taken account of. Interestingly, in light of his position that we participate in making-true what can only be a reality-for-us, he does not say, 'when all the evidence is in', as Charles Sanders Peirce might, but when every person has had their experiences and has given their views of them.[34] For our purposes, it is also important to note that he resoundingly rejects skepticism as a refusal to participate in the task of weaving the various moral claims already existing in the world into the unity of a stable system, which he takes to be the proper goal of a philosophical ethics. In *The Will to Believe*, he does not even flinch from calling such a deliberate rejection of systematic philosophical skepticism in regard to the reality and accessibility of truth, a decision he reaches on purely dogmatic grounds.[35]

James ultimately finds that philosophical ethics plays too thin a note in the rich and varied symphony that includes an 'infinite scale of values'.[36] He thinks that in strenuously trying to overcome the abundance of evils and suffering in the world, we would be overcome by the depth of the tragedy that is inseparable from life if we did not have religious faith in a God. For the earlier four sections of 'The Moral Philosopher', he strictly limited himself to what can be finitely experienced and to the insecurity of choosing the best possible universe of good when we cannot know for certain in advance which particular universe *is* the best. He even rejects the possibility of a scientific ethics and urges instead recourse to literature because it 'is confessedly tentative and suggestive rather than dogmatic'.[37] But then in the last section, he turns dogmatic himself, proclaiming triumphantly that since those of a strenuous type of character will always outlast the more easy-going type, 'religion will drive irreligion to the wall'. His final conclusion is that 'the stable and systematic moral universe for which the ethical philosopher asks is fully possible only in a world where there is a divine thinker with all-enveloping demands'.[38]

How does this differ from the dogmatic temper he had described a few pages earlier as one which rejects the growing, unsettled state of morality for absolute rules or pronouncements? James' lack of skepticism ultimately leaves him vulnerable to prematurely accepting as fact interpretations of phenomena that are congenial to his own needs rather than investigating alternative explanations. Nowhere is this more apparent than in regard to religious experiences. He admits that the mystical states he describes in *Varieties* can be explained medically as pathological conditions, ones in which certain intense and unusual experiences such as are induced by drugs, shock, or the physiological conditions of dying are interpreted according to the subject's beliefs or superstitions.[39] But he denies that they can be fully explained this way, not because he can demonstrate anything in the state over and above what has already been explained medically or psychologically, but by introducing an additional criterion: namely, the nature of the consequences for life that follow from the experience.

3 The Appeal to Consequences for Life in *The Varieties of Religious Experience*

James could find no other escape from the debilitating effects of nihilism than belief in an afterlife. His existential anguish is palpable as he declares that 'insecurity of all well-being, failure, pain and suffering are pivotal human experiences'.[40] Our lives are fraught with 'illness, danger, nausea, melancholy—[and] an irremediable sense of precariousness'.[41] It is because the healthy-minded ignore or easily dismiss from their minds the prevalence in this life of tragic death from 'freezing, drowning, entombment alive, wild beasts, worse men, and hideous diseases' that

Anti-Dogmatism as a Defense of Religious Belief 39

their approach can never be taken seriously.[42] For sick-minded souls, the enjoyment of life is poisoned as long as it unfolds against the background of 'the great spectre of universal death, the all-encompassing blackness'.[43] From such experiences, the need for a God arises.[44]

These conclusions are prepared for by James' method of analysis. Mostly, he goes with personal feelings and private consolations as best embodying what he calls his empirical method. He even characterizes his goal in *Varieties* as 'rehabilitating the element of feeling in religion and subordinating its intellectual part'.[45] Our only guides for judging whether the consequences of believing that our experiences have put us in touch with something beyond give us sufficient evidence for these claims are 'our general philosophic prejudices, our instincts, and our common sense'.[46] Even when he begins with current scientific views, as soon as he cannot find verifiable causes for some experience, he hypothesizes theological or mystical causes instead of withholding judgment. Grasping at the insight that the scientific method cannot sufficiently explain all the facts[47] and believing that even when it does so, it interprets the unknown after the manner of the known,[48] James feels justified in filling in the gaps with his own beliefs. A truly scientific approach doesn't blindly invent mechanisms to explain mysterious events, however, but proposes hypotheses requiring 'a vast program of work to be done in the way of verification'.[49] As a philosopher, James holds himself to this same scientific standard, but he weakens its meaning to such an extent that it hardly restricts his will to believe.

He thinks it is legitimate, for example, to appeal to 'the unseen' or mysticism to explain otherwise unexplainable bursts into consciousness of mysterious phenomena[50] not reducible to subliminal aspects of consciousness. He grants that 'the significance and value of a human event or condition must be decided on empirical grounds exclusively'. But by 'empirical' he means radially empirical: that is, by its results for bettering human life. He says, for example, that 'if *the fruits for life* of the state of conversion are good, we ought to idealize and venerate it' whether it is a merely natural or a supernatural phenomenon.[51] A century later, Dr. Melvin Morse has provided such evidence of the improvement of human life by tracking down adults who, as children, had near-death experiences of a life continuing beyond this world and found that the experience did in fact brighten their lives forever. His research with adults who have had near-death experiences shows that they have also been transformed by the experience, exhibiting 'a greater zest of life and virtually no fear of death'.[52] Since any belief—no matter how ludicrous it may appear to someone else—can have for the person holding it a salutary effect on their lives and that of others, what restraints, if any, has James imposed on unsubstantiated beliefs, fantastical or not?

By judging beliefs solely by their consequences, their 'fruits for life', most particularly by their consequences in promoting a better way of life for oneself and others, James demonstrates his whole-hearted anti-dogmatism but at the price of encouraging nonsense.[53] Any belief can lead to good behavior. Those who swear by Elvis-sightings could indeed demonstrate their claims by living good lives as a consequence of that belief. And those who believe in evolution as a model for the biological sciences could provide grounds for rejecting the theory if they happen to live self-destructively because of a perceived indifference to human values in the natural world of evolutionary processes. There are at least two reasons why those who are sympathetic to James' philosophy of radical empiricism do not recognize or admit these flaws in the application of his criterion. The first is an ambiguity in James' own use of his criterion of the 'consequences for life'.

According to the pluralism of James' radical empiricism, we are doubly partial in our interpretations of experience: we can only select a few aspects out of all of reality or of the multiplicity of phenomena available to pay attention to and we can only do so from some particular angle of vision for the sake of some subjective interest.[54] These aesthetic or subjective limitations of perception and the beliefs we develop as a result require the pragmatic method as a way to arbitrate between conflicting interpretations and between particular beliefs and the reality which they are supposed to disclose. The sensible world is the paradigmatic reality for most of us. Because this is so, we can use the pragmatic method as a criterion according to which

> before I can think you to mean my world, you must affect my world; before I can think you to mean much of it, you must affect much of it; and before I can be sure you mean it *as I do*, you must affect it *just as I should* if I were in your place.[55]

This criterion is rather straightforward if we want to find out whether we both mean the same thing when we say that we cook by means of a microwave oven, or whether this object in front of us is indeed such an oven, but becomes less useful as we move from beliefs about physical realities to religious and moral beliefs.

The problem is that we do not inhabit just one kind of reality, but function within various levels of reality. Even given the coercive force of the physical world which impresses itself on our senses whether we will it or not, as when I slam my fingers in a car door, in a 'less real or relative sense . . . *reality means simply relation to our emotional and active life, . . . whatever excites and stimulates our interest is real*'.[56] James concludes that moral and religious truths are therefore real for those who find them to be 'emotionally and exciting objects'.[57] And the belief in an afterworld or in a sacred realm accessible in altered states of consciousness is surely among the most emotional and exciting beliefs we can hold. It follows that the sensations that might induce the belief that someone is having an out of body experience, or a mind-altering encounter different in kind to normal perception, which are experiences of great emotional resonance, need only be triggered by unfamiliar but all-engrossing sensational hints and yet be sufficient to be extended by imagination or analogy to be taken as a reality of a certain sort. Whether the reality as believed in and the reality that is taking place is the same is a question of interest only to those who can imagine that having an experience and having an experience of a definite, demonstrable kind or object are not the same thing.

A second reason for not recognizing the weakness of James' criterion of the consequences for life that follow from believing something is an ambiguity in the meaning of experience. The pragmatic criterion requires the assumption that false beliefs will be demonstrated to be false in the course of experience. But James also acknowledges that some proofs take more than one life-time to work themselves out. In the meantime, one can happily persist in unsuspected error or folly. Even more serious an objection is that if the content or referent of one's belief is irrelevant or not directly apprehensible, then on what grounds are the consequences being judged as 'good' or 'better'? It is just because the good life as perceived and lived by one person can be judged as bad, harmful, or destructive by other persons that ethics, psychology, social criticism, religious beliefs, and the laws of civil society were developed. These all have explicit or implicit standards as to what constitutes the good life. I am not denying that James also develops such standards, but only pointing out that they were not derived from his own pragmatic method nor appealed to in *Varieties*. Moreover, in *Varieties* he explicitly rejected the claim 'that there can be one intrinsically ideal type of human character, nor any need for theoretically determining truth apart from utility'.[58] Ideal types 'vary according to the point of view adopted'.[59] His test of religious phenomena deliberately abandons all theological criteria and judges by practical common sense and the empirically pragmatic method.[60] This comes perilously close to saying: 'You'll know it when you see it.'

Against the majority of the academic and scientific professions, James thinks that two hypotheses best satisfy the evidence he has been describing. The evidence concerns 'certain kinds of incursions from the subconscious region'. It suggests that something ideal beyond mere human consciousness can cause regenerative changes in individual lives.[61] He thinks that the hypothesis that best explains these phenomena is a religious one; namely, 'that there exists a larger power which is friendly to [us] and to [our] ideals'.[62] The two hypotheses that the given 'facts require is that the power should be both other and larger than our conscious selves'.

Do the facts actually require or prove these hypotheses? In the *Varieties of Religious Experience* James is careful not to claim more certainty than the evidence permits. He lists three possible conditions that would lend plausibility to the desired conclusion, but is careful not to call them facts. What is important about stating these conditions is that they cohere as an intelligible theory and one must have an intelligible theory or at least a particular hypothesis in order to test it by the experimental method. He is warding off the contention by those dogmatic adherents of the scientific method who deny that *any* coherent theory can be formulated about supernatural or transcendent causes. David Hume, for example, famously denied that the reality of miracles, events contrary to the laws of nature, could even be coherently stated as a reasonable proposition. James' three conditionals are:

> If, then, there be a wider world of being than that of our every-day [sic] consciousness, if in it there be forces whose effects on us are intermittent, if one facilitating condition of the effects be the openness of the 'subliminal' door, we have the elements of a theory to which the phenomena of religious life lend plausibility.[63]

This amounts to little more than the claim that if extra-human forces exist, then the religious phenomena he has been describing could plausibly be understood as revealing these forces. But, of course, since whether they do in fact exist is what we need to ascertain, this line of reasoning doesn't get us very far. James has seized on a new phenomenon that the psychology of his day was elaborating as the missing empirical evidence that could provide the scientific backing for religious claims that has remained so elusive. The door which opens to both the supernatural and the natural world, which partakes of both, is the region of the subliminal or the unconscious.

4 The Clash of Classic and Romantic Imaginations

James explains this subliminal, or what we would today call the unconscious region of the mind, in an article commemorating the life and work of Frederic Myers, his good friend and co-worker in the field of parapsychology.[64] In this article, he first tries to induce a certain openness of mind, a willingness to entertain uncommon hypotheses, by contrasting two approaches to mental science, which he calls the classic-academic and the romantic. These two approaches are distinguished by their different uses of the imagination. The traditional or classic-academic type of imagination admitted only physical facts and studies of the brain and left metaphysical questions to philosophers. James poetically calls attention to the reductivist character of normal science and its dependence on the metaphor of transparency. He says that 'it has a fondness for clean pure lines and noble simplicity in its constructions. It explains things by as few principles as possible and is intolerant of either nondescript facts or clumsy formulas.' He continues in a deflationary vein: 'The facts must lie in a neat assemblage, and the psychologist must be enabled to cover them and "tuck them in" as safely under his system as a mother tucks her babe in under the down coverlet on a winter night.'[65] Consequently, the scientific imagination can only encompass the normal range of human psychic phenomena and deal with what can be simply and elegantly explained. What doesn't fit is ignored.

By contrast, the romantic type of imagination, which is more gothic than classic, looks beyond the clean, orderly world of conventional consciousness to take in its darker regions. According to James, some of these new candidates for psychological description are 'fantastic, ignoble, hardly human, or frankly non-human . . . The menagerie and the madhouse, the nursery, the prison, the hospital, have been made to yield their material.'[66] Consequently, the mind has been found to be infinitely more complex than had earlier been imagined. Most psychologists, having lingering prejudices for the nobler simplicities, shrink from hypnotism, mesmerism, clairvoyance, mediums, and out-of-body experiences. Myers understood all these phenomena as aspects of the Subliminal Self.

Is it dogmatic to deny the possibility of spirit return from beyond the grave and short visits to an afterworld during out-of-body experiences? Human history is replete with such reports. Once consciousness emerged long ages ago in human organisms, death has been our constant companion. Realization brings with it recognition of the death of friends and enemies alike, anticipation of our own demise, and vigorous rejection of death as an affront to our desire for continued existence. Disembodied spirits of the dead, both desired and feared, were encountered everywhere in pre-modern times. Beseeching, welcoming, or placating them were common ritualistic features of religions in cultures around the world. But after the disenchantment of the world carried out by Nietzsche, Marx, and Freud, it is more difficult to credit these phenomena as anything more than human, all-too-human denials of our deepest fears and wishful expressions of our strongest desires.

Such a priori rejection of the possibility of the experience of life beyond death is an expression of dogmatism, according to James. But the uncritical acceptance of spirit life as a demonstrated reality is also ruled out by his pragmatic method. Having early been beset with doubts and recognizing the legitimacy of Chauncey Wright's cool scientific demonstrations of the indifference of the physical world to human needs and desires, James made it his life-long task to demonstrate the reality of a world of co-operating spirits separated from the everyday world of experience by the thinnest of veils that was sometimes penetrated. The experiential point of entry had to be both demonstrable according to the accepted protocols of experimental method on the one hand, and properly other-worldly on the other.

In the Foreword to *Closer to the Light*, Raymond Moody reports that Dr. Melvin Morse has found such a point of entry in an area of the brain close to the right temporal lobe which he says 'is genetically coded for near-death experiences' and in *Cleansing the Doors of Perception*, Huston Smith says that mind-altering substances which he calls entheogens 'hold the possibility of opening the doors of perception to the sacred unconscious'.[67] The evidence of subliminal experiences satisfied James' scientific requirements as to the real possibility of such a point of entry in this world, as a certain area of the brain does for Morse, and altered states of consciousness brought on by entheogens do for Smith, but the needed demonstration of the reality of the world beyond this world which penetrated from the other side was, for James, on shakier ground. It was attested to by mediums and their clients through seances. The near-death experiences are reported to Morse by his patients, and Smith describes his own experiences and what others report of what happens after taking mescaline and other drugs. In all these cases, what needs to be established, according to James, is whether the self-reporting of receiving communications from beyond or of having 'psychedelic theophanies' are what they seemed to be.

Although it may be an issue for those who do not share his belief in the many levels of reality beyond the merely mundane, for James, there is no a priori reason not to accept the experiences as described by those who have them. Indeed, many of the mystical experiences described by James in the *Varieties* sound like the sense of the sacred experienced by Smith. They may even be found attributable to the same combination of chemical processes in the brain with some tradition of religious beliefs, language, and imagery. But whether the referents of such experiences exist in just the ways they are perceived or the content of the experience is disclosive of the reality as it is interpreted or understood by the one having the experience, is another issue. James reluctantly concludes the *Varieties of Religious Experience* with the admission that '[f]acts . . . are yet lacking to prove "spirit return"'.[68] Morse and Smith think they do have such facts. James' philosophy of radical empiricism does not dogmatically exclude either the reality of the experiences or the interpretation given them. Neither does it ratify either without experimental evidence. But do his pragmatic criteria for ascertaining the truth of such claims really eliminate false assertions?

I use criteria in the plural because James gives several different explanations of the pragmatic method. These include the marriage function of traditional beliefs with novel happenings, the pragmatic hermeneutic circle, and a leading that is worthwhile. Since a belief is that on which we are prepared to act, and if having acted on it, our expectations are met, then such a belief is by that process justified, so long as it is not contradicted by further experiences or by what we already know to be the case (unless our new experience causes us to revise and rearrange the store of beliefs we already have).

But James does not distinguish between the evidentiary values of claims about the existence or non-existence of external objects like tigers or Harvard's Memorial Hall, which can be predicated and then reached in space and time by anyone who cares to try, and religious beliefs in unseen objects like gods or spirits, which are attested to only indirectly by the character of the lives of those who believe in them. How odd this is can be seen if we used the religious criterion for tigers in India, which could be proved simply by acting as though they existed; for example, by writing stories about them, collecting the food they supposedly eat and describing their habitats, dancing in tiger-like movements, and always acting as though they existed, but without ever having to actually come into the presence of one and providing directions that anyone else could also follow and get the same results. We know that such circumstantial evidence is enough for many people to believe in the Loch Ness monster or in Big Foot, but James thought that the pragmatic method would be able to distinguish true from false beliefs.

Despite James' recognition that mystics' experiences did not carry with them any factual evidence of their interpretation of what it was they were experiencing, he is less scrupulous when the interpretation is left deliberately vague. He claims, for example, that the evidence of the religious experiences he has been reporting 'unequivocally testifies to [the fact] that we can experience union with *something* larger than ourselves and in that union find our greatest peace'.[69] Perhaps this is because he wants to undermine the monotheistic bias of the mystics he has been presenting but does not want to cast doubt on their claims to transcend the limits of this world. He presses the point that the facts do not require the existence of a singular, all-powerful deity, but only that some power or powers larger than our conscious selves are friendly to human beings and our ideals.

He himself is more comfortable with a pluralistic hypothesis of multiple higher beings who require our cooperation in order to save the world. Better to leave some parts of the world unsaved and some persons irretrievably lost through our failures, than to believe in an Absolute God in whom all things will come right. Since such an Absolute power needs nothing from us, belief in his existence will fail to elicit our utmost efforts and thus fail to serve as an all-inspiring ideal of conduct. This is important because conduct is observable, while the identity of the object of mystical experience is not.

Even those who have had an experience of the same sort can have an interest in making explicit the conditions which bring such experiences about. James calls this effort

> following up the suggestions nascently present in them, working in the direction they seem to point, clearing up the penumbra, making distinct the halo, unraveling the fringe, which is part of their composition, and in the midst of which their more substantive kernel of subjective content seems consciously to lie.[70]

This effort to unravel the fringe, to investigate the conditions responsible for religious experiences, would be a science of religions in the only sense in which James takes religion, namely as personally experienced. Morse, for example, does allude to some scientific studies to bolster his position. Do his explanations provide stronger evidence of the conditions responsible for religious experiences than James did a century ago?

Morse says that '[s]olar storms which generate bursts of electromagnetic radiation have been shown to affect human behavior', and '[p]ower-line electromagnetism has been linked to an increase in suicides and a decrease in neurochemicals serotonin and dopamine which control such things as sleep and mood'.[71] After adding some stories of electric currents inducing limb regeneration, Morse says 'I mention these studies to demonstrate that this "unseen power" has in fact been well researched.'[72] Neither the precise scientific studies of which these are the conclusions nor studies which challenge these conclusions are cited or discussed. As readers, we do not have enough evidence to decide whether these studies have been well researched or not. Even if they were found to be well verified, they wouldn't demonstrate the truth of his claims.

Despite his disavowal of relying on merely anecdotal evidence, the book is filled with just such reports, together with speculation about possible explanations. To give just one example. After reporting a patient's story of a near-death experience she had while suffering from scarlet fever, Morse says: 'She had a strong feeling that it had led to her rapid healing.'[73] He then asks whether it really did and answers 'I think it triggered an electromagnetic charge that stimulated her body's immune system.'[74] That's it. She thinks so and he thinks so and it might have been due to an electromagnetic charge because Dr. Becker, a bio-electric researcher, says such things could happen, and after all, 'the human body is a machine driven by energy'.[75] These surmises could be formulated into a testable hypothesis and then tested, but they have not been.

Charles Sanders Peirce thinks there is little to constrain those sanguine beliefs which are not contradicted by experience. Even a lifetime of experiential checks on our willingness to believe whatever suits us best does not dampen our enthusiasm. 'Where hope is unchecked by any experience,' according to Peirce, 'it is likely that our optimism is extravagant.'[76] He goes so far as to argue that there may even be an evolutionary advantage to certain fallacious tendencies of thought insofar as such pleasing and encouraging visions buoy up our spirits, independently of their truth. But for those like Peirce, for whom the truth of their beliefs is a concern, a habit of mind 'is good or otherwise, according as it produces true conclusions from true premises or not'. James certainly wanted to believe just as strongly as Morse does, but as someone who well knew our propensity to believe what we wanted to believe, he also wanted—at least in his better moments—better evidence than self-reporting, no matter how many times these were multiplied. It is this holding out for evidence, as much as his willingness to support even unpopular hypotheses and improbable beliefs, that makes James' approach non-dogmatic. And as such, it is a healthy antidote to an unrestrained will to believe. But when it comes to what counts as experiential evidence, the shape-shifting aspect of experience from subjective apprehension to intended object and then back again to subjective feel is finally too ambiguous to discriminate the demonstrable from the merely desirable. James undercuts even the minimal requirements he gives of what would constitute a critical science of religions when he says that it not only takes personal experiences as its subject matter, but that its critical reconstructions should also 'square itself with personal experiences' without adding, as John Dewey does, that the reconstructed experience is a transformation of, not simply a reproduction or repetition of, the original experience.[77]

James brackets his proposal for a science of religions between two withering criticisms of philosophy and science as having any right to adjudicate religious claims or pass judgment on the reality of religious experiences. In Chapter 18, he rejects 'the pretensions of philosophy to found religion on universal reason' because logical reasoning is limited to claims of universal validity and religion is a matter of feelings and personal experiences.[78] The divine presence vouched for in mystical experiences is a factual claim based on feelings, which are not subject to the veto of abstract reasoning. And in Chapter 20, he worries that the materialist bias of the sciences makes it all too likely that they will fail to recognize the truth of religious beliefs. He counters this by limiting the scope of science to questions of objectivity and situating religion within the realm of subjective experiences, in which alone reality is to be had.[79] Religious experience is, finally, declared impervious to both philosophic and scientific attacks.[80] Why, then, bother to appeal to a science of religions at all?

According to James, the science of religions can only answer some of our intellectual needs.[81] It cannot replace or defeat psychic or religious experiences. It can only make some of the claims made about such experiences more or less plausible. But philosophy and science will only have something positive to contribute to determining the objective truth of religious claims when they cease to be dogmatic and become experimental. Only when they abandon metaphysics and reject a priori reasoning,[82] only when they cease trying to coerce beliefs by the force of their arguments and instead humbly adopt the hypothetical stance,[83] will they have anything of value to offer to religious discussions.

A science of religions, as James conceives it, would 'abandon metaphysics and deduction for criticism and induction'.[84] In its critical function it would eliminate the local and accidental by determining what is common and essential in religious beliefs.[85] This includes removing historic encrustations from dogma and worship and anything incongruous with the natural sciences. In its empirical function, it will examine the widest variety of religious experiences. What is left will be treated as a hypothesis to be tested both positively and negatively. Mere symbolism and over-beliefs can by this means be distinguished from what is to be taken literally. James hopes that because they have been arrived at non-dogmatically by an experimental method, these hypotheses can then mediate among conflicting religious beliefs and at last bring about consensus of opinion where now there is only dissension and acrimony.

However, James' own anti-dogmatic assumptions, radically empiricist principles, and concrete findings make it highly unlikely that such a science could effectively perform its functions. He has vindicated his claim that pragmatism has no rigid canons of what shall count as proof, but only by holding fast to his own prejudice or dogma that his investigations of reports of religious experience 'unequivocally testify to' the fact 'that we can experience union with *something* larger than ourselves and that in that union find our greatest peace'.[86] Since he has already questioned the possibility of there being only one type of ideal human character and holds as a postulate of the empirical method that conclusions are always matters of relation, changing with changing circumstances and beliefs, how can such a hoped-for science ever mediate successfully between such a non-negotiable claim and any other?[87] Any verdict reached 'will vary according to the point of view adopted'.[88] After re-emphasizing that the science of religions is utterly dependent on personal experiences in all their variety, James flatly denies that any verbal formulation can capture the truth and fact of lived religious experiences.

But what is the use of an impartial science of religions formulating a common body of doctrine which is unobjectionable to science if 'religion must be considered vindicated in a certain way from the attacks of her critics' insofar as it already exerts 'a permanent function, whether she be with or without intellectual content?'.[89] Does James even mean to hold religious experience accountable to scientific confirmation or refutation if he already feels that personal religious experiences are intrinsically subjective and non-interchangeable? His attempts to institute a science of religions falters on his own anti-dogmatism, which secures its status by eliminating all doctrines and all verbal formulations as being so much hollowness and irrelevancy, and therefore eliminating anything remotely testable by experimental methods.[90]

5 An Alternative Hypothesis

John Dewey could never have subtitled a book on *The Varieties of Religious Experience* as James did: namely as *A Study in Human Nature*. In his own book on *Human Nature and Conduct*, which is subtitled *An Introduction to Social Psychology*, religious experiences are not even among the human experiences he examines.[91] In *Experience and Nature* the reason why this is so becomes clear. Dewey turns on its head James' invocation of the anguish, pain, and suffering that the melancholic person is sensitive enough to acknowledge and attribute to the irremediable evil of the world, a feeling of personal failure from which James thought that 'the need of a God very definitely emerges'.[92] Dewey instead blames cynicism, indifference, and pessimism for preventing people from acknowledging that common experience has sufficient resources for intelligently directing one's life and that we need no extrinsic standards of judgment or value for overcoming evils and deficiencies.[93]

Disillusionment with life and tragic failure are attributed to losing touch with concrete experience, rather than with its full acceptance. Where James criticizes philosophies and religions that focus on happiness as the meaning of life for ignoring the very real evils that are just as much a part of life, Dewey blames them for obscuring 'the potentialities of daily experience for joy and for self-regulation'.[94] Both James and Dewey want, in Dewey's words, to create and promote 'respect for concrete human experience and its potentialities', but differ greatly in what they think constitutes experience and its intelligent appropriation.

The problem with both materialists and spiritualists, according to Dewey, is that they convert traits of experience that are operational and relational into entities. James' subliminal explosions bursting through the boundaries of consciousness to take palpable form as glimpses of a parallel spiritual world is an example of what Dewey calls 'ghosts walking underground'.[95] Dewey agrees that it is a mark of intelligence to strive 'to make stability of meaning prevail over the instability of events', but this effort is too often 'dropped from the province of art and treated as the property of given things'.[96] Only when the precarious, perilous, and uncertain nature of existence is treated as a scandal offensive to our longing for stable, sure, regular, and harmonious experiences as James does, only when 'the existing mixture of the regular and dependable with the unsettled and uncertain' is treated as two separate realms does the need arise to create a parallel world above, below, or behind the world of everyday experience to house one of them.[97] Out of this conversion of different aspects of the world into different worlds of existence is created the contrasting philosophies feeding off these dualisms such as spiritualism/materialism, transcendentalism/positivism, rationalism/sensationalism, and idealism/realism.[98]

James is appalled at the eventual disintegration of ourselves and those we love. Nor can he reconcile himself to the evils, suffering, and cruelty that recur with numbing regularity throughout life. Dewey's laconic response to these revulsions is that nothing lasts forever. In mind-numbing understatement, he says that this realization 'is discomfiting when applied to good things, to our friends, possessions and precious selves', and continues 'it is consoling also to know that no evil endures forever'.[99] He fears that attitudes such as James expresses distract people from choosing what goods to pursue and what evils to transform by developing ideals to inspire and guide conduct and instead lead them into seeking 'a refuge, an asylum for contemplation' in other-worldliness.[100] James, in his turn, thinks that the experience of intractable evil and suffering and the inevitability of one's own death will be paralyzing to sensitive natures like his own, who need reassurance that their efforts to eradicate evil will not finally be in vain and their lives will not be snuffed out forever. As we have seen, he characterized these two approaches to life as that of the sick soul and that of the healthy soul.

Whether the sick soul more truly grasps the actual world as it is concretely experienced, as James thought, or the healthy soul does, as Dewey thought, they both agreed as pragmatists that the truth should not be determined by personal need or preference alone, but only as tempered by observation and experiment.[101] But Dewey rejects outright the search for a refuge in other-worldliness by choosing instead to grapple with the problems and sorrows of the present world. James, despite his rejection of such refuges when described as merely contemplative, chooses to believe in the comforts provided to the sick soul by active interventions from beyond in preference to the requirements of Dewey's robustly healthy soul. Such are our choices.

Notes

1. R. A. McDermott, Introduction to W. James (1986) *Essays in Psychical Research* (Cambridge, MA: Harvard University Press), p. xix.
2. W. James (1901) 'Frederic Myer's Service to Psychology' in *Essays in Psychical Research*, p. 197.
3. W. James (1984) *The Varieties of Religious Experience* (New York: Penguin American Library), pp. 433, 455–6.
4. W. James (1975) *Pragmatism* (Cambridge, MA: Harvard University Press), pp. 32–3.

52 William James on Religion

5. Ibid., p. 32.
6. Ibid., p. 43–4.
7. Ibid., p. 32.
8. C. H. Seigfried (1990) *William James's Radical Reconstruction of Philosophy* (Albany: State University of New York Press), pp. 238–9.
9. W. James (1976) *Essays in Radical Empiricism* (Cambridge, MA: Harvard University Press), p. 81.
10. W. James (1975) *The Meaning of Truth* (Cambridge, MA: Harvard University Press), pp. 6–7. James' claim that relations are directly experienced is defended in C. H. Seigfried (1978) *Chaos and Context: A Study in William James* (Athens, OH: Ohio University Press).
11. James, *The Varieties of Religious Experience*, p. 151.
12. James, *Pragmatism*, p. 44.
13. James, *The Meaning of Truth*, p. 47.
14. Ibid., p. 47.
15. Ibid., p. 49.
16. I am using pragmatism and humanism as equivalent. For James' unsuccessful attempts to distinguish them, see Seigfried, *William James's Radical Reconstruction*, pp. 282–8.
17. James, *The Meaning of Truth*, p. 49.
18. Ibid., p. 49.
19. James, *Pragmatism*, p. 122; Seigfried, *William James's Radical Reconstruction*, pp. 231, 250, 297. See also *Pragmatism*, p. 108.
20. James, *Pragmatism*, p. 34.
21. Ibid., p. 35.
22. Ibid., pp. 38–9.
23. Ibid., p. 37.
24. Ibid., p. 39.
25. Ibid., p. 43.
26. James, *The Varieties of Religious Experience*, pp. 522, 507.
27. Ibid., p. 447.
28. For James' inability to accept women and other marginalized ethnic and racial groups as fully human, see chapter 6, 'The Feminine Mystical Threat to the Scientific-Masculine Order', in C. H. Seigfried (1996) *Pragmatism and Feminism: Reweaving the Social Fabric* (Chicago: University of Chicago Press), pp. 111–41.
29. See C. H. Seigfried (2000) 'The Philosopher's "License": William James and Common Sense' in K. Oehler (ed.) *William James: Pragmatism* (Berlin: Akademie Verlag), pp. 93–110. James always characterizes philosophers as male and takes mysticism as a more typically female experience. See Seigfried, *Pragmatism and Feminism*, pp. 131–41.
30. James, *The Varieties of Religious Experience*, p. 510.
31. As Sami Pihlström argues, and the preceding pages explain, James' humanized pragmatism means that no higher perspective on truth and falsity is available to us than our own best, most critical practices. However, it also seems clear that the warrant James seeks would be epistemically as well as religiously convincing. I am arguing that James fails to prove his religious claims according to his own well-founded pragmatist criteria. Pihlström's

recognition of 'a deep structural analogy between pragmatically reconstructed transcendental arguments and Jamesian will to believe arguments' seems a promising way to reconstruct James' position to make it more plausible. S. Pihlström (2008) *'The Trail of the Human Serpent is Over Everything': Jamesian Perspectives on Mind, World, and Religion* (Lanham, MD: University Press of America), pp. 46–7.
32. Quoted in R. B. Perry (1935) *The Thought and Character of William James*, Vol. 2 (Boston: Little, Brown), p. 455.
33. W. James (1979) *The Will to Believe* (Cambridge, MA: Harvard University Press), p. 141.
34. He actually says 'the last man'.
35. James, *The Will to Believe*, p. 20.
36. Ibid., p. 160.
37. Ibid., pp. 158–9.
38. Ibid., p. 161.
39. James, *The Varieties of Religious Experience*, p. 413.
40. Ibid., p. 138.
41. Ibid., p. 136.
42. Ibid., pp. 363–4.
43. Ibid., p. 139.
44. Ibid., pp. 139–41.
45. Ibid., p. 501.
46. Ibid., p. 327.
47. Ibid., p. 236n1.
48. Ibid., p. 235.
49. Ibid., pp. 235–6.
50. Ibid., p. 236n.
51. Ibid., p. 237.
52. R. A. Moody, foreword, in M. Morse with P. Perry (1990) *Closer to the Light* (New York: Villard Books), p. xii; M. Morse with P. Perry (1990) *Transformed by the Light* (New York: Villard Books), p. ix.
53. James, *The Varieties of Religious Experience*, p. 413.
54. See chapter 7, 'Interpretive Theory and Praxis', in Seigfried, *William James's Radical Reconstruction*, pp. 173–207.
55. James, *The Meaning of Truth*, pp. 23–4.
56. William James (1981 [1890]) *The Principles of Psychology* (Cambridge, MA: Harvard University Press), Vol. 2, pp. 923–4.
57. Seigfried, *William James's Radical Reconstruction*, p. 192; James, *The Principles of Psychology*, Vol. 2, p. 935.
58. James, *The Varieties of Religious Experience*, 374, 377.
59. Ibid., p. 376.
60. Ibid., p. 377.
61. Ibid., p. 523.
62. Ibid., p. 525.
63. Ibid., pp. 523–4.
64. W. James (1986 [1901]) 'Frederic Myer's Service to Psychology' in *Essays in Psychical Research* (Cambridge, MA: Harvard University Press), pp. 192–201.

54 *William James on Religion*

65. James, *Essays in Psychical Research*, p. 193.
66. Ibid., p. 194.
67. Moody, *Closer to the Light*, p. xi; and H. Smith (2000) *Cleansing the Doors of Perception* (New York: Jeremy P. Tarcher/Putnam), pp. xvi, 78.
68. James, *The Varieties of Religious Experience*, p. 524.
69. Ibid., p. 525.
70. James, *The Meaning of Truth*, p. 29.
71. Morse, *Closer to the Light*, p. 137.
72. Ibid., p. 141.
73. Ibid., p. 150.
74. Ibid., p. 150.
75. Ibid., p. 151.
76. C. S. Peirce (1982) *Pragmatism: The Classic Writings*, ed. H. S. Thayer (Indianapolis: Hackett), p. 64.
77. James, *The Varieties of Religious Experience*, p. 456.
78. Ibid., p. 436.
79. Ibid., pp. 498–9.
80. Ibid., p. 507.
81. In a companion essay to this one, I question James' sanguine belief that religious beliefs have nothing to fear from scientific scrutiny. I also argue that Dewey took up James' naturalistic religious project and exposed his biased assumptions and faulty reasoning, while also missing his own subjective assumptions in regard to science. See C. H. Seigfried (2012) 'Distinguishing Myth from Reality: Are Pragmatic Tools Sufficient?', *Revue Internationale de Philosophie*, 66 (260), Special issue on William James, pp. 187–205.
82. James, *The Varieties of Religious Experience*, p. 455.
83. Ibid., p. 511.
84. Ibid., p. 455.
85. Ibid., p. 456.
86. Ibid., p. 525.
87. Ibid., p. 374.
88. Ibid., p. 376.
89. Ibid., pp. 510, 507.
90. Ibid., p. 457.
91. J. Dewey (1957 [1922]) *Human Nature and Conduct* (New York: Modern Library). He does mention religious experience in passing when he criticizes James' defense of taking moral holidays, pp. 242–3, and, like James, he thinks that institutional religion fosters dogmatism and intolerance, pp. 301–2.
92. James, *The Varieties of Religious Experience*, p. 138n2.
93. J. Dewey (1988) *Experience and Nature*, in *Later Works*, Vol. 1: 1925 (Carbondale and Edwardsville: Southern Illinois University Press), p. 41.
94. Ibid., p. 41.
95. Ibid., p. 65.
96. Ibid., p. 49.
97. Ibid., pp. 52–3.
98. Ibid., p. 46.
99. Ibid., pp. 63–4.

100. Ibid., p. 51.
101. Although James thought that whether one was a sick or a healthy soul was more a matter of temperament than choice, and that either approach can lead to union with the divine, he rated the sick or twice-born soul more highly in that its outlook on life was wider and completer and it did not evade evil (James, *The Varieties of Religious Experience*, p. 488n1).

3
The Varieties and the Cognitive Value of Religious Experiences

Niek Brunsveld[1]

When analyzing William James' philosophy of religion, we often turn to his explicit writings on religion, e.g. in his *The Varieties of Religious Experience*,[2] and to his theoretical views on cognition, experience, and epistemology, such as in *The Principles of Psychology, A Pluralistic Universe*, and *Essays in Radical Empiricism*.[3] There is much debate, however, on what James' views are on such basic issues as consciousness, experience, and truth.[4] This chapter establishes whether, from a pragmatist perspective, religious experiences can have cognitive value. Instead of turning to James' theoretical writings on these issues, however, I analyze his more empirical *The Varieties of Religious Experience: A Study in Human Nature* in answering this question.

In order to see whether James' perspective on the cognitive value of religious experiences is tenable with regard to its basic notions of truth and experience, I will evaluate it on the basis of Hilary Putnam's pragmatic pluralist perspective on truth and experience. Putnam's pragmatic pluralist perspective on truth and experience depends strongly on James' philosophy, especially with regard to Putnam's views on philosophy of mind.[5] As we will see, however, Putnam and James differ about whether religious experiences should in principle be taken as similar to experiences of other aspects of reality. To Putnam, as we will see, experiences are transactions between human beings and their environment. When it comes to religious experiences, however, he makes an exception.[6] This analysis of James' *Varieties* allows us to see whether religious experiences can be transactions between people and their environment in a way similar to other, non-religious experiences.

In *The Varieties*, James does not reflect on the notions of truth and experience as systematically as he does in other works, such as *Essays in Radical Empiricism*,[7] 'A World of Pure Experience',[8] and *Pragmatism*.[9]

What is pivotal about an analysis of these issues in his *Varieties* is that this provides a perspective on James' notion of cognitive value with regard to religious experience, as inferred from his use of cognitive aspects of religious experience.

Analyzing James' seminal work in this manner attests to the possibility of approaching religious experiences and religious propositions in a manner not discontinuous with other, non-religious experiences and propositions. This should provide a fruitful perspective on how, contrary to Putnam's viewpoints on the same matter, religious experiences *are* transactions between the religious believer and her surroundings from a pragmatist perspective.

1 Preliminary Remarks about James on the Truth-value of Religious Experience

In analyzing James' perspective on the truth-value of religious experiences in *The Varieties*, it is pivotal to realize that this perspective is not necessarily congruous with his explicit views on truth and experience in other, more theoretical writings. Furthermore, it should be remembered that my interest here is not so much a full-blown analysis of James' views on truth and experience, or even a comprehensive view of these notions in *The Varieties*. Rather, this chapter means to show whether and how, in that work, religious experiences have cognitive value.

A first delimitation of my analysis is that I will not turn to James' explicit writings on truth and experience,[10] but rather to his more implicit views on the cognitive value of religious experiences in *The Varieties*. Only to a small extent will it provide insights into James' views on truth with regard to (religious) experience. It will, however, provide us with a perspective on the relationship of religious experience to truth, and thus allows answering the question about whether religious experiences have cognitive value, and are transactions similar to experiences other than religious ones.

We should also turn briefly to the term 'religious experience'. I understand experience both ontologically and phenomenologically. An 'experience' can denote the experienced object, such as the experienced 'cat' when perceiving my cat, as well as the event of experience in which we perceive an object or a property, such as 'experiencing my cat' when perceiving my cat.[11] With Putnam, I would argue that we should not delimit 'experience' to a state internal to the mind.[12] Extrapolating on that notion, I would argue that religious experiences, if there are any, should also be conceived of as events that involve a transaction between an individual and the individual's surroundings.

In this analysis, I take the meaning of 'religious experience' to go beyond a theistic understanding of the same.[13] Although James has a well-known understanding of religion as 'the belief that there is an unseen order, and that our supreme good lies in harmoniously adjusting ourselves thereto',[14] he himself is aware of the difficulties of defining religion.[15] Among other reasons because he does not want to force the definition onto his study subjects, he does not discuss those subjects who, in his view, have described a religious understanding of their experience but who would reject such a claim themselves, under the rubric of *religious* mystical experiences but rather under 'mystical experiences without explicit religious significance'.[16] Though James had a rather clear picture of what it is to be religious, for his study into the notion of mystical religious experiences the debate is not about what counts and what does not count as religious but rather about whether mystical religious experiences have epistemic import. In a similar vein, my investigation delves not into the nature of religion but into the cognitive value of what we take as religious experiences.[17]

2 James on Truth and Experience in *The Varieties*

With the delimitations of this investigation into James' notion of the truth-value of religious propositions in mind, I turn to an analysis of how experience functions in determining the truth of religious propositions in James' thinking on religious experience. What I will establish here is whether and how experiential access to religious aspects of reality, in James' view, allows for religious propositions to have truth-value.

In coming to understand James' views on the role of truth and experience in the various forms of mystical (religious) experience, we come to an analysis of the truth-value of these experiences. A number of aspects will turn out to be central to this analysis: James' stress on the role of experience and feeling, not philosophy and rationalism, in cognition;[18] James' contemplations concerning the convincingness of religious experiences to those subject to them, but possible unconvincingness to those not subject to them; and James' conviction that a '[m]an's thinking is organically connected with his conduct',[19] which has important repercussions on how conceptual and practical abilities relate. As we will see, these aspects connect intimately with Putnam's pragmatic pluralist perspective on the role of conceptual and practical abilities in truth and experience.

2.1 James' Study of Mystical and Religious Experiences in *The Varieties*

James sets out to study religious experiences from a psychologist's point of view, which he holds implies among other things that 'not religious institutions, but rather religious feelings and religious impulses must be its subject'.[20] To James, individual experiences are at the root of religions.[21] The personal religious experiences and the beliefs that have come to be held on the basis of them have primacy over the institutional religious beliefs: 'In critically judging of the value of religious phenomena, it is very important to insist on the distinction between religion as an individual personal function, and religion as an institutional, corporate, or tribal product.'[22] It is with the former that James engages in this work, since these are the authentically 'religious' experiences, not tainted with a-religious and anti-religious powers.[23]

According to James, 'personal religious experience has its root and centre in mystical states of consciousness'.[24] He takes mystical experiences to have two necessary and a further two recurrent aspects.[25] Subjects of mystical experiences hold that the experience cannot be adequately expressed. To understand it, one must have experienced it oneself, much like having a particular feeling. This is what James calls a mystical experience's 'ineffability'. The second necessary component is its 'noetic quality', which points at the cognitive or intellectual aspects of such experiences. Even though their content is hard to communicate, mystical experiences have intellectual qualities. The further two aspects that often go with mystical states of consciousness are their brevity and their passive nature, the latter of which denotes the fact that even though subjects can sometimes invoke mystical states of consciousness, once he or she has such a state it feels to the subject as if his or her 'own will were in abeyance'.[26]

James claims that his is first of all a *descriptive* analysis of the phenomenon of mystical religious experiences. In answering the question 'What are the religious propensities?',[27] one seeks to answer what the nature of something is, how it came about, and what its constitution, origin, and history are.[28] The various examples of religious and non-religious mystical states of consciousness that James addresses speak of the impression they have left on the subjects of their truth, and of the revelatory import that subjects cannot but ascribe to it. And James sees no reason, on beforehand, to question that this be so. It is from such a 'purely existential point of view'[29] that James sets out to study the phenomena. This is in rather stark contrast with Putnam's tendency to take religion as not directed at reality.

2.2 Truth and Experience in Mystical Experiences without Explicit Religious Weight

James starts out with a principally descriptive analysis of 'some typical examples'[30] of mystical experiences that 'claim no special religious significance'.[31] There are various degrees of mystical experiences of this kind. A first more 'rudimentary' such experience consists of having a 'deepened sense of the significance of a maxim or formula'[32] swept over one. James then describes two kinds of mystical experience of a 'dreamy state', i.e. 'sudden invasions of vaguely reminiscent consciousness',[33] which we would call *déjà-vus*, and a feeling of finding oneself surrounded with meaning and truths, both of which form a second, more 'pronounced' class. A more radical kind of mystical experiences, for which subjects increasingly fail to find appropriate descriptions, include those in which the subject loses all senses of time and space, and self. James dismisses the idea that these states are necessarily pathological.[34] A further class that James turns to, and with which he claims to have some experience himself, is those experiences generated by intoxicating substances.

As to the content of these mystical experiences without explicit religious import, James notes that

> [l]ooking back on my own experiences, they all converge towards a kind of insight to which I cannot help ascribing some metaphysical significance. The keynote of it is invariably a reconciliation. It is as if the opposite of the world, whose contradictoriness and conflict make all our difficulties and troubles, were melted into unity. ... [I]t is a monistic insight, in which the *other* in its various forms appears absorbed into the One.[35]

This conforms to James' findings on what others have reported about the content of their mystical experiences.[36] There is a sense of conflicts being settled, both in a metaphysical and in what one could call a moral sense. What, in a non-mystical state of consciousness, are deemed opposite aspects of reality is one and the same in these mystical states.[37] Where good and bad are thought to be on equal footing in non-mystical states, mystical experiences reveal 'the nobler and better'[38] aspect of reality to soak up and absorb the less noble and inferior one.

On the basis of James' descriptions, we can conclude that James takes it as a matter of fact that mystical states of consciousness during which subjects have these experiences[39] can be induced by various means, such as chloroform, nitrous oxide, anesthetics,[40] but also 'a warm glow of light'.[41] Thus, he does not deny that these experiences may come about through abnormal physical circumstances. Yet, this does not persuade him to deny that the alternate experiences of reality themselves (e.g. experiences of being one with the Unseen) are real, and that the alternate aspects of reality experienced (e.g. a reality whose opposites have united) may be real. Let us turn to these two observations.

For the cognitive value of the mystical experience, James' views imply, first, that the alternate experience of reality itself is real.[42] No matter how the experience has been triggered, it is nevertheless an experience. To James, as said, experiences have primacy over our philosophical deliberations, and thus also over our philosophical deliberations about what is to count as a real experience. James contends that we have no a priori reasons to dismiss the experience as a real experience just because it has been brought about through unconventional means. '[O]ur normal waking consciousness, rational consciousness as we call it, is but one special type of consciousness, whilst all about it, parted from it by the filmiest of screens, there lie potential forms of consciousness entirely different'.[43] There is no reason for privileging, on beforehand, one sort of experience, e.g. the experience of the naturalistic kind, over another, such as the mystical experience. Although this does not imply that experiences can then function unimpeded as sufficient warrant for beliefs about reality, since our perceptions are corrigible and can therefore be flawed,[44] it does show that in James' view a subject's perceptions should be taken at face value, i.e. as experiences with at least some cognitive import.

Secondly, the alternate aspects of reality that these mystical experiences suggest may be real. As there is no a priori reason for privileging experiences of the naturalistic kind over mystical experiences, just like the experiences themselves cannot be dismissed, the reality that the subjects experience cannot be written off a priori either, e.g. by reference to the manner in which it was perceived. 'No account of the universe in its totality can be final which leaves these other forms of consciousness quite disregarded.'[45] James is aware, of course, of the diversity of mystical experiences, their inexpressibility, and their inconclusiveness: 'How to regard them is the question—for they are so discontinuous with ordinary consciousness. Yet they may determine attitudes though they cannot furnish formulas, and open a region though they fail to give a map.'[46] Until we have reasons to assume that the insights are flawed, we have no reasons to presume that the reality they induce is not real. These views on the cognitive value of religious experiences turn the rationalist's argument around, a finding to which we will turn shortly.

2.3 Truth and Experience in Mystical Experiences with Explicit Religious Weight

The continuum of mystical experiences stretches from those without religious pretensions to those that are said to have special religious significance. This latter group, instances of which James holds not to be uncommon, centers on those mystical states of consciousness that include a 'sudden realization of the immediate presence of God'.[47] In between are mystical experiences of nature's and cosmic unifying reality. In my analysis of James' descriptions, I will focus on the perceptual and cognitive value that is attributed to these states of consciousness, i.e. on the question of whether and how these experiences are real and veridical, and if they can function in attaining true insights into (religious) reality.

Before turning to experiences that are placed, by their subjects, in particular religious traditions, James quotes a number of passages that speak of mystical experiences that seem to be triggered and fueled by the outdoors, and that have cosmic significance. James holds that these examples should at least convince his audience that there are mystical states of 'an entirely specific quality',[48] and that these have a significant impact on those subject to them. The passages that he quotes speak, in one way or another, of the cognitive insights that these experiences generate, e.g. 'I know ... that all the men ever born are also my brothers and the women my sisters and lovers',[49] and 'the spiritual life [...] is a life whose experiences are proved real to their possessor'.[50] This connects to what it means for them to be of an 'entirely specific quality'. In addressing this quality, James introduces, approvingly it seems, psychiatrist R. M. Bucke's term 'cosmic consciousness', with which Bucke means to convey that subjects in these mental states are conscious 'of the cosmos, of the life and order of the universe'.[51] The enlightenment, as Bucke calls it, is intellectual. It provides knowledge of the eternal scheme of things, and into the moral order of the universe.[52] Instead of addressing this supposed cognitive aspect of mystical experiences, James turns first to examples of religious experiences from particular religious traditions.

In James' analyses of mystical experiences with religious pretensions, as he calls this group, issues of knowledge, reason, and intellect are again central, and he addresses them somewhat more explicitly here. In mentioning of the yoga traditions in India, he quotes the nineteenth-century yoga theorist Swami Vivekananda who describes the state that the yogi can attain, called *samâdhi*, as providing cognitive insights that go beyond reason, as receptive to the 'Truth', especially about our state in the universe.⁵³ James further contends that the Vedantic belief that one can judge whether someone has really attained *samâdhi* by the subject's subsequent practices is similar to his views on judging religion's value, since it is the empirical test that 'its fruits must be good for life'.⁵⁴ According to James, Buddhists know this state of consciousness *samâdhi* too, but they also take there to be higher states of consciousness, known as *dhyâna*. However, unlike in the case of *samâdhi*, higher states of *dhyâna* consciousness lose their intellectual aspect. Instead, 'indifference, memory, and self-consciousness are perfected'.⁵⁵ About this James contends, however, that in this higher state of consciousness memory and self-consciousness cannot be similar to the same faculties in non-mystical or lower mystical states, as in this latter state they *are* connected to intellect. I take it that he believes it is 'doubtful' what memory and self-consciousness come down to in the case of higher states of consciousness, because, in his view, these faculties are always tied up with the intellect, whereas there they are separated.

In James' lengthy quotation from al-Ghazālī's autobiographical writings on the latter's personal experiences with Sufi methods of mysticism, the issue of knowledge through mystical consciousness is central. Al-Ghazālī differentiates between, on the one hand, learning about, and having the actual experiences of being absorbed in God on the other. Since the experience goes beyond perception of forms and figures one cannot, without sin against God, i.e. without betraying the true reality that one has experienced, give an account of the experience the subject has had. Therefore, the learnings of Sufi can never yield to the non-mystic the insights that Sufis themselves have. It is this 'incommunicableness' of the insights of mysticism that James zooms in on. Though the mystical religious experiences themselves are instances of communication between a (higher) reality and the mystic, the mystic cannot fully communicate the insights gained through the experiences to the non-mystic.⁵⁶ James holds that, therefore, the insights based on mystical experiences are truths to the mystic, not the non-mystic, and that these insights are more similar to insights based on sensations than those based on conceptual thought.⁵⁷ Just like sensations, one must have the mystical experiences oneself in order to understand them.

Both the sensory aspect of religious experiences and their cognitive import are basic to James' description of particular Christian mystical practices.⁵⁸ By making one 'ideal thing', such as an imaginary picture of Christ, fully occupy the mind through meditation, the mystic can detach himself or herself from other, outer sensations. Mystical experiences, in these imagery cases, can be communicated to others. However, higher states of consciousness where all sensory aspects have gone, even the imaginary representations in the mind, are 'insusceptible of any verbal description'.[59] James introduces St. John of the Cross' 'dark contemplation' as representative of what he takes to be the unanimity of mystical teachings on this ineffability. While the mystic receives knowledge in its most direct manner, translating it into language cannot do justice to the actual religious experience. Another lengthy quote of St. Teresa's *The Interior Castle* is to underline that for a mystic the truth of, and the truths transported by, the religious experience, such as God being in the mystic and the mystic in God, are at the same time incommunicable and undeniable.

As to the contents of the truths transported through both the sensory and the non-sensory experiences, James holds that these are various. They can be about this world, e.g. about nature, history, the future, meaning, etc. James holds, however, that 'the most important revelations are theological or metaphysical',[60] with which he means that they pertain to matter beyond the thisworldly order. While many may dismiss the insights generated by these religious experiences because of supposed pathological conditions of the mystics, James holds that only an inquiry into their fruits for life can tell us something about their value. Although James holds that mystical experiences have had much positive impact on the lives of many mystics, he also concedes that the positive impact would be misguided if the experiences themselves were erroneous.[61] In an attempt to come to an answer to the question of whether mystical consciousness can establish the truth of religious convictions, James provides a generalization of the 'outcome of the majority of them'.[62] James' summaries[63] lead him to conclude that 'the general traits of the mystic range of consciousness'[64] are pantheism, optimism, anti-naturalism, twice-bornness, and otherworldliness.[65] As the content of these states is not of our concern here, I proceed to the question of whether and how these experiences are thought to be veridical.

James' general stance seems to be that 'there is about mystical utterances an eternal unanimity which ought to make a critic stop and think'.[66] James explores the *authority* of religious experiences to mystics, and its repercussions for critics. While those who do not have the experiences cannot be expected to see their veracity, the fact that those who have those experiences *do* see their veracity counters the critic's claim that only non-mystical experiences can be veridical.[67] As mystical experiences are as much direct experiences of reality as many of our sensational experiences of reality are, and as the beliefs that the mystic holds on the basis of these experiences are therefore as 'rational' as ours are, the mystic is at least allowed to be convinced by these experiences, and to hold the beliefs that he or she has formed on the basis of them true. To James, however, this gives the mystic no right to presume that mystical experiences should have the same authority over those who have not had the experiences. Because these mystical experiences do not appeal to outsiders in the manner that they do to mystics, what they can justifiably evoke in the non-mystical mind is a 'presumption' concerning a possible world-view and possible truths. Furthermore, these experiences are only relatively commonly directed towards the earlier-mentioned philosophical outlooks,[68] but even if they were more unanimous this would not be a compelling reason to take them as authoritative. As they stem from a region of the mind that contains both the 'seraph and the snake', '[t]o come from thence is no infallible credential'.[69] Just as we need to test the experiences we have on the basis of our non-mystical senses in order to justifiably base beliefs on them, non-mystics have to test the mystical experiences by empirical method. James maintains, thus, that what his analysis has shown is that the non-mystical experience is just one manner of approaching the world, and that we cannot a priori dismiss mystical insights.

2.4 Religious Experiences and Truth

James thus insists on the potential veracity of religious experiences, and their cognitive import to those who have these experiences. On the other hand, he holds that the experiences themselves cannot be communicated fully with those who have not had them. What interests us here is not the content of the mystical experiences, such as whether the mystic consciousness is indeed pantheistic and optimistic, but what James takes to be the cognitive relevance of these experiences. It will then become apparent what James' presuppositions concerning perception and truth are with regard to religious experiences.

One of the most telling parts regarding the question basic to our investigation states that

> [i]t must always remain an open question whether mystical states may not possibly be such superior points of view, windows through which the mind looks out upon a more extensive and inclusive world. The difference of the views seen from the different mystical windows need not prevent us from entertaining this supposition. The wider world would in that case prove to have a mixed constitution like that of this world, that is all. ... We should have to use its

experiences by selecting and subordinating and substituting just as is our custom in this ordinary naturalistic world; we should be liable to error just as we are now; yet the counting in of that wider world of meanings, and the serious dealing with it, might, in spite of all the perplexity, be indispensable stages in our approach to the final fullness of the truth.[70]

It would seem that, behind these words, there lives for James a hope that the world as a mystical, religious state of mind knows it may be just as adequate, or perhaps even *more* true to the whole of reality, than the non-mystical mind's understanding.[71] If this hope were what had to justify the idea that the mystical state possibly has a more extensive and inclusive window to the world, then James' view would not be of use to the question of this chapter as to the potential transactional nature of religious experiences. His hope might have triggered James' stress on the possible superiority of this outlook, but what grounds his views on the indispensability of mystical experiences is the argument that mystical experiences possibly provide adequate or even superior access to the wider reality.[72]

James' conclusion that in our aim to understand the complex universe we should take into account not only the non-mystical but also the mystical experiences, I believe, is based on (1) the contention that, even if their outcomes are more diverse than the paradigm experiences that the sciences use, we have no a priori reasons to exclude particular experiences from our inquiries, on (2) the belief that we can approach both these kinds of experiences in a fallibilist manner, which allows us to in principle reject or accept certain upshots of particular (religious) experiences, on (3) the notion that what the (truth-)value of these experiences is should be tested in light of the wider experiences that we have, and on (4) the claim that for a full grasp of this world's complexities, it will be detrimental to limit one's studies to just one form of experience.

These views turn the rationalistic argument around. The rationalistic anti-religious argument holds that only those beliefs that are grounded in evidence are justified,[73] yet James' views imply that we have no a priori reasons to dismiss the possible insights that mystical experiences may generate. Rather, we should assess them, much like beliefs that we hold on ordinary experiences, by way of empirical tests: within the wider range of our experiences, how do these beliefs hold up? Furthermore, the rationalist take on what are to count as justified beliefs is too narrow to accommodate even our ordinary beliefs.[74] James also rejects rationalistic intellectualism in religion, which does not manage to take into account the human experiences of reality either. What comes first, James holds, is human feeling, be it towards the sensational part of reality or the non-sensational, religious aspects. The rationalistic arguments about the existence of a particular divine entity cannot do justice to this. Religious beliefs are not based on these rational arguments, but on subconscious, non-rational aspects of our mind's thinking.[75]

From James' descriptions of religious experiences and their cognitive impetus, an ambiguous perspective on truth emerges.[76] On the one hand, truth is connected to what is of most value. Not only do James' descriptions breathe the supposition that we should take religious experiences seriously because so many people have deemed them so valuable to their lives, James also explicitly mentions the 'utility' of religion.[77] On the other hand, however, James' notion of truth, here, is bound to the results and adequacy of our cognitive practices. Within this latter notion of truth, at times what is stressed is the more pragmatist notion, of empirically testing the religious experiences by looking at the fruits that they bear. At other times a more realist notion of truth as correspondence with reality is basic, e.g. where the truth-value of beliefs in absence of evidential support is discussed.[78] In both cases, however, it applies not only to naturalistic issues but also to religious ones. As James holds that religious experiences are experiences of reality, furthermore, their truth-value consists in an interaction of the propositions with reality.

As we have seen, however, although truth is applicable to the issue of religious experiences, this does not imply that these experiences, and the beliefs they generate, are necessarily communicable. Whereas, in the case of beliefs generated by communally accessible aspects of reality these can be authoritative for those who have not had the same experiences, the private experiences of the mystic do not allow for such weight. The truth of religious propositions based on these private experiences thus cannot be evaluated in a manner comparable to the truth of propositions based on publicly accessible experiences. It is this aspect of truth and experience in religious experiences that we need to square with the pragmatic pluralist perspective on the truth-value of propositions.

3 Truth and Experience in *The Varieties* and Putnam's Pragmatic Pluralism

We have uncovered the implicit views on the cognitive value of religious experiences in James' *Varieties*. In scrutinizing the notions of truth and experience basic to these views, I evaluate them in light of Putnam's Jamesian pragmatic pluralist perspective on truth and experience. The reasons for doing this are twofold. Putnam's philosophy of mind and language leans strongly on important aspects of James' thinking on experience, but has also incorporated important other, notably Wittgensteinian notions of *truth*. Furthermore, Putnam's pragmatic pluralism is considered a central pragmatist perspective on truth and experience today.[79] Thus, I assess James' views on the cognitive value of religious experiences in light of Putnam's pragmatic pluralist notions of truth and experience.

3.1 Evaluation in Light of Putnam's Pragmatic Pluralist Truth

Putnam's pragmatic pluralism takes truth to be a functional, plural notion rather than a substantial, singular notion, which means that there is no single property that can be ascribed to every true proposition. A comprehensive account of Putnam's views on truth goes beyond the goals of this chapter's argument.[80] What is essential regarding the argument, however, is that instead of gaining the property of truth, propositions already have or do not have it, because of the interactional relation of these propositions with reality. This is an important pragmatist aspect of Putnam's position. What makes his position a pluralist one is that what this interaction consists of depends on the various practices that make up human reality.

In this picture, the conceptual abilities that we have concerning a particular discourse are interdependent on the particular practical abilities that we have within that field. As Putnam puts it: 'We learn what mathematical truth is by learning the practices and standards of mathematics itself, including the practice of *applying* mathematics.'[81] But it works the other way around as well, in that we learn how to work within such a field by learning what the concepts (such as simplicity and coherence) amount to.

Mathematical assertions are exemplary of how true propositions are propositions that are in accordance with reality without their objectivity depending on a correspondence to supposed objects. As a true proposition is true because of a specific interaction of a person's conceptual abilities and reality, pragmatic pluralism implies that it is possible to communicate the proposition and its truth-value. In this picture, truth is essentially non-solipsistic since it consists of an interactional relation of a proposition with particular aspects of reality, a relation which depends on our linguistic and other practices, which in turn depend on a community.

As we saw, the analysis of James' views on religious experiences shows that in his view veridical religious experiences are experiences of reality, which have cognitive import. Because of their interactional relation with reality, religious propositions that go back onto religious experiences therefore potentially have truth-value. While this is in line with the pragmatic pluralist perspective on truth, there also is a potential problematic aspect of James' views on the cognitive value of religious experiences, viz. his contention that religious experiences are ineffable. Other than in the case of experience, to which I turn below, Putnam rejects important aspects of James' notion of truth, even if he reads James carefully, and therefore uncovers a more nuanced view of James on truth than others have ascribed to him (namely that 'truth is what works').[82]

In James' view, religious experiences are essentially ineffable in the sense that the individual who has the experience cannot communicate the experience fully to another person. Contrary to non-religious experiences, there thus is a solipsistic quality to religious experiences. The question is what the consequences are for the truth-value of religious propositions if they are based on these ineffable experiences. From the analysis above it shows that religious experiences cannot function in the same manner as non-religious experiences can in showing the truth-value of the propositions based on them, since religious experiences are mostly individual affairs and since their full extent cannot be explicated to those who have not had them. To James, then, religious experiences ultimately seem to be private or solipsist events, since they cannot be communicated to others. If that is the case, then the question is whether the religious propositions based on them are also ineffable.

When turning to the contention that religious experiences are ineffable, then, what does it say about the notion of truth if the religious experiences can be true while at the same time incommunicable? If the belief that an experience has generated is true if, in one way or another, it is in accordance with or adequate to reality,[83] then this would imply that even though the mystic has in an extraordinary manner seen how and why this belief is indeed in accordance with reality, then it should from a pragmatic pluralist perspective in principle be possible for a non-mystic to come to see this truth also, provided that the aspects of reality accessible to the mystic are not *categorically* different from those accessible to the non-mystic.[84] This coheres with James' notion that the fruits of the religious experiences, among which are the religious propositions people hold on the basis of them, can be evaluated in a fallibilist manner, namely in 'the laboratory of life'. Thus, the ineffability of the experiences has no detrimental consequences for the truth-value of the propositions. Rather, the reality of religious experiences, even if ineffable, impairs the reductionist contention that only non-religious experiences could have cognitive value.

I take it that James implies that the experience itself is ineffable while the propositions held on the basis of them can in principle be communicated. Although we should conclude that in James' view religious experiences are ineffable, in a pragmatic pluralist perspective true religious *propositions* based on them *are* in principle effable. As the ineffability of religious experiences thus need not conflict with the communicability of religious propositions, James' views on the cognitive value of religious experiences fit the pragmatic pluralist perspective on truth as an interactional notion.

3.2 Evaluation in Light of Putnam's Pragmatic Pluralist Experience

James' notion of religious experience may thus be individualistic or even ultimately solipsistic in the sense that religious experiences are thought to occur to individual mystics, not to groups of mystics, and that they cannot be communicated fully to others. Nevertheless, the propositions based on these experiences can in principle be communicated. The question with regard to the religious experiences themselves, however, is whether the perspective on experience in *The Varieties* coheres with the pragmatic pluralist perspective on experience.

Without being able to attend to Putnam's pragmatic pluralist perspective on experience comprehensively,[85] we can state that it connects to the actual manner in which we have experiences rather than imposing a meta-philosophical view on it that reduces experiences to experiences of objects in the brain. It acknowledges a plurality of irreducible experiences, relative to the conceptual and experiential schemes that we employ. In Putnam's view, experiences are epistemologically basic transactions between ourselves and our surroundings. Putnam:

> As Dewey might have put it, perception is transactional. We are aware of ourselves as in interaction with our experiential objects. I am aware of a series of visual, tactile, etc., perspectives on the chair without ceasing to perceive the chair as an object that does not change as those perspectives change.[86]

In the pragmatic pluralist perspective, thus, experience consists of a transaction between an individual and his or her surroundings. For his views on experience Putnam relies strongly on a number of significant features of James' thinking, such as the views that experience is direct, and that it is conceptualized. This explains why there is more agreement between James' notion of (religious) experience and the pragmatic pluralist view on experience.

For the pragmatic pluralist perspective on the truth-value of religious propositions, James' view on the notion of experience or perception with respect to religious experiences implies the following. It has made it plausible that there is no a priori reason to dismiss religious aspects of reality, or, for that matter, to refute experiences of religious aspects of reality. These experiences may be as real as any other experience of natural aspects of reality. Furthermore, just like the latter kind of experiences may be improved and corrected, religious experiences can in principle be amended.

This accords well with pragmatic pluralism's take on experience as direct but corrigible.[87] Whether an experience is 'real' depends not on whether it is true. Whether these experiences give the subjects real insights into the aspects of reality *is* connected to those insights being true. These two aspects of James' notion of experience, i.e. his notion of experience as in principle real, but not necessarily veridical, and his corresponding unwillingness to limit experiences, on beforehand, only to the non-mystical, naturalistic experiences, attest to a view on religious experiences as potentially cognitive experiences.

4 Concluding Notes: The Cognitive Value of Religious Experiences

Instead of having argued about James' position regarding truth and experience on the basis of an analysis of his explicit writings on the subject, I sought to take James' insistence on the practical relevance of one's perspective on truth and his belief that experience and feeling should be the primary source of (religious) knowledge seriously by showing what his notions of truth and experience amount to in the more practical issue of the abundance of religious experiences. As such, this has allowed us to reflect on what the role of religion, and religious experience in particular, may consist in when it comes to a pragmatic pluralist view on the truth-value of religious propositions.[88]

Congruent with the pragmatic pluralist perspective on experience, James' perspective on religious experience as it emerges from *The Varieties* is that these are transactions between the experiencing individual and reality. James shows that we have no a priori reasons for discarding religious experiences as hallucinatory or non-veridical. In taking these experiences at face-value, i.e. in approaching them in a manner that one would generally approach any experience, James explores their potential cognitive value. We can conclude that as transactions between a knowing subject and reality, religious experiences—if they occur, i.e. if they are experiences in the real sense of the word—have cognitive value.

Notes

1. I am indebted to the Fulbright Center for a grant that aided in conducting part of my PhD research at Harvard University in the fall semester of 2010, during which I wrote a first version of this chapter. I thank David Lamberth and Parimal Patil for valuable comments on my argument, and the members of Harvard Divinity School's Colloquium on Theology, Religion, Ethics, Politics and Sociology, under supervision of Francis Fiorenza, for valuable feedback when I had the opportunity of presenting an earlier version of this chapter to them. Finally, I thank my dissertation supervisors, Christoph Baumgartner and Dirk-Martin Grube.
2. W. James (1963 [1902]) *The Varieties of Religious Experience: A Study in Human Nature*, ed. J. Ratner (New York: University Books).
3. W. James (1981 [1890]) *The Principles of Psychology* (Cambridge, MA: Harvard University Press); W. James (1977 [1909]) *A Pluralistic Universe* (Cambridge, MA: Harvard University Press); W. James (1976 [1912]) *Essays in Radical Empiricism* (Cambridge, MA: Harvard University Press).
4. In this regard, see e.g. Owen Flanagan's discussion of one of the central concepts to James, consciousness, in O. Flanagan (1997) 'Consciousness as a Pragmatist Views it' in R. A. Putnam (ed.) *The Cambridge Companion to William James* (Cambridge: Cambridge University Press), pp. 25–48, esp. p. 29. Flanagan's is a noteworthy perspective on James' notion of consciousness, including the problems with seeming inconsistencies or changes of mind throughout James' intellectual career. See also the discussion between David Lamberth and Hilary Putnam on James' notion of truth. See H. Putnam (1997) 'James's Theory of Truth' in Putnam (ed.) *The Cambridge Companion to William James*, pp. 166–85; see also H. Putnam (2005) 'James on Truth (again)' and D. C. Lamberth (2005) 'James and the Question of Truth: A Response to Hilary Putnam' in J. R. Carrette (ed.) *William James and 'The Varieties of Religious Experience': A Centenary Celebration* (London: Routledge), pp. 172–82 and 221–34, respectively.
5. See e.g. H. Putnam (2000) *The Threefold Cord: Mind, Body, and World* (New York: Columbia University Press), esp. pp. 43–92.
6. An analysis of Putnam's viewpoints on the role of experience in religion would reach beyond the limits of this chapter. I refer to my 'One Religious Truth? Assessing Religious Propositions in a Secular Society' in N. Brunsveld and R. Trigg (eds.) (2010) *Religion in the Public Sphere. Ars Disputandi Supplement Series 5* (Utrecht: Igitur Publishing), pp. 199–210.
7. James, *Essays in Radical Empiricism*.
8. W. James (1904) 'A World of Pure Experience', *The Journal of Philosophy, Psychology and Scientific Methods*, 1(20), 533–43.

9. W. James (2008 [1907]) *Pragmatism. A New Name for Some Old Ways of Thinking* (Rockville: Manor), pp. 85–100.
10. For an analysis of James' notion of truth, see D. C. Lamberth (1999) *William James and the Metaphysics of Experience* (Cambridge: Cambridge University Press), pp. 205–9.
11. Cf. David Lamberth on James' notion of experience in ibid., pp. 26ff.
12. See Putnam, *The Threefold Cord*, pp. 93–108.
13. I take it that James' use of the notion of religion is just one of the uses of the notion of religion today. As we will see, his view amounts to the idea that religious statements and beliefs are about such an unseen order. We may find, however, that statements and beliefs, such as about issues in the natural sciences, in historiography, in morality, in the existential-religious etc. may be called religious, that is if they are motivated by or based on a religious outlook. It is nevertheless a rather common view, today also, that religion pertains to some kind of unseen order, and for now we can take James' views as applicable to this view.
14. James, *The Varieties of Religious Experience*, p. 53. This is itself a more substantial view than his earlier presupposition that '[r]eligion, ... as I now ask you arbitrarily to take it, shall mean for us the feelings, acts, and experiences of individual men [sic] in their solitude, so far as they apprehend themselves to stand in relation to whatever they may consider the divine' (ibid., p. 31).
15. See e.g. ibid., pp. 26–31.
16. Cf. ibid., pp. 389–93.
17. See my remarks in the Introduction for the various fields of inquiry and reasoning this may pertain to.
18. Cf. E. K. Suckiel (1996) *Heaven's Champion: William James's Philosophy of Religion* (Notre Dame: University of Notre Dame Press). See also James' letter to Mrs. James, Castebelle, April 13, 1900, in James, *The Varieties of Religious Experience*, p. 533.
19. James, *The Varieties of Religious Experience*, p. 442.
20. Ibid., p. 3.
21. Cf. ibid., pp. 334–9; cf. also Joseph Ratner in his introduction to James' *Varieties*, ibid., p. vii.
22. Ibid., pp. 334.
23. In this respect, James writes that '[a] survey of history shows us that, as a rule, religious geniuses attract disciples, and produce groups of sympathizers. When these groups get strong enough to "organize" themselves, they become ecclesiastical institutions with corporate ambitions of their own. The spirit of politics and the lust of dogmatic rule are then apt to enter and to contaminate the originally innocent thing ... and to some persons the word "church" suggests so much hypocrisy and tyranny and meanness and tenacity of superstition that in a wholesale undiscerning way they glory in saying that they are "down" on religion altogether' (ibid., pp. 334–5). Cf. also James' claims about the heterodoxy of the 'genuine first-hand religious experience' (ibid., p. 337) and John Dewey's worries about the same in the first part of John Dewey (1960 [1934]) *A Common Faith* (New Haven: Yale University Press).
24. James, *The Varieties of Religious Experience*, p. 379.
25. Cf. ibid., pp. 380–2.

26. Ibid., p. 381.
27. Ibid., p. 4.
28. Cf. ibid., p. 4.
29. Ibid., p. 6. 'Existential', here, pertains to the historical and physical facts, not to a religio-existential dimension.
30. Ibid., p. 382.
31. Ibid., p. 382.
32. Ibid., p. 382.
33. Ibid., p. 384.
34. Cf. ibid., pp. 384–6 for James' arguments against James Crichton-Browne's views on the same.
35. Ibid., pp. 388–9.
36. Cf. e.g. ibid., p. 387.
37. Below, I return briefly to a discussion of the monism in this view as opposed to James' pluralism in other writings.
38. James, *The Varieties of Religious Experience*, p. 388.
39. James' use of consciousness, here, is close to that of having a particular mental state, which, I take it, in turn is necessarily connected to experience. Cf. Flanagan, 'Consciousness as a Pragmatist Views it', esp. p. 29. Flanagan's is a noteworthy perspective on James' notion of consciousness, including the problems with seeming inconsistencies or changes of mind throughout James' intellectual career.
40. Cf. the various 'typical examples' of mystical experience James gives in James, *The Varieties of Religious Experience*, pp. 382–8.
41. Ibid., p. 397, quoting J. Trevor.
42. It might seem that 'the alternate experience of reality itself *can* be real' would be more appropriate, here, than '*is* real', since the former expression would allow for some experiences to be veridical and for others to be non-veridical, while the latter would take all experiences to be veridical. However, we should not forget that to James, as to Putnam, experiences are not incorrigible, which is true for experiences of the naturalistic kind as well as for mystical experiences (cf. ibid., p. 428). This means that experiences, though real, may be flawed. Thus, since an experience is real if it is an experience, and not only if it is a veridical experience, since, in other words, an experience is already a real experience if it is an experience, not only if it is a 'true' or unflawed experience, we should stick to the phrase that 'the alternate experience of reality itself is real'.
43. Ibid., p. 388. As said, I take it that where it says consciousness we can read 'mental state of experience'.
44. I come back to this below.
45. James, *The Varieties of Religious Experience*, p. 388.
46. Ibid., p. 388.
47. Ibid., p. 393.
48. Ibid., p. 398.
49. Ibid., p. 396, quoting Walt Whitman.
50. Ibid., p. 397, quoting J. Trevor.
51. Ibid., p. 398, quoting R. M. Bucke.
52. Cf. the lengthy quotations of R. M. Bucke in ibid., pp. 398–9.
53. See ibid., p. 400.

54. Ibid., p. 401.
55. Ibid., p. 401.
56. James does not discuss whether the mystic can communicate these insights to other mystics, but it could be that this is deemed equally impossible, since the reason why these insights are incommunicable is that one has to have had the experience oneself to understand the insights. Perhaps it is easier, however, for a mystic to communicate his or her insights gained through a mystical experience to another mystic, since both have had experiences of a relatively comparable nature.
57. Cf. James, *The Varieties of Religious Experience*, p. 405, see also p. 380.
58. Cf. ibid., pp. 406–13.
59. Ibid., p. 407.
60. Ibid., p. 410.
61. Here it seems that James has an ambiguous outlook on truth. On the one hand, he holds that whether something (an insight generated by the mystical experience) is true depends entirely on its fruits, while on the other, he allows truth to be independent of its fruits (the inspiration itself can be not true). I will return to the issue of whether truth does or does not depend entirely on the fruits it generates shortly.
62. James, *The Varieties of Religious Experience*, p. 416.
63. Ibid., pp. 416–22.
64. Ibid., p. 422.
65. Three pages later, James takes back much of what he says here about the unanimity of mystical experiences. Cf. ibid., pp. 424–5.
66. Ibid., pp. 419.
67. James holds that

    (1) Mystical states, when well developed, usually are, and have the right to be, absolutely authoritative over the individuals to whom they come.
    (2) No authority emanates from them which should make it a duty for those who stand outside of them to accept their revelations uncritically.
    (3) They break down the authority of the non-mystical or rationalistic consciousness, based upon the understanding and the senses alone. They show it to be only one kind of consciousness. They open out the possibility of other orders of truth, in which, so far as anything in us vitally responds to them, we may freely continue to have faith (ibid., pp. 422–3).

68. As said, James takes back much of what he said earlier about the abundance of agreement among mystical experiences in ibid., pp. 424–5.
69. Ibid., p. 426.
70. Ibid., p. 428.
71. It is clear that James was attentive to religious questions himself. See e.g. Suckiel, *Heaven's Champion*, chapter 1, who argues that despite his ambivalence about being religious himself, James nevertheless took religion to be one of the most important aspects of life. Furthermore, James believed that being religious would help a person live a morally better life. See W. James (1891) 'The Moral Philosopher and the Moral Life', *International Journal of Ethics*, 1(3), 330–54. Cf. also M. R. Slater (2009) *William James on Ethics and Faith* (Cambridge: Cambridge University Press), chapters 3 and 4.

72. For reasons discussed above, James holds that whether one experience is superior to the other should always remain an open question. This does not mean that one should never opt to *act* upon the conclusions one draws on mystical rather than on natural experiences. That this may sometimes be necessary can be defended on the basis of James' argument in James, *The Will to Believe*. Very briefly put, James' argument there is that in certain situations, i.e. in the case of genuine options which are live and whose settling should and cannot be postponed, answering certain questions, i.e. questions for the answer to which no evidential support is available, requires a will to believe, i.e. a willingness to take a point of view without evidence for it (which in turn would give a person the right to a (religious) belief—hence James' statement, in *Pragmatism*, that he preferred to see the arguments as an argument for the *right* to believe; James, *Pragmatism*, p. 124; cf. Slater, *William James on Ethics and Faith*, p. 19). In case of those genuine options, for which we have no 'intellectual grounds' to decide, and for which non-mystical experiences provide no hypotheses or directions, it would be justified to choose to rely on the hypotheses or directions that one can draw from mystical experiences.
73. Of course, what these evidential grounds come down to varies among rationalists. Cf. W. K. Clifford (1986 [1877]) 'The Ethics of Belief' in G. McCarthy (ed.) *The Ethics of Belief Debate* (Atlanta: Scholars Press), pp. 19–36, of which William James' *The Will to Believe* is meant as a firm rebuttal, for one influential, rationalist stance.
74. Cf. James, *The Varieties of Religious Experience*, p. 73. See Suckiel, *Heaven's Champion*, esp. chapter 1, for James' struggle against intellectualism in a largely scientific environment.
75. Cf. James, *The Varieties of Religious Experience*, pp. 73–4. See H. Brown (2000) *William James on Radical Empiricism and Religion* (Toronto: University of Toronto Press), esp. chapter 1, for an account of James' endeavor to bring in subjectivity in epistemology.
76. See H. S. Levinson (1981) *The Religious Investigations of William James* (Chapel Hill: University of North Carolina Press), esp. pp. 220–30, for a discussion of the meanings of the term 'truth' in James' days and ours.
77. Cf. James, *The Varieties of Religious Experience*, pp. 377, 505–7.
78. Cf. Suckiel, *Heaven's Champion*, chapter 5, for a discussion of what is often thought to be an ambiguous notion of truth in James' works, amongst which *The Varieties*.
79. See e.g. S. Pihlström (2006) 'Putnam's Conception of Ontology', *Contemporary Pragmatism*, 3(2), 1–13; D. Copp (2006) 'The Ontology of Putnam's *Ethics without Ontology*', *Contemporary Pragmatism*, 3(2), 39–53; and C. Travis (2005) 'The Face of Perception' in Y. Ben-Menahem (ed.) *Hilary Putnam* (Cambridge: Cambridge University Press), pp. 53–82.
80. See Putnam, *The Threefold Cord*, esp. pp. 43–92; and H. Putnam (2004) *Ethics without Ontology* (Cambridge, MA: Harvard University Press), pp. 52–69. Cf. Brunsveld, 'One Religious Truth?' for a concise introduction to the issue of pragmatic pluralist truth.
81. Putnam, *Ethics without Ontology*, p. 66.
82. Cf. R. A. Hertz (1971) 'James and Moore: Two Perspectives on Truth', *Journal of the History of Philosophy*, 9(2), 213. Putnam's pragmatic pluralism conflicts

e.g. with James' notion that concepts acquire meaning through external relations rather than having meaning through their intrinsic relation with that to which they refer. See Putnam, 'James's Theory of Truth'; Putnam, 'James on Truth (again)'; and David Lamberth's criticism in Lamberth, 'James and the Question of Truth: A Response to Hilary Putnam'.

83. Cf. Putnam, 'James's Theory of Truth', pp. 166–85; Putnam, 'James on Truth (again)', pp. 172–82; and Suckiel, *Heaven's Champion*, esp. chapter 5, for a discussion of James' realist tendencies in his notion of truth.

84. Perhaps a non-mystic can gradually close in on those aspects of reality that the mystic has encountered instantly. The non-mystic would close in on them not from an extraordinary experience but by discarding those beliefs that after testing them have proved inadequate.

85. See H. Putnam (2012) 'Sensation and Apperception' in S. Miguens and G. Preyer (eds.) *Consciousness and Subjectivity* (Heusenstamm: Ontos Verlag), pp. 39–50; and Putnam, *The Threefold Cord*, pp. 43–92. Cf. Travis, 'The Face of Perception' for an introduction to Putnam's notion of experience.

86. Putnam, *The Threefold Cord*, p. 159.

87. See ibid., pp. 43–92.

88. It has also given us insights into James' views in epistemology and philosophy of perception from an unusual angle, i.e. not from his explicit theorizing on the same but from the more practical engagements with the issue of religious experiences.

4
Pragmatic Realism and Pluralism in Philosophy of Religion

Sami Pihlström

As suggested in the Introduction to this volume, there is, for pragmatists, no such thing as a single, absolute, privileged, or overarching perspective from which religious issues ought to be viewed, but a plurality of relevant philosophical approaches, reflecting the plurality of our practices of life. This plurality must be taken seriously even when it comes to exploring such an abstract issue as *the problem of realism*, as applied to religious belief and religious language. I hope to elaborate on this idea through my examination of William James' peculiar form of *pluralism*.

I will proceed as follows. First, I will outline James' perspective on the realism vs. antirealism opposition as well as the plurality of Jamesian pluralisms in some more detail, showing how Jamesian pragmatic pluralism grounds religious (theological) metaphysics in ethics and suggesting that this approach in an important way goes beyond the realism vs. antirealism debate (as it is conventionally understood in contemporary philosophy of religion). Pluralism is the key pragmatist principle to be applied to this debate. Finally, I will argue that James' pragmatic pluralism must not blind us to the reality of evil and suffering, nor to what may be called the 'tragic' dimension of pragmatism. On the contrary, what we may call James' 'realistic spirit' accommodates a realistic attitude to the many faces of such evil. A brief concluding section will then draw the discussion to a close.

1 The Tension between Realism and 'Humanism' in James' *Pragmatism*

The great classical pragmatists Charles S. Peirce, William James, and John Dewey all defended views that are, arguably, *to some extent realistic but to some extent non-realistic*—if not straightforwardly anti-realistic, at least in some sense idealistic or constructivist. Yet, none of these classical pragmatists was a *relativist* in any clear sense, although James' notorious views on truth as something that is good or satisfactory to believe, as spelled out in Lecture VI of *Pragmatism* (1907), as well as its sequel, *The Meaning of Truth* (1909), have often been (mis)read as flatly subjectivistic.[1] The tensions we can find in James' thought regarding realism and its various alternatives illuminate the way in which the realism issue has been and still is at the heart of the pragmatist tradition more generally, and must therefore be taken very seriously in pragmatist philosophy of religion as well.

The fact that James has often been read as an anti-realist or subjectivist is explained by the fact that he does say in so many words that our interests and what we find satisfactory play a crucial role in determining what is, 'for us', true and what is real—but he also affirms that there is a reality out there that our truths are in agreement with. So there seems to be a tension between realism and idealism in Jamesian pragmatism, though in a manner somewhat different from the other classical pragmatisms.[2] This tension is readily applicable to James' philosophy of religion.

In his essay, 'Pragmatism, Realism, and Religion', Michael R. Slater defends James against a number of widespread misunderstandings.[3] I find his treatment of James problematic enough to require some critical comments that will highlight the Jamesian application of the pragmatic method in the philosophy of religion and thus lead us to our investigation of the specifically Jamesian version of pragmatically pluralist yet realist philosophy of religion.

Slater seeks to show that James' pragmatism not only is compatible with realism (including religious realism) but is even a species of *metaphysical realism*. James, we are told, 'combines a "humanist" account of truth with a commitment to metaphysical realism', while also defending 'a pragmatic version of the correspondence theory of truth'.[4] We should agree with Slater about the latter point, provided that the correspondence theory is not understood as being necessarily connected with metaphysical realism. That is, far from being a naïve subjectivist or relativist, James clearly starts from the commonsense idea that truth involves some sort of agreement between our 'ideas' (or beliefs, statements, theories, etc., overlooking the question of what the primary 'truth-bearers' are) and reality, seeking to specify this notion of agreement pragmatically, in concrete experiential terms.[5] Slater offers sufficient textual evidence for this reading, and there is no need to repeat that evidence here. However, the claim that James is a metaphysical realist, even in a general sense, is inaccurate. Setting this matter straight will lead us to our major issue in this chapter.

Much of what is controversial here depends on what exactly we should mean by 'metaphysical realism'. Slater's definition of this notion follows the one given in a recent philosophy dictionary: according to the metaphysical realist, 'there is a world of mind-independent objects'.[6] Slater thus rejects Hilary Putnam's threefold characterization of metaphysical realism as the commitment to the following theses: (1) the world consists of a definite set of mind- and scheme-independent objects and properties; (2) the world can in principle be described by means of a single complete true theory, that is, there is an 'absolute conception of the world', formulated from an ideal 'God's-Eye View'; and (3) truth is a non-epistemic correspondence relation between our statements (or whatever the ultimate truth-bearers are) and the mind-independent entities and facts of the world.[7] Now, while there certainly is a sense in which James does accept the realist view that there is a mind-independent world, and the related account of truth as agreement with such a world, he can hardly be taken to endorse even the relatively broad notion of metaphysical realism understood as the commitment to there being 'a world of mind-independent *objects*' (my emphasis). This is because James finds the very notion of an object dependent on human purposes. This is especially clear in the seventh lecture of *Pragmatism*, where he argues that reality is something we (help to) create, to which we inevitably make an 'addition'—something 'still in the making'—and that anything we may call a *thing* is 'carved out' by us in and through our purposive practices.[8]

Moreover, even James' theory of truth, albeit starting from the idea of 'agreement' (as Slater correctly shows), is not a version of the correspondence theory, insofar as the latter is viewed (as it is by most metaphysical realists) as an essentially non-epistemic account of truth. That is, metaphysical realists and correspondence theoreticians would not accept the Jamesian epistemic characterization of correspondence (agreement) in terms of confirmation and experiential satisfaction[9] as a characterization of the proper sort of correspondence required by a realist theory of truth. Furthermore, a metaphysically realist philosopher like D. M. Armstrong, postulating not just correspondence but an asymmetrical, metaphysically cross-categorial 'truthmaking' relation from the world to true propositions,[10] would hardly view such a metaphysically benign version of correspondence realistic at all.

A much more helpful description of the Jamesian conception of truth could be achieved by emphasizing the fact that James, unlike our standard metaphysical realists, refuses to draw a principled distinction between the *meaning* of truth and the *criteria* of truth. Even strong metaphysical realists may regard the latter as epistemic, but for James the very meaning of truth is epistemic all the way down, and inseparable from our pragmatic criteria of arriving at truths. Metaphysical realists can hardly accept this as a correspondence theory of truth proper, but James deliberately—and in my view with good reason—blurs the distinction between meaning and criteria, pragmatically proposing that the meaning of truth largely lies in the epistemic criteria we employ for arriving at the truth. There is no pragmatic meaning of truth available *in abstracto*; what the concept of truth means for us is inseparable from the plurality of epistemic practices we engage in in order to reach truths.

According to Slater, while truth is an *'event'* (original emphasis) and 'happens to an idea or statement', as James often says, 'what ultimately *makes* our beliefs and statements about reality successful is their agreement with reality'.[11] This is correct, but then again agreement itself is understood in terms of satisfaction, of concrete 'leadings' from one bit of experience to another. It should be realized that the kind of success relevant here is epistemic. Moreover, the 'making' involved here is a kind of truthmaking, insofar as truth itself amounts to success, but it is very different from, say, Armstrong's metaphysically realistic notion of truthmaking.[12] Slater admits that James takes truth to be an epistemic concept, but 'epistemic *precisely on account of its relation to reality*'.[13] A metaphysically realist correspondence- or truthmaking-theoretician, such as Armstrong, would have none of this. For such philosophers, the 'relation to reality' that truths have must be non-epistemic in order to be sufficiently realistic.

It is to Slater's merit that he is one of the very few commentators on James who perceive that there are Kantian-like 'transcendental arguments that are basic to his pragmatism', one of them being the realistic bunch of arguments seeking to show that 'if beliefs or statements about reality are to be either meaningful or true, there must first be a reality to which they refer', and that 'in order for a belief or statement about some reality to be true it must also *agree* with that reality'.[14] The existence of a mind-independent reality is argued to be a necessary condition for the possibility of truth.[15]

Slater admits that James has difficulties in balancing his realist and 'humanist' ideas,[16] even at times 'undercutting his commitment to realism' by suggesting that 'reality is somehow altered or reconstructed through our cognitive interactions with it'.[17] This is a revealing formulation, because in my view it is right here that James arrives at what is essential in his 'realism', namely, its subordination to (what I have elsewhere called) *transcendental pragmatism*.[18] We need not read James as claiming that we alter or reconstruct reality through our cognitive interactions with it in any causal, factual, or empirical sense; these alterations and reconstructions—or the dependence of reality on us and our cognitive powers—are, rather, in Kantian terms 'transcendental'. It is only (roughly) in the sense in which the spatio-temporal framework and the categories, such as causality, are established by us, or imposed by us on the world that we are able to experience, according to Kant, that reality is, for James, dependent on us or altered by us in cognition. Our 'worldmaking', to borrow a term of Nelson Goodman's more recent neopragmatism which is in some ways analogical to James' pragmatism,[19] is transcendental, not factual—although neither James nor Goodman is willing to put the matter in precisely these terms. Nevertheless, just as Kant was able to defend *empirical realism* within, and indeed held that it is made possible by, his *transcendental idealism*, James is able to endorse a form of empirical (though not metaphysical) realism within his transcendental pragmatism. We may agree, then, with Slater when he argues that we need both realism and humanism about truth.[20] But it is important to see that the kind of realism that we may maintain compatibly with humanism is empirical realism, and the kind of humanism we may maintain compatibly with realism is transcendental humanism (or, better, transcendental pragmatism).

The same Kantian or quasi-Kantian reflections apply to what James has to say about religion and 'religious reality'. Our postulation of 'an unseen religious order'[21] is, we might say, transcendentally—rather than causally or empirically—dependent on our religious life. What this means is that it is our religious life, and the experiences it may give rise to, that makes possible the specific kinds of religious meanings that such a postulation may conceptualize.

Slater perceptively notes the analogy between Kant and James:

> In a move similar to Kant's in the *Critique of Practical Reason*, James argues that while the basis of morality is autonomous from religion, our desire to lead 'morally strenuous' lives and to offer an account of moral objectivity cannot plausibly be satisfied unless we postulate God's existence. James' view, in brief, is that we cannot fully awaken our moral capacities and sustain them at their highest level without

believing that our moral obligations are ultimately grounded in a moral standard that transcends any merely human standard.[22]

However, again, this is both correct and incorrect. For Kant, or for James, morality cannot be based on a religious standard, because morality, in order to be genuine morality at all, must be autonomous (instead of, in Kantian terms, 'heteronomous'). However, leading a truly moral life, or trying to make sense of such a life, leads us to postulate divine powers. Slater's discussion of James' 'way of simultaneously acknowledging both the autonomy of morality and the necessity of religious commitment for realizing certain moral goods' could be significantly enriched, if he had explicitly phrased his reading of James in terms of Kant's notion of the postulates of practical reason, and if he had connected *this* with his accurate observation that there are transcendental arguments in James.[23]

Hence, it is plausible to propose that James may be read as arguing transcendentally when suggesting (according to Slater) that 'there are moral goods that can only be gained (if at all) by supplementing our world-view with metaphysical and religious beliefs',[24] and that this might even amount to a pragmatic-transcendental argument ultimately grounding metaphysical and religious postulations upon ethical premises. Moreover, a related transcendental account of religious realism as subordinated to transcendental pragmatism—and to the appreciation of the irreducible plurality of our religious lives and moral outlooks—would strengthen the reading of James as a religious realist by setting his peculiar kind of realism in its proper pragmatic context.

James, we should now emphasize, is not merely a pragmatist but also (among other things) a pluralist. As Slater also notes, 'James's pragmatism entails a commitment to *pluralism* at both the theoretical and practical levels.'[25] This pluralism is both religious, respecting individuals' (as well as nations' and historical epochs') particular 'over-beliefs', and ethical, emphasizing tolerance toward different ways of life.[26] Slater says we need to defend a combination of realist and pluralist pragmatism in order to 'account for the potential reality of some of the objects of religious belief, experience, and devotion [...] while rejecting the narrow exclusivism characteristic of many realist approaches to religion'.[27] This is obviously a pragmatically desirable goal. Indeed, this is one of the main reasons for taking James seriously in contemporary philosophy of religion and for getting his realism right; in this sense, my discussion of James' pluralism in the next section comes relatively close to Slater's views.

2 James' Plurality of Pluralisms

As we saw, Slater recognizes not only (somewhat problematically) the presence of a form of realism in James but also the equally important presence—and crucial importance—of James' pragmatic pluralism. This requires further elaboration.

In my *Pragmatic Pluralism and the Problem of God* (forthcoming, 2013), I argue that the problem of realism vs. anti-realism (just like other philosophical oppositions relevant to our understanding of religion, including the one between evidentialism and fideism),[28] receives new interpretations when seen from a pragmatically pluralist perspective, because religion is then understood as a human practice (or set of practices) with certain inherent aims and goals, responding to a plurality of human needs and interests, serving important human values. Its meaning for us, as well as its metaphysical and epistemological status based on its human meaning(fullness), is then not reducible to any privileged referential relationship to a mind- and practice-independent reality.[29]

The 'promise' pragmatism makes in the philosophy of religion can, I believe, be pragmatically cashed out in terms of James' pluralism. According to James, the problem of monism vs. pluralism is the deepest and 'most pregnant' in philosophy.[30] In Lecture IV of *Pragmatism*, he applies the pragmatic method to the problem of 'the one and the many'. The pragmatist must inquire into the multitude of ways in which the world can be taken to be 'one' (or 'many'). Such an inquiry reveals that the world is 'one' in a number of different ways. The world is, first, one subject of discourse. There are, secondly, continuities (that is, cases of things 'hanging together') in the world. There are, thirdly, 'lines of influence' of various kinds—including, James' fourth point, causal lines of influence and causal unity based thereupon. Even more importantly, there is, fifthly, 'generic unity' in the world: things belong to different classes of *genera*, existing 'in kinds'.[31] James' sixth and seventh dimensions of 'oneness' are the unity of purpose and aesthetic unity. The eighth and philosophically perhaps the most controversial dimension is, finally, the notion of 'the one knower'—that is, the Hegelian monistic idealists' Absolute, a popular metaphysical postulate in the late nineteenth and early twentieth century, which James sets out critically to examine at some length.

James argues, famously, that the pragmatist prefers the pluralistic and empiricist approach to the monistic and rationalistic postulations celebrating the Absolute whose only pragmatically acceptable cash-value, according to James, is the occasional 'moral holiday' it might grant us.

The debate with monistic idealists', including particularly F. H. Bradley's and Josiah Royce's, views was one of the most important controversies James engaged in toward the end of his philosophical career. This is how he concludes the discussion of the one and the many in *Pragmatism*:

> 'The world is one,' therefore, just so far as we experience it to be concatenated, one by as many definite conjunctions as appear. But then also *not* one by just as many definite *dis*junctions as we find. The oneness and the manyness of it thus obtain in respects which can be separately named. It is neither a universe pure and simple nor a multiverse pure and simple. And its various manners of being one suggest, for their accurate ascertainment, so many distinct programs of scientific work. Thus the pragmatic question 'What is the oneness known-as? What practical difference will it make?' saves us from all feverish excitement over it as a principle of sublimity and carries us forward into the stream of experience with a cool head.[32]

Monism and pluralism must, hence, be treated pragmatically: no rationalistic metaphysics dogmatically set up in advance of our piecemeal, practice-oriented inquiries into the quite different ways in which the world can be said to be 'one' or 'many' can do the job of settling the issue. Applying the pragmatic method, James arrives at what may be characterized as the ethical superiority of pluralism over monism:

> Pluralism [...] has no need of this dogmatic rigoristic temper [of monism]. Provided you grant *some* separation among things, some tremor of independence, some free play of parts on one another, some real novelty or chance, however minute, she is amply satisfied, and will allow you any amount, however great, of real union. How much of union there may be is a question that she thinks can only be decided empirically. The amount may be enormous, colossal; but absolute monism is shattered if, along with all the union, there has to be granted the slightest modicum, the most incipient nascency, or the most residual trace, of a separation that is not 'overcome.' Pragmatism, pending the final empirical ascertainment of just what the balance of union and disunion among things may be, must obviously range herself upon the pluralistic side.[33]

We must not fail to see that there are a number of different pluralisms at work in James' pragmatism. In one important sense, pluralism amounts to a *metaphysical* theory (set against the postulation of the Absolute), according to which there are, instead of one single 'knower', 'bits and pieces' of 'pure experience' pretty much everywhere; it is therefore inseparable from James' radical empiricism, according to which pure experience is the 'neutral stuff' (beyond the subject–object dichotomy) out of which the world is 'made'.[34] James' theory can definitely be read in this way, and his metaphysical opposition to the monistic idealists' Absolute is a key element of his position, especially in *A Pluralistic Universe*. According to pluralism, as characterized in that late book, 'the substance of reality may never get totally collected' and 'some of it may remain outside of the largest combination of it ever made'.[35] Multiplicity is pragmatically preferable to all-inclusiveness—both scientifically and ethically.

However, just as James argues in *Pragmatism* that the world can be 'one' or 'many' in a variety of different ways, there are other ways of being a pluralist. I want to emphasize an alternative to purely metaphysical accounts of pluralism: it could be suggested that pluralism, for James, is not only, or not even primarily, a metaphysical doctrine (presupposing radical empiricism) but a *metaphilosophical* one, insisting on the possibility of a plurality of different 'correct' metaphysical positions, and thus coming closer to the general argument of *Pragmatism*, as well as the later defense of 'internal realism' and 'conceptual relativity' (or even explicitly 'pragmatic pluralism') by Hilary Putnam and other neopragmatists.[36] This metaphilosophical pluralism, closely related to the issue of realism vs. anti-realism already discussed above, can also be called *meta-metaphysical*, as it is concerned with the very nature and the correct (pragmatic) methodology of ontology or metaphysics, replacing the assumption of there being a single absolute conception of reality (or, as Putnam often puts it, the idea of a 'God's-Eye View') by the notion of several acceptable ontologies, each serving different pragmatic purposes. The Jamesian view, spelled out in Lecture VII of *Pragmatism*, in particular, that objects do not exist 'ready-made' but only relative to our purposes or categorization comes in an important respect very close to Kantian transcendental idealism, which is also opposed to strong realism: the world is not knowable *an sich*; any humanly knowable or experienceable structure it may have is imposed on it by us.[37] Yet, in addition to James' general distaste for the Kantian transcendental vocabulary and methodology, there is a crucial difference to Kant: pluralism. There are, instead of just one transcendental structure of experience, several acceptable, or even several 'true' or 'correct', ontological structures, each based on human practices and their inherent purposes, or the needs they serve. For instance, science and religion—to take the obvious case relevant here—may be argued to serve different human purposes and hence categorize reality in different, even incommensurable ways.[38]

In fact, it is hard to see how the purely metaphysical doctrine of radically empiricist pluralism, closely analogous to the view labeled 'neutral monism', defended by Ernst Mach and Bertrand Russell, among others, could be seriously regarded as 'pluralistic' at all. It is not obvious that such a metaphysical version of monism—a form of substance monism[39]—could actually be a form of pluralism. At least it would presuppose the kind of metaphysical realism we saw Slater attribute to James. On my alternative reading, we should, rather, maintain the possibility for such monism(s) only within a pluralism of different metaphysical alternatives that all need to be pragmatically examined and evaluated within a more inclusive pluralism. Arguably, James' metaphysical pluralism (radical empiricism), *qua* substance monism, is incompatible with his meta-metaphysical pluralism, which seeks to argue against such monistic ontologies that would seem to presuppose a God's-Eye View on the world. James' Kantianism, I like to think (though conclusive textual evidence is very hard to find), ultimately prevails over the empiricism he inherited from the British empiricist classics like David Hume. In order to be pragmatic pluralists in the meta-metaphysical sense, we should drop the metaphysical overtones of radical empiricism and embrace the kind of transcendental pragmatism I have suggested is a pragmatic heir of Kantian transcendental idealism.

There is, then, a plurality of pluralisms. There are both metaphysical and (at the meta-level) conceptual, methodological, and metaphilosophical versions of pluralism. Moreover, there is also a crucially important *ethical* (and even political) aspect to Jamesian pluralism. This, arguably, is eventually the key to his reconciliation of realism and anti-realism in the philosophy of religion. Let me explain.

James' version of the pragmatic method can be understood as the 'meta-metaphysical' principle that the conceivable ethical aspects and implications of different metaphysical views, ideas, and issues ought to be taken seriously when evaluating the content of those views, ideas, and issues, as well as their acceptability.[40] When employing the pragmatic method, the Jamesian pragmatist examines metaphysical problems from an ethical perspective. James shows us what this means in the case of such traditional controversies as those concerning, for example, the notion of substance, free will vs. determinism, theism vs. atheism (or materialism), and monism vs. pluralism. The metaphysical truth of pluralism is itself ethically grounded. Pluralism, we may say, is a pragmatic constraint on, or even a necessary precondition of, pragmatically serious metaphysical inquiry. No pragmatically adequate investigation of the ways the world must be (or must be taken by us to be) can ignore the plurality of ethically relevant purposes, perspectives, or contexts of conceptualization and categorization that Jamesian pluralism emphasizes. In metaphysics as much as ethics, there are different human 'voices' to be heard, very different ways people (need to) take the world to be (cf. below). This has direct bearing on James' treatment of the issue of realism in the philosophy of religion.

Although this is not James' own way of putting the matter, I want to re-emphasize that his proposal to defend the reality of God by pragmatic means in *Pragmatism* and elsewhere presupposes a version of Kantian-like transcendental idealism (compare my response to Slater's metaphysically realistic reading of James in the previous section): the world is not absolutely independent of us but is, instead, responsive to our ethical (or more generally valuational) needs and interests, or 'in the making' through an open-ended plurality of such needs and interests.[41] *We*—religious believers and non-believers—structure our reality in terms of what our practice-embedded (especially moral) agency requires; there is no pre-structured, 'ready-made' world that we could meaningfully engage with, as for us there is no 'God's-Eye View'—even to the question concerning God's reality. The world we find ourselves living in is structured by us—not merely by our 'cognitive faculty', as in Kant, but also by our various practical interests and purposes.[42] Pluralism, once again, is the key difference to Kantian constructivist metaphysics here: the world is ontologically 'structured' from a plurality of different perspectives. Yet, this structuring is at least analogous to the dependence of empirical reality on the structure imposed by the transcendental subject in Kantian transcendental philosophy (transcendental idealism).

In order to carry this line of thought through, we also need a pluralistic reconstruction of the transcendental subject itself, presumably in terms of social practices. The world-structuring transcendental subject(ivity) is itself perspectival, not an 'all-enveloping noetic unity',[43] but an open-ended set of practice-engagements based on socially positioned and historically emerging individuals' needs and purposes, which themselves develop through human history. The present chapter cannot undertake such a rearticulation of transcendental subjectivity, however. (A further question, not to be taken up here either, concerns the structuring of this subjectivity itself: *who* is responsible for the— again ethically relevant—task of reconceptualizing transcendental subjectivity into this new shape?)[44]

3 Pluralism, Relativism, and the Pragmatic Method

If my approach is taken seriously, then it turns out that pragmatism and Kantian transcendental methodology will have to be synthesized, and this synthesis will be most valuable because it enables us to pay attention to the emergence of another, even more important synthesis, namely, the one between metaphysics and ethics. Any truly pragmatist philosophy of religion must incorporate an inseparable integration of metaphysical and ethical commitments—or, better, it should advance an ineliminably metaphysical position defended (and in the end only defensible) by means of ethical considerations starting from our moral practices and from the requirements morality sets us. This follows from the pragmatist's premise that religion is ultimately a human practice, or a set of practices. We equally need to avoid both the monistic metaphysics of atheism (materialism) and the equally monistic position of absolute idealism, both of which would, in Jamesian terms, be examples of an overly abstract 'vicious intellectualism'. The latter's postulation of the Absolute, while it may grant us 'moral holidays', is as problematic ethically as the former's mechanistic, purely physical, deterministic 'block universe'. Both eliminate genuine human subjectivity and responsibility by eliminating all chance and novelty from the world.

These reflections also bear on the task of normatively legitimating religious ways of thinking. We may never be able to justify our religious (or non-religious, or any deep) commitments in a fully objective manner, to all parties potentially concerned, to the open-ended plurality of individual standpoints we must take seriously.[45] We also have to take seriously the moral task of justification itself before we can even begin arguing for, or against, theism. This is, above all, to accept the primacy of the ethical point of view we are continuously challenged to occupy—and thus the autonomy of morality in relation to everything else, including religion—but it is this very primacy that renders that point of view itself deeply metaphysical, inseparably and ubiquitously embedded in everything that goes on in our human lives, in everything (including God) we may be able to postulate, or to come to regard as real, from within those lives. It is in this sense that we might speak about the 'co-dependence' (mutual dependence) or perhaps 'co-constitutivity' of metaphysics and ethics in Jamesian philosophy of religion (and Jamesian pragmatist philosophy more generally).

I have suggested above that pragmatic pluralism must be taken to a 'meta-level'—both in metaphysics and in the philosophy of religion. Instead of ending up with radical relativism (as too straightforward forms of pragmatism may threaten to), the present discussion may, I hope, have taken some steps toward a healthy pragmatic pluralism in the philosophy of religion. The theism vs. atheism issue, any more than other deep metaphysical issues, cannot be adequately settled from a single, privileged perspective but requires a plurality of perspectives, pragmatically balanced and harmonized in terms of their potential functional workability in the (would-be) believer's overall account of the ethico-metaphysical problem of God as a problem of his or her personal life and reflective moral understanding. The philosophy of religion, if pragmatically adequate, must hence be thoroughly *antireductionist*. This is one of the messages of James' pluralism.

Arguably, then, James' pluralism is the true heir of the pragmatic method, especially in its applications to the philosophy of religion (and, extrapolating from this case study, more generally as well). Peirce characterized the pragmatic method, or the pragmatist maxim, as a method of 'making our ideas clear'.[46] He required that we should consider the conceivable practical results the objects of our ideas (beliefs, theories, concepts, or conceptions) might have in the course of experience in order to find out the true meaning of those ideas. James transformed this originally scientific method of conceptual clarification into a more *weltanschaulich* method of making our ideas pragmatically relevant in terms of human experience at large, moral and religious experience included. Here, in the case of religion, it is crucially important to take into account not just the *diverse religious experiences* that individuals have had and may have, but also the diversity and plurality of conceptual, theological, and philosophical approaches to those experiences, that is, the richness of philosophical and theological traditions through which people have tried to understand and organize their religious lives and problems. What this means is that no single philosophy of religion, not even James' own pluralism or pragmatism, can offer us an overarching, privileged perspective on the deeply problematic phenomenon of religion. We really do need a plurality of perspectives. This is one of the key implications of Jamesian pragmatism: we must be prepared to employ conceptual frameworks and philosophico-theological interpretations of religion different from, and even in tension with, pragmatism itself, in order fully to account for the pragmatically relevant differences in people's religious options and problems. We need, then, a truly pluralistic pragmatism in the philosophy of religion. We also need *genuine acknowledgment of otherness*—of different religious outlooks and different theological and/or philosophical (meta-theological) approaches. This is what we may get, if we apply the pragmatic method in its Jamesian formulation.

While, for instance, we may follow James in arguing that the monistic idealists' Absolute is ethically unacceptable and that metaphysical and religious pluralism makes better sense of a melioristic moral struggle for a better world, we should also keep our eyes open to the possible ethical virtues such monistic postulations might have. That is, we should not dogmatically reject them without pragmatically considering them, or perhaps even experimenting with them in our religious or non-religious lives. Furthermore, the anti-essentialist and anti-foundationalist pragmatist can hardly just say that pragmatism itself is 'essentially' pluralistic (although I may have come close to saying precisely that in the above discussion of Jamesian pluralism). More monistic versions of pragmatism (e.g. possibly, Peirce's) need to be acknowledged as well, as they also play a pragmatically valuable role in advancing certain human purposes—for example, scientific, if not religious or metaphysical or ethical. Our meta-level pluralism, then, should be connected with our acknowledgment of the ethical grounds of metaphysics:[47] pluralism is an expression of acknowledging the inevitable dependence of metaphysical inquiry on the inquirers' concrete individual, ethically— and even politically—loaded perspectives (including their individual 'philosophical temperaments'). Individuals may, for instance, weigh in their different ways the different criteria that can be used for determining the acceptability of metaphysical views, and there cannot be any absolute or universal algorithm for this weighing. To accept this pluralism *is* to be a pragmatist, in the Jamesian sense, that is, to be prepared to put metaphysical and theological ideas into action by evaluating them ethically in individuals' lives—social lives of course included. This, in short, is to employ the pragmatic method in one's metaphysical and religious considerations.

The problem we finally arrive at is, then, how to distinguish such pluralistic applications of pragmatism and the pragmatic method from relativism, from the shallow doctrine that 'anything goes'—regarding religion or anything else. Which philosophical or theological 'voices' should be heard, and which ones should be silenced? What does it mean, after all, that we 'hear' (or fail to hear) a philosophical or theological voice? These questions constitute a fundamental problem that must eventually be connected with the issue of *reflexivity*. When listening to *other* (metaphysical, philosophical, religious) voices in addition to pluralism, don't we have to say that pluralism itself is just one (or, rather, many!) of the many different correct philosophical views? Yes, we do have to accept this, at least in a sense. However, pluralism does not entail a shallow 'anything goes' relativism; or, better, any relativism we may be pragmatically entitled to embrace is itself only relatively and contextually acceptable. Above all, reflexivity is responsibility. Even if no 'voice' is absolute and infallible in human affairs, we can intelligently inquire into the pragmatic acceptability of any particular perspective.

Moreover, as the remarks above on James' relations to the problem of realism and to the Kantian issues of transcendental philosophy hopefully make clear, James himself was no shallow relativist at all, even though he is sometimes taken to be one.[48] He was, in the pragmatic sense of the term, as fully a 'realist' as anyone—especially when it comes to acknowledging the full reality, and the religious significance, of human suffering, mortality, and evil. This aspect of his realism still needs explanation and further elaboration.

4 The Religion—and Ethics—of a 'Sick Soul'

Let us, then, finally examine what may be regarded as the 'realistic spirit' of James' thought, especially as applied to the (pluralistic) reality of evil and suffering. The piecemeal and pluralistic approach in the philosophy of religion as well as in philosophy generally that James defends throughout his major works should not just be understood as a view emphasizing the plurality of 'positive'—happy, interesting, exciting, meaning-bestowing, significant—experiences that human beings have in their (secular and/or religious) lives. On the contrary, the 'negative'—unhappy, absurd, threatening, or even tragic—experiences are at least as important as the positive ones.

Pace Slater's metaphysically realistic interpretation of James (see section 1 above), it would be much more interesting to compare James' special kind of realism to the 'realistic spirit' that Cora Diamond attributes to Ludwig Wittgenstein,[49] at least if we purge Diamond's position from its anti-metaphysical and 'therapeuticist' aspects.[50] The ethical recognition of the full reality of evil and suffering is a crucial element of this realism, which, hence, is ultimately grounded in ethics, in the proper philosophical and experiential attitude we should take to other people around us, to the human 'voices' we must hear in the world. For the same reason, this form of realism is also pluralistic: there is no essence of evil and suffering but an irreducible individuality in them, very different voices, different 'cries of the wounded'.[51] Presumably Leo Tolstoy touches this polyphonic understanding of suffering as his narrator opens *Anna Karenina* by maintaining that all happy families are happy in the same way whereas unhappy families are each unhappy in their own specific way.

Based on this pluralism inherent in suffering, we may further suggest that James' realistic spirit, as applied to evil and suffering, is also a realism with *relational identities*. As James' radical empiricism—also called 'natural realism' by James himself—accepts the reality of relations, we should make the even more radical observation that, from the perspective of Jamesian realistic spirit, there is no non-relational existence at all. In particular, our own identities are relational: we are what we are—the kind of experiencing subjects we take ourselves to be—only through our relations to other human beings in a common world with different human needs and interests always already in place. This position has obvious ethical and political significance.[52]

As an illustration of what I propose to call the realism of the 'sick soul'—as distinguished from, for example, metaphysical or scientific realism, which would presumably go better together with the 'healthy-minded', in James' terminology—let us finally turn to James' views on the sick soul and moral holidays.

Here, my discussion differs from many other treatments of pragmatist philosophy of religion and moral philosophy due to what might be called its *via negativa* methodology. I am *not* trying to positively characterize, or to interpret James' characterizations of, such notions as the 'good life', or the 'goods' or 'fruits' of religious life and religious experiences—even though I do regard (Jamesian) pragmatism as a highly valuable perspective on these concepts and topics as well. On the contrary, I want to examine the nature of ethically acceptable religious outlooks by drawing attention to evil, suffering, melancholy, and tragedy. I agree with those who have emphasized the *tragic dimension of pragmatism*—the need to 'catch the deeper, darker tones of human articulation'[53]—in contrast to those who see pragmatism as a 'mere' philosophy of the good. (We might call the latter kind of pragmatists 'healthy-minded', adopting James' terminology from a different context.)[54] Meliorism, to use another Jamesian term, in my view *presupposes* (instead of overcoming) a serious attitude to the reality of evil, the acknowledgment, made in a 'realistic spirit', that we may not in the end be able to make the world a better place, even though we must try. There is, then, a tragic element inherent in pragmatic meliorism itself. While I am not entirely convinced that the notion of tragedy provides the best possible characterization of the Jamesian position regarding evil and suffering (see below), I do believe that James' concept of a sick soul,[55] and especially his account of the ethical and religious relevance of this concept, captures a great deal of what has been meant by the 'tragic sense of life'.[56]

James' concept of a moral holiday, formulated in the context of his pragmatic critique of the Absolute (cf. above), is highly significant here. We are lucky to have avoided (at least many) tragic moral choices, for instance; this is a kind of 'holiday' we may view ourselves as enjoying. This instance of 'moral luck' enables us to take a relatively relaxed and happy attitude to moral life. Just as we do not have to worry about our daily duties when enjoying a vacation, we need not (at least not all the time) worry about our not having helped the Jewish families that desperately tried to avoid deportation to concentration camps in the 1940s. At least we haven't done anything we should feel guilty about regarding this historical event we were not part of; so we can sit back and enjoy our moral holiday. Those who were less lucky—those who were there when they shouldn't have been—are 'punished', in a sense, by a bad conscience, or more severely by the need to make a tragic choice that will haunt them for the rest of their lives. Alternatively, we might say that we may be inclined to accept the 'fact' of what has been called moral luck without much worrying about it, if we are (in James' terms) 'healthy-minded' thinkers; only the sick souls are truly concerned with this issue, and only for them is the reality of moral luck a phenomenon that makes their moral lives problematic from the start.

This is how James describes the 'moral holiday' in *Pragmatism*, in relation to the Hegelian idealists' in his view ethically and metaphysically appalling postulation of the Absolute:

> What do believers in the Absolute mean by saying that their belief affords them comfort? They mean that since in the Absolute finite evil is 'overruled' already, we may, therefore, whenever we wish, treat the temporal as if it were potentially the eternal, be sure that we can trust its outcome, and, without sin, dismiss our fear and drop the worry of our finite responsibility. In short, they mean that we have a right ever and anon to take a moral holiday, to let the world wag in its own way, feeling that its issues are in better hands than ours and are none of our business.
>
> The universe is a system of which the individual members may relax their anxieties occasionally, in which the don't-care mood is also right for men, and moral holidays in order,—that, if I mistake not, is part, at least, of what the Absolute is 'known-as,' that is the great difference in our particular experiences which his being true makes, for us, that is part of his cash-value when he is pragmatically interpreted. [...] If the Absolute means this, and means no more than this, who can possibly deny the truth of it? To deny it would

be to insist that men should never relax, and that holidays are never in order.[57]

However, the fundamental Jamesian argument, ultimately, is of course *not* that we are entitled to take our moral holiday, either because of having been 'morally lucky' or for any other reason, but rather that there are in the end no moral holidays available to us. There is no possibility for any genuine rest or relaxation in moral matters. This is also the reason why moral luck is a phenomenon that troubles us.

In *The Varieties of Religious Experience* (1902), James tells us that the sick souls are those who, in contrast to the 'healthy-minded', maintain that 'the evil aspects of our life are of its very essence, and that the world's meaning most comes home to us when we lay them most to heart'.[58] The sick souls, then, are those 'who cannot so swiftly throw off the burden of the consciousness of evil, but are congenitally fated to suffer from its presence'.[59] Reflecting on the reality of evil and suffering, we may become 'melancholy metaphysicians',[60] acknowledging human helplessness and sadness even when life seems happy and easy. James concludes:

> The method of averting one's attention from evil, and living simply in the light of good is splendid as long as it will work. It will work with many persons [...]. But it breaks down impotently as soon as melancholy comes; and even though one be quite free from melancholy one's self, there is no doubt that healthy-mindedness is inadequate as a philosophical doctrine, because the evil facts which it refuses positively to account for are a genuine portion of reality; and they may after all be the best key to life's significance, and possibly the only openers of our eyes to the deepest levels of truth.[61]

Therefore, James suggests, '[t]he completest religions would [...] seem to be those in which the pessimistic elements are best developed'—that is, 'religions of deliverance', according to which one has to 'die to an unreal life' in order to be 'born into the real life'.[62]

The concept of a sick soul is, for James, a concept to be employed in the description and explanation of certain kind of religious attitudes and ways of living and thinking. This, we might say, is a description and/or explanation based on a 'realistic spirit'. It incorporates a realistic attitude to evil and suffering we experience, or see others as experiencing, around us. However, given the close relation between religion and ethics in James (and pragmatism more generally), the concept of a sick soul can, I believe, be used in ethical contexts bracketing the actual religious aspects of, say, conversion. We may say that the sick soul takes extremely seriously—ethically seriously, and therefore 'realistically'— the evil and suffering around him or her in the world even if he or she never experiences this as a *religious* problem. The sick soul, then, acknowledges that (as James puts it toward the end of *Pragmatism*, without using this specific terminology) 'something permanently drastic and bitter' may always be in store for us, however successfully we fight against evil and suffering. The specific kinds of realism and pluralism available in Jamesian philosophy of religion, therefore, are highly significant even beyond the philosophy of religion proper.

In his posthumously published work, *Some Problems of Philosophy* (1911), James contrasted pluralism and monism in terms of the problem of evil as follows:

> Evil, for pluralism, presents only the practical problem of how to get rid of it. For monism the puzzle is theoretical: How—if Perfection be the source, should there be Imperfection? If the world as known to the Absolute be perfect, why should it be known otherwise, in myriads of inferior finite editions also? The perfect edition surely was enough. How do the breakage and dispersion and ignorance get in?[63]

Accordingly, the theoretical approach of monists (e.g. Hegelian idealists) leads to the theodicy problem, while the practical approach of the pluralists (including James himself) starts from the acknowledgment that evil is real—not to be explained away or justified—and focuses on the task of 'how to get rid of it'. In *Pragmatism*, James argued against 'the airy and shallow optimism of current religious philosophy' that what suffering human beings experience '*is* Reality':

> But while Professors Royce and Bradley and a whole host of guileless thoroughfed thinkers are unveiling Reality and the Absolute and explaining away evil and pain, this is the condition of the only beings known to us anywhere in the universe, with a developed consciousness of what the universe is.[64]

A Leibnizian theodicy, in particular, postulating a 'harmony' of the universe, amounts to 'a cold literary exercise, whose cheerful substance even hell-fire does not warm'; hence, the idealist and optimist philosophers James argues against are, he says, 'dealing in shades, while those who live and feel know truth'.[65]

James' *Pragmatism* actually opens its very project of advancing a melioristic philosophy with a discussion of the reality of evil. Even in the final pages of the book James returns to evil, suffering, loss, and tragedy:

> In particular *this* query has always come home to me: May not the claims of tender-mindedness go too far? May not the notion of a world already saved *in toto* anyhow, be too saccharine to stand? May not religious optimism be too idyllic? Must *all* be saved? Is *no* price to be paid in the work of salvation? Is the last word sweet? Is all 'yes, yes' in the universe? Doesn't the fact of 'no' stand at the very core of life? Doesn't the very 'seriousness' that we attribute to life mean that ineluctable noes and losses form a part of it, that there are genuine sacrifices somewhere, and that something permanently drastic and bitter always remains at the bottom of its cup?
>
> I cannot speak officially as a pragmatist here; all I can say is that my own pragmatism offers no objection to my taking sides with this more moralistic view, and giving up the claim of total reconciliation. [...] It is then perfectly possible to accept sincerely a drastic kind of a universe from which the element of 'seriousness' is not to be expelled. Whoso does so is, it seems to me, a genuine pragmatist.[66]

It is this very same moral seriousness that has been emphasized in the contemporary discourse on evil by Susan Neiman, Richard Bernstein, and others.[67] Our moral life with other human beings in this world full of suffering is inevitably tragic. This is because, given our human finitude, we will never be able fully to overcome the irreducible plurality of evil and suffering; yet we must always, melioristically, try. Our moral seriousness is based on this realistic realization of the tragic dimension of life that is part of our pragmatic pluralism itself. This is what the sick soul realizes, and this is what makes the sick soul's perspective on life superior to the 'healthy-minded' person's perspective—even when the sick soul himself or herself is 'morally lucky' to enjoy relatively nondemanding ethical situations.

The concept of the sick soul has been discussed by commentators in great detail, but the complete ethical aspects of this notion still remain to be worked out. The sick soul, indeed, never enjoys a moral holiday but is fundamentally serious and melancholic. His or her basic attitude to the world and life or she experiences is the one of melancholy. His or her *world*—not just his or her attitude to the world he or she lives in—is fundamentally melancholic. Furthermore, it could even be argued that ultimately only the sick soul is, or can be, 'genuinely religious' (and perhaps genuinely ethical, too). A religious attitude, however enjoyable the positive fruits of religion may be, is melancholic, thus affirming the seriousness of life at a level at which only religious responses are available to one's ultimate questions and concerns.

Being a sick soul is, moreover, to be fundamentally—*melancholically*—conscious of and concerned with one's—and generally human—mortality and finitude, as well as with the contingent traces one's actions (as well as omissions) leave in the world. Hence, the notion of a sick soul is finally closely related to the *irrevocability* of evil and suffering—an issue that has also been emphasized in recent discussions of pragmatist moral philosophy and philosophy of religion.[68] Everything, including the Holocaust, is forever real. Our ultimate concern in morality may be that whatever we do, or fail to do, leaves irrevocable traces into whatever futures, or future presents, we or our fellow human beings will inhabit.[69] Any human act (or omission) is radically contingent, excluding a myriad of possible worlds. Moral luck is a pervasive phenomenon, and its pervasiveness may make the demands of morality either illusory or, perhaps even worse, too tragic to live with. The sick soul melancholically reflects on this state of affairs, finding no peace in such reflection, realizing the impossibility of ever taking a genuine moral holiday.

There is, then, a tension deeply involved in the sick soul's ethical (and/or religious) engagement with the world. The sick soul recognizes, and acknowledges our need to continuously recognize, both *finitude* (human mortality and the resulting contingency) and a kind of *infinity* (irrevocability)—that is, our inability to ever heal all the wounds there are, to wipe suffering away in its plural forms. On the one hand, we always inevitably leave a trace to the world; on the other hand, we will some day be gone and nothing will remain. Both the traces and the threatening nothingness pose us an existential challenge that may (possibly) be met only religiously, if at all.[70]

5 Conclusion

A final metaphysical issue remains to be considered—and to be left for another occasion for further scrutiny. As is well known, James' pragmatism emphasizes actual and concrete life experiences in comparison to Peirce's original version of the 'pragmatic maxim', which focuses on the *conceivable*—possibly never actualized—practical effects that the objects of our ideas might have. If Peirce's 'real generals' are real—if there are real *possibilia*, for instance[71]—then it could be argued that not only the actual facts and events of human history but also the mere possibilities that were never actualized are 'irrevocable' in the tragic sense described above. Then, not only actual horrors such as the Holocaust but the irreducible plurality of all possible horrors would be irrevocably part of our ethical orientation to the world we live in and would need our 'realistic' moral attention. We should, reminded by what is actual, be aware of what is possible for us. As has been often remarked, the Holocaust showed what human beings are capable of. So its horror is not merely in what actually happened, even though that is as horrible as anything can be, but also in what *may* happen. Sometimes the actual may simply shock us, as Peircean Secondness, in such a manner that we may be unable to even reflect further on any mere possibilities, but even amidst such shock effects there is room for the further realization that even something worse *could* have happened. We are always capable of more; even though we are finite and contingent beings, there is no upper limit to the suffering we can in principle inflict on other human beings, and therefore no upper limit to the demands of the cries of the wounded we must never shut our ears to.

This adds one more existential dimension to the picture of pluralism, and to the picture of the special kind of realism (or 'realistic spirit') that goes together with pluralism in Jamesian pragmatism. I am not claiming that the dimensions of Jamesian pluralism I have identified and emphasized are *the* correct ones, or even *the* most important ones, however. There is—for pragmatist readers of James, at least—a plurality of correct readings of James, each good, or pragmatically useful, for its own purposes. For example, early in this chapter, I tried to show that Slater's picture of James, while correcting many of the catastrophic inaccuracies of James scholarship, is too much a picture of a metaphysical realist to represent the real James. Furthermore, while my own Kantianized 'transcendental James' with a realistic attitude to evil may not be *the* real James, either, I do believe that a rereading of James as a kind of transcendental pragmatist illuminates the troubles he had with realism and idealism, while also providing us with ample conceptual resources for making sense of his unique combination of realism, pluralism, and humanism.

To return to where we started in section 1 above, I should like to conclude by noting that I obviously agree with Slater, then, that '[t]here is much in James [...] that is philosophically interesting and defensible, and much that might variously strengthen or challenge our prevailing philosophical assumptions'.[72] I am only suggesting that the best of James, and even the best of his (religious) realism, can be brought out by (re)interpreting him as a pluralistic transcendental pragmatist instead of a metaphysical realist. This strategy is actually in accord with Slater's own pluralistic proposal to 'take James in piecemeal fashion rather than taking him wholesale'.[73] This meta-level interpretive pluralism is, presumably, the only acceptable methodology for the pragmatist reader of James, who is as fallibilist in his or her interpretations as in any other beliefs and who recognizes James' own (many) voices as being among those we must ever more carefully learn to listen to.[74]

Notes

1. References to James' writings will, if not indicated otherwise, be to *The Works of William James* (1975–88), 19 vols, eds. F. H. Burkhardt, F. Bowers, and I. K. Skrupskelis (Cambridge, MA and London: Harvard University Press). *Pragmatism: A New Name for Some Old Ways of Thinking* appeared in this edition in 1975 and *The Meaning of Truth: A Sequel to* Pragmatism in 1978.
2. For a detailed analysis of the tension between realism and its alternatives in classical and contemporary pragmatism, see S. Pihlström (1996) *Structuring the World: The Issue of Realism and the Nature of Ontological Problems in Classical and Contemporary Pragmatism* (Acta Philosophica Fennica 59, Helsinki: The Philosophical Society of Finland). For my previous engagements with James' philosophy of religion, in particular, see S. Pihlström (2008) *'The Trail of the Human Serpent Is over Everything': Jamesian Perspectives on Mind, World, and Religion* (Lanham, MD: University Press of America).
3. M. R. Slater (2008) 'Pragmatism, Realism, and Religion', *Journal of Religious Ethics*, 36, 653–81. Slater has recently offered a more comprehensive version of his argument in M. R. Slater (2009) *William James on Ethics and Faith* (Cambridge: Cambridge University Press), but I will focus on the 2008 paper here.
4. Slater, 'Pragmatism, Realism, and Religion', p. 655.
5. See James' response to various critics of *Pragmatism* in the essays collected in *The Meaning of Truth*.
6. R. Audi (ed.) (1999), *Cambridge Dictionary of Philosophy* (Cambridge: Cambridge University Press). See Slater, 'Pragmatism, Realism, and Religion', p. 658n5.
7. In addition to Putnam's many works, see Pihlström, *Structuring the World*, chapters 3–4. It should be noted that Putnam has recently once again reconsidered his views on realism: see several essays in H. Putnam (2012) *Philosophy in an Age of Science* (Cambridge, MA and London: Harvard University Press).
8. See James, *Pragmatism*, pp. 121–3.
9. See Slater, 'Pragmatism, Realism, and Religion', p. 661.
10. D. M. Armstrong (2004) *Truth and Truthmakers* (Cambridge: Cambridge University Press).
11. Slater, 'Pragmatism, Realism, and Religion', p. 662.
12. See S. Pihlström (2009) *Pragmatist Metaphysics: An Essay on the Ethical Grounds of Ontology* (London and New York: Continuum), chapter 2.
13. Slater, 'Pragmatism, Realism, and Religion', p. 665.
14. Ibid., pp. 663–4n16.
15. Ibid., p. 665.

16. James' occasional references to 'humanism' must be set in the context of his exchange of ideas with F. C. S. Schiller, the somewhat more radical British pragmatist who called his view 'humanism'. This is not the right place to examine their similarities and differences in any detail.
17. Slater, 'Pragmatism, Realism, and Religion', p. 665.
18. Cf. Pihlström, 'The Trail of the Human Serpent Is over Everything'; and S. Pihlström (2013) *Pragmatic Pluralism and the Problem of God* (New York: Fordham University Press), for the suggestion that there must be something analogous to transcendental idealism at work in James' pragmatism, if, e.g., his essentially ethical argumentation in favor of theistic metaphysics is supposed to get off the ground.
19. See N. Goodman (1978) *Ways of Worldmaking* (Indianapolis: Hackett). Goodman, having been told that his views resembled those that James had defended decades earlier, famously once quipped that James quoted him without mentioning the source.
20. Slater, 'Pragmatism, Realism, and Religion', p. 666.
21. Ibid., p. 667.
22. Ibid., p. 670.
23. Ibid., p. 654. Cf. also Pihlström, *Pragmatist Metaphysics*, chapter 7; *Pragmatic Pluralism and the Problem of God*, chapter 1; as well as the reflections in this essay below.
24. Slater, 'Pragmatism, Realism, and Religion', p. 671.
25. Ibid., p. 674 (original emphasis).
26. Ibid., pp. 668, 674.
27. Ibid., p. 676.
28. See also the Introduction to this volume.
29. Note that this by no means precludes rational criticism of religious ways of thinking; on the contrary, such criticism itself is served by an enhanced understanding of the ways in which religion functions in our practices—or *is* a practice. Pragmatist philosophy of religion is obviously committed to the traditional *normative* task of the philosophy of religion, seeking to critically evaluate, and not just to explain and understand, religious beliefs and practices from a non-committed perspective. The science vs. religion dialogue, in particular, vitally needs a comprehensive and tolerant account of both scientific and religious practices and their diverging conceptions of rationality and intellectual (as well as ethical) responsibility. A lot has gone wrong in this dialogue, as is witnessed by the controversies over teaching evolution in schools in the United States, the increasing conflicts between radical, fundamentalist Islam and the Western world, the equally increasing hostility toward even moderate Islam in various countries, and other unfortunate developments. Pragmatism—particularly Jamesian pragmatism—promises to advance a much more deeply understanding approach to the issues of science vs. religion, offering us pluralism and tolerance without succumbing to uncritical relativism, according to which 'anything goes'. For a more comprehensive defense of pragmatist philosophy of religion along these lines, see Pihlström, *Pragmatic Pluralism and the Problem of God* (cited above).
30. James examines this problem at some length in Lecture IV of *Pragmatism*, as well as his late work, *A Pluralistic Universe* (1909), both available in *The Works of William James* (1975 and 1979, respectively).

102   William James on Religion

31. This should be sufficient to set to rest the oft-heard allegation that James' pragmatism is simply nominalistic. He does believe that universals or generals, especially 'kinds', have an important philosophical role to play, insofar as they are pragmatically cashed out.
32. James, *Pragmatism*, p. 73.
33. Ibid., p. 79. See also James' discussion of pluralism in his posthumous work, *Some Problems of Philosophy* (1911), chapters 7–8: 'Pluralism [unlike monism or absolute idealism] is neither optimistic nor pessimistic, but melioristic. The world, it thinks, may be saved, on condition that its parts shall do their best. But shipwreck in detail, or even on the whole, is among the open possibilities.' And further: 'Towards this issue, of the reality or unreality of the novelty that appears, the pragmatic difference between monism and pluralism seems to converge. That we ourselves may be authors of genuine novelty is the thesis of the doctrine of free-will.' W. James (1996 [1911]) *Some Problems of Philosophy* (Bison Books edition, ed. E. K. Suckiel, Nebraska and London: University of Nebraska Press), pp. 142, 145. Among the key problems of monistic idealism is, then, that it is fatalistic (sacrificing real novelty and chance) and leads to the problem of evil (ibid., pp. 138–9).
34. In addition to *A Pluralistic Universe*, cf. W. James (1912) *Essays in Radical Empiricism*, also included in *The Works of William James* (1977). James' position here has also been described as 'piecemeal panpsychism' or 'panexperientialism'. Here I will set aside the interpretive issue of whether James is, in some sense, a panpsychist or not.
35. When quoting from James' *A Pluralistic Universe* (2008), I am using the new edition edited and introduced by H. G. Callaway (Cambridge: Cambridge Scholars Press), which contains the editor's useful notes and his discussion of the different meanings of pluralism. For the quotation, see p. 21. Note also that in this passage and elsewhere, James understands—somewhat puzzlingly—pluralism as a species of 'pantheism', a spiritualist view that, unlike monism, understands the 'spiritual substance' of the universe not as an 'all-form' but as an 'each-form', rejecting the 'intellectually neat' picture of monistic idealism with its Absolute (see p. 28). In particular, the problem of evil, James argues, haunts absolutist conceptions of the spiritual universe (ibid., p. 72).
36. See H. Putnam (1990) *Realism with a Human Face*, ed. J. Conant (Cambridge, MA and London: Harvard University Press); and H. Putnam (2004) *Ethics without Ontology* (Cambridge, MA and London: Harvard University Press). (As noted above, Putnam's most recent volume, *Philosophy in an Age of Science*, reconsiders some of these views.) Cf. also R. B. Goodman, 'Some Sources of Putnam's Pluralism', in M. Bahgramiam (ed.) (2012) *Reading Putnam* (London and New York: Routledge), pp. 205–18, for a recent discussion of the different versions of, and the historical background influences (including James) of *Putnam*'s pluralism. Goodman also speaks about there being a 'plurality of pluralisms' (p. 205) and notes that pluralism can be seen as a species of realism (p. 206)—both extremely important observations also regarding the argument of the present chapter.
37. Note that pragmatism thus rejects *metaphysically realistic metaphysics* but not necessarily metaphysics as such, because metaphysics can itself be interpreted pragmatically as an inquiry into the 'human world' and its

(categorization-dependent and thus in the end pragmatically constructed) structure. See Pihlström, *Pragmatist Metaphysics*. It must be kept in mind that the 'world-structuring' the pragmatist metaphysician is interested in is never merely ontological but also epistemic (and, as will emerge in due course, also ethical). See also the previous section. If the phrase, 'imposed on it by us', sounds too traditionally Kantian, as I am sure it will sound to many pragmatist readers, try the following replacement (kindly suggested by David Hildebrand): 'a natural outcome of our lived experience'. The latter retains as much transcendentality as is necessary in a Jamesian pragmatist context.

38. Another (related) difference between Kant and James, not to be further discussed here, is the fact that, according to James, our experience always contains elements that cannot be conceptually classified or categorized. However, admitting that no categorization is final or total is not to reject categorization completely. Radical empiricism itself is *a* way of categorizing reality, however anti-conceptualistic.

39. In order properly to use such a label here, we should pay attention to James' criticisms of the notion of substance in *Pragmatism*, Lecture III (see also Pihlström, *Pragmatist Metaphysics*). Clearly, pluralism, for James, cannot just be, say, the view that there is a plurality of substances, as the concept of a substance must itself be pragmatically examined, and it may even be put to work within pluralism by emphasizing its different functions as, say, both the bearer of properties and the unchanging permanence amidst all changes.

40. See Pihlström, *Pragmatist Metaphysics*, for an extended argument for this interpretation.

41. I am here deliberately redescribing transcendental idealism by employing Jamesian terminology. Orthodox Kantians (as well as Jamesians) will find my Jamesian rearticulations of Kant problematic; however, my main interest lies in systematic issues in the philosophy of religion, pragmatically considered, rather than in detailed historical questions. Some work has, however, been done on the historical relations between Kant and James: see, e.g., S. Pihlström (2006) 'Synthesizing Traditions: Rewriting the History of Pragmatism and Transcendental Philosophy', *History of Philosophy Quarterly*, 23, 375–90. Let me also note that Peter Byrne (1998), in his *The Moral Interpretation of Religion* (Edinburgh: Edinburgh University Press), explicitly compares Kant's moral argument for God's existence with James' 'will to believe' argument (see chapter 7). My approach is quite different, though, because (unlike some of the other contributors to this volume) I am not here focusing on 'The Will to Believe' (but, rather, on *Pragmatism*) and because I view James' own ideas 'transcendentally'; cf. section 1 above.

42. Or, to put the point in a more properly Jamesian manner, these needs, interests, and purposes are always already at work within our cognitive faculty itself; there is no pure cognition independently of practical orientation in the world. This is pretty much what pragmatism is all about: any experience, cognition, or representation we are capable of is inseparably embedded in human practices, or habits of action. See also Wayne Proudfoot's discussion (in his contribution to this volume) of James' view that our world-picture needs to construe reality 'congruously with our spontaneous powers'.

43. This is one of James' descriptions of the Absolute in Lecture IV of *Pragmatism*.
44. I deal with these issues concerning the pragmatist ontology of subjectivity in Pihlström, 'The Trail of the Human Serpent Is over Everything', chapter 5. See also S. Pihlström (2009) 'Pragmatism and Naturalized Transcendental Subjectivity', *Contemporary Pragmatism*, 6, 1–13, for a more comprehensive discussion of this particular topic, in relation to more standard pragmatist accounts of subjectivity.
45. For James' 'will to believe' argument and its relevance in contemporary philosophy of religion, see the other chapters of this volume, especially Guy Axtell's and Dirk-Martin Grube's essays.
46. Peirce's famous essay, 'How to Make Our Ideas Clear' (1878), is reprinted, among other places, in *The Essential Peirce* (1992), Vol. 1, eds. N. Houser et al. (Bloomington and Indianapolis: Indiana University Press).
47. See again Pihlström, *Pragmatist Metaphysics*.
48. What is more, I definitely do not think that any reading of James is as correct as any other; on the contrary, I have above argued against some of the mischaracterizations of James that I find in Slater's interpretation. Yet, again, we should not be too easily led to believe that any one interpretation of James is correct; here, again, pluralism should reign. There may be a plurality of correct readings of James, but this does not mean that there is no distinction between better and worse readings.
49. See C. Diamond (1991) *The Realistic Spirit* (Cambridge, MA and London: MIT Press). Putnam also finds this conception of realism important (though not uncontroversial) both as a reading of Wittgenstein and as a general philosophical approach. Cf., e.g., his essays on Wittgenstein in Putnam, *Philosophy in an Age of Science* (cited above).
50. For a critical comment on too strongly (dogmatically) therapeutic readings of Wittgenstein and the pragmatists, see S. Pihlström (2012) 'A New Look at Wittgenstein and Pragmatism', *European Journal of Pragmatism and American Philosophy*, 4, URL: www.journalofpragmatism.eu (accessed 17 July 2012).
51. As one of the few recent theorists of evil inspired by pragmatism, Richard Bernstein, explains (without specifically referring to these Jamesian considerations), there is no essence of evil; rather, evil can take very different forms in different historical situations. See R. Bernstein (2002) *Radical Evil: A Philosophical Interrogation* (Cambridge: Polity Press); and R. Bernstein (2005) *The Abuse of Evil* (Cambridge: Polity Press). For a more Jamesian approach to the problem of evil, see Pihlström, *Pragmatic Pluralism and the Problem of God*, chapter 5.
52. On the importance of James' conception of relational identities, see J. Medina (2010) 'James on Truth and Solidarity: The Epistemology of Diversity and the Politics of Specificity' in J. J. Stuhr (ed.) *100 Years of Pragmatism: William James's Revolutionary Philosophy* (Bloomington: Indiana University Press), pp. 124–43.
53. V. Colapietro (forthcoming 2012) 'The Tragic Roots of Jamesian Pragmatism', forthcoming in *Journal of Speculative Philosophy*, ms., 19.
54. W. James (1958 [1902]) *The Varieties of Religious Experience: A Study in Human Nature* (New York: New American Library), Lectures IV and V.

55. This concept is explored by James in ibid., Lectures VI and VII. Compare Russell B. Goodman's characterization in R. B. Goodman (2012) 'Encountering Cavell: The Education of a Grownup' in N. Saito and P. Standish (eds.) *Stanley Cavell and the Education of Grownups* (New York: Fordham University Press), pp. 62–3: 'I soon concluded that what James calls "the sick soul" in *Varieties of Religious Experience* is a form of the lived skepticism that Cavell describes in his essays on Thoreau, Coleridge, and Wordsworth. I found that, like Cavell and Heidegger, James searches for an "intimacy" between self and world.' While I will avoid comparisons between James and the other thinkers invoked by Goodman here, I very much sympathize with the idea that the sick soul attempts to find a kind of 'intimacy' he or she never fully succeeds in finding. (Cf. also Proudfoot's chapter in this volume.)
56. We should duly note that the phrase, 'pragmatism and the tragic sense of life', was coined by Sidney Hook in his book with the same title: see S. Hook (1974) *Pragmatism and the Tragic Sense of Life* (New York: Basic Books). However, I am not going to deal with Hook's (largely Deweyan rather than Jamesian) version of pragmatism in any detail here. The fact that the phrase, 'the tragic sense of life', originates with Miguel de Unamuno, should also be acknowledged. James is, clearly, a thinker with a philosophical temperament very close to this famous Spanish thinker and essayist.
57. James, *Pragmatism*, Lecture II.
58. James, *Varieties*, p. 114.
59. Ibid., p. 116.
60. Ibid., p. 121.
61. Ibid., pp. 137–8.
62. Ibid., p. 139.
63. W. James (1977 [1911]) *Some Problems of Philosophy: A Beginning of an Introduction to Philosophy*, eds. F. H. Burkhardt, F. Bowers and I. K. Skrupskelis (Cambridge, MA and London: Harvard University Press), p. 138. See also James, *Varieties*, p. 115.
64. James, *Pragmatism*, pp. 20–1.
65. Ibid., pp. 20, 22.
66. Ibid., pp. 141–2.
67. See S. Neiman (2002) *Evil in Modern Thought: An Alternative History of Philosophy* (Princeton, NJ: Princeton University Press); Bernstein, *Radical Evil* and *Abusing Evil* (cited above).
68. Cf. here Claudio Viale's excellent paper, 'Royce and Bernstein on Evil' (submitted ms., forthcoming); as well as Colapietro's above-cited essay, 'The Tragic Roots of Jamesian Pragmatism', where Colapietro returns to Hook's conception of the tragic sense of life by noting that the losses felt as tragic are irrevocable, and unredeemable. Viale's discussion should make us rethink the conventional conception of Josiah Royce (as a pragmatist postulating the Absolute) as a thinker seeking to offer us a theodicy, even though theodicy does seem to be threatening the ethical acceptability of Royce's position, too. Royce's reflections on irrevocability and sorrow are highly relevant to the Jamesian concerns of the present essay, even though I haven't tried to comment on Royce at all here. (Cf. also another recent manuscript by Claudio Viale: 'William James' Conception of Religion in Josiah Royce's Mature Thought: Three Approaches'. I should note that while I am largely sympathetic to Viale's

careful explorations of James and Royce, the kind of secularized and ethical characterization of the sick soul that I have offered in this chapter—going beyond James' own views to some extent—is in a mild tension with Viale's claim that there is no '*moral* salvation' available for the sick souls: 'morality never cures' [ms., pp. 9–10]. This is undoubtedly true if we focus on what James actually says about the possibility of salvation the sick soul faces, but if we take into account not just the *Varieties* but also *Pragmatism* and other late works, we will be forced to admit that the philosophical view of religion available to the Jamesian pragmatist is itself thoroughly ethical, to the extent that any religious metaphysics that is humanly possible must, as I have argued above, have ethical grounds, even if religion itself—or the notion of salvation in particular—cannot be reduced to ethics. Life in general is a moral struggle for Jamesian pragmatists; viewing religion and morality as parts of the same overall project of finding meaning in life is not to maintain any specific conception of salvation—a topic I am glad to leave for theologians to discuss further.)
69. I am indebted to Hans Joas' comments on this idea at the conference, *Pragmatism and the Theory of Religion*, in Erfurt, Germany, in February, 2012.
70. While this chapter has not explicitly addressed James' views on death and mortality (for my earlier discussions of that topic, see S. Pihlström (2002) 'William James on Death, Mortality, and Immortality', *Transactions of the Charles S. Peirce Society*, 38; reprinted in an expanded form in S. Pihlström, '*The Trail of the Human Serpent Is over Everything*', chapter 3), it seems to me clear that human mortality—or, more generally, vulnerability and potential helplessness—is a key source of the sick soul's attitude to the world: 'The fact that we *can* die, that we *can* be ill at all, is what perplexes us, the fact that we now for a moment live and are well is irrelevant to that perplexity. We need a life not correlated with death, a health not liable to illness, a kind of good that will not perish, a good in fact that flies beyond the Goods of nature.' (James, *Varieties*, p. 121.)
71. For Peirce's writings—early and late—defending 'scholastic realism', see *The Essential Peirce*, both volumes.
72. Slater, 'Pragmatism, Realism, and Religion', p. 655.
73. Ibid., p. 678.
74. Early versions of this material were partly presented in the symposium, *Monism, Pluralism, and Metaphysics*, at the University of Tampere, Finland (August, 2010), and at the conference, *William James and the Transatlantic Conversation: Pragmatism, Pluralism, and the Philosophy of Religion* (University of Oxford, UK, September, 2010). I should like to thank the organizers of these events (Leila Haaparanta and Heikki J. Koskinen, and Martin Halliwell and Joel Rasmussen, respectively), as well as the audiences for critical suggestions. There is a minor overlap between this chapter and my contribution appearing in the volume based on the Oxford conference (eds. Halliwell and Rasmussen, Oxford University Press, forthcoming). Some parts of the material also slightly overlap with the essay I recently wrote for another conference volume (that is, the one to be based on the conference, *Pragmatism and the Theory of Religion*, Max-Weber-Kolleg, University of Erfurt, Germany, February, 2012), eds. Magnus Schlette et al. In addition, the topic of this

essay is more comprehensively discussed in chapter 4 of my above-cited monograph, *Pragmatic Pluralism and the Problem of God* (2013). Moreover, I am indebted to Vincent Colapietro, Russell B. Goodman, David Hildebrand, Hans Joas, Heikki A. Kovalainen, Wayne Proudfoot, Henrik Rydenfelt, Thomas Schmidt, Claudio Viale, and many others for highly valuable comments and discussions on the topic of this chapter.

Part II

5
'The Ethics of Belief' Reconsidered[*]

Susan Haack

What is the relation of epistemic to ethical appraisal? Possible answers include:

(1) that epistemic appraisal is a sub-species of ethical appraisal—henceforth, for short, the **special-case thesis**;
(2) that positive/negative epistemic appraisal is distinct from, but invariably associated with, positive/negative ethical appraisal—the **correlation thesis**;
(3) that there is, not invariable correlation, but partial overlap, where positive/negative epistemic appraisal is associated with positive/negative ethical appraisal—the **overlap thesis**;
(4) that ethical appraisal is inapplicable where epistemological appraisal is relevant—the **independence thesis**;
(5) that epistemic appraisal is distinct from, but analogous to, ethical appraisal—the **analogy thesis**.

I hope this list exhausts the serious options.[1] But refinements will be needed to take account of the fact that each of the positions listed has both a completely general form ('for every dimension of epistemic appraisal'), and a variety of specific forms (e.g., 'where epistemic appraisal of someone as completely, or to some degree, justified, or as unjustified, in believing that ... is concerned'). The correct account may be different with respect to different dimensions of epistemic appraisal. But the logical relations among the positions listed are the

---

[*]Reprinted by permission from *The Philosophy of R. M. Chisholm*, edited by Lewis Edwin Hahn, La Salle, IL: Open Court Publishing Company,1997. Copyright © 1997 by the Library of Living Philosophers.

same whether one considers each in its general form, or each in the same specific form. The special-case thesis is incompatible with any of the others. The correlation thesis is incompatible with the overlap thesis and with the independence thesis. The analogy thesis, however, though incompatible with the special-case thesis, is compatible with the correlation thesis, with the overlap thesis, and even with the independence thesis.

In 'Firth and the Ethics of Belief', published in 1991, Chisholm writes that since 1938, when he and Firth both enrolled in Ralph Barton Perry's seminar on value theory, 'Firth's inclination was to say that [epistemic justification] is merely an analogue [of ethical justification]; and my inclination was to say that it is a subspecies [...] I still find myself inclined to accept the original view'.[2] For most of this essay I shall concentrate, like Chisholm and Firth, specifically on the relation of epistemic to ethical justification. Here, as I see it, the special-case thesis is too strong, the analogy thesis (not false but) too weak; the relation of epistemic to ethical justification is as stated in the overlap thesis: less intimate than partial identity, more intimate than analogy.

Interwoven with my arguments for this specific version of the overlap thesis will be some speculations of a more historical character: that in the celebrated debate between Clifford and James, it is their shared failure to distinguish epistemological from ethical justification that creates the false impression that one must choose *either* the morally over-demanding account proposed in 'The Ethics of Belief', *or* the epistemologically over-permissive account proposed in 'The Will to Believe'. And interwoven with these speculations will be an argument that locates Chisholm closer to the Jamesian side of that debate, significantly more permissive epistemologically than Clifford—and somewhat more permissive epistemologically than myself.

Finally, I shall turn my attention briefly to the relation of epistemic to ethical appraisals of character which, I shall suggest, seems more intimate than the relation of epistemic to ethical justification. This will suggest a friendly, if revisionary, reinterpretation of what is plausible in Clifford's, and Chisholm's, talk of 'the ethics of belief'.

***

Like Chisholm, I take for granted the essentially evaluative character of epistemological concerns, the focus on what makes evidence *better* or *worse*, what determines to what degree a person is *justified in* a belief, how inquiry *should be* or *is best* conducted. But when one thinks about the different ends on which epistemological and ethical appraisal are focused, it looks likely that their relation is to be expected to be at least as complex and oblique as the relation of knowledge to human flourishing. This expectation is confirmed by reflection on such questions as: Is all knowledge conducive to human flourishing, or is there some knowledge we should be better off without? Is it always morally, as it is epistemologically, best to seek out all available evidence, or are some means of obtaining evidence unethical? Is it always harmful to believe unjustifiedly, or is it sometimes harmless or even beneficial?[3]

If it is possible that there should be cases where a person believes unjustifiedly, but where the appropriate moral appraisal is favorable or indifferent, the claim that to say that a person believes unjustifiedly is *eo ipso* to make an unfavorable moral appraisal—henceforth, the special-case thesis$_J$—is false. Unless, therefore, it is incoherent to claim that believing unjustifiedly is sometimes simply harmless, or, as some philosophers have done, that there is moral merit in faith, or in a husband's believing that his wife is faithful even if the evidence indicates otherwise, the special-case thesis$_J$ is false. And, whether or not they are true, such claims are surely coherent.

This argument is not quite conclusive, however, for a defender of the special-case thesis$_J$ might reply that the coherence of these descriptions is insufficient to refute his thesis; in the cases described, he might argue, there is a *prima facie* moral failing (believing unjustifiedly), but it is so slight as to be negligible, or has been overridden by weightier considerations (the moral value of trust between husband and wife, for example).

Another argument against the special-case thesis$_J$ appeals to the fact that 'morally ought' implies 'can', and hence that 'epistemically ought' cannot be a subspecies of 'morally ought', since it does not imply 'can'; for believing, and hence believing unjustifiedly, is not in any straightforward sense voluntary.

If this argument were conclusive, it would rule out, not only the special-case thesis$_J$, but also the correlation thesis$_J$ and the overlap thesis$_J$. But it is not conclusive. Chisholm observes that, though indeed one cannot stop believing that p or start believing that p *now*, no more can one fulfill all one's [as the special-case thesis$_J$ would have it, all one's other] moral obligations *now*; what is required is only that one *can in due course*.[4] Of course, the sense in which one can't just stop believing or start believing that p now is quite unlike the sense in which one can't, say, answer all one's correspondence now; the difficulty isn't that one hasn't time just now to stop or start believing that p, but that one can't simply stop or start believing that p at any time. Believing that p is a condition one finds oneself in, not something one does. However, as Chisholm pointed out in an earlier discussion of this issue,[5] one *can* sometimes bring it about that in due course one believes ...; one can sometimes *induce* a belief, by bringing about the circumstances in which that condition is likely to arise. One cannot believe at will; nevertheless, sometimes the wish is father to the thought,[6] and this may be enough for moral appraisal to be applicable.

A better argument against the special-case thesis$_J$ is this. A person is epistemically unjustified in believing that p just in case his evidence isn't good enough. But he can't be morally at fault in believing that p unless his belief is wilfully induced. And his evidence may not be good enough even in cases where his belief is not wilfully induced. So it is possible that there should be cases where a person is epistemically unjustified but not morally at fault; and the special-case thesis$_J$ is false.

Before I turn to the correlation thesis$_J$, however, I need to consider a reinterpretation of the special-case thesis$_J$ more recently suggested by Chisholm. 'The distinguishing feature of *ethical* duty', Chisholm writes in a paper published in 1991, 'is not to be found in the considerations that impose that duty. Rather, an ethical duty is simply a requirement that is not overridden by any *other* requirement.'[7] And so, he argues, when an epistemic requirement is not overridden by any other requirement, it is one's ethical duty. Even if this account of what it is to be an ethical requirement were acceptable, this would be insufficient to establish the special-case thesis$_J$; for it would show only that *some* epistemic requirements—those which are not overridden by other requirements—are ethical. And, in any case, it seems that 'ethical' has been persuasively redefined, as 'any normative requirement not overridden by some other requirement'; that this is a *re*-definition becomes apparent when one considers that it implies, for example, that any requirement, of prudence, say, or of aesthetics, would thereby be classified as ethical provided only that it is not overridden by any other requirement.[8]

According to the correlation thesis$_J$, although to say that a person believes unjustifiedly is not *eo ipso* to say that he is morally at fault, nevertheless, whenever a person believes unjustifiedly, he *is* morally as well as epistemologically at fault. Two arguments against this thesis immediately suggest themselves. If it is ever *true* (not merely, as the first argument considered against the special-case thesis required, possible) that believing unjustifiedly is beneficial or harmless, or if it is *ever* false (not necessarily, as the second argument considered against the special-case thesis required, always) that a person is responsible for believing unjustifiedly, then the correlation thesis$_j$ is false.

There are cases in which a person's believing unjustifiedly is harmless or even beneficial. My believing, on inadequate evidence, that the apples I just selected are the best in the supermarket, is, like many inconsequential beliefs, harmless. Again, if a patient's believing, on inadequate evidence, that he will recover from his illness significantly improves the chances that he *will* recover, then he may properly be appraised neutrally from a moral point of view.[9]

Cases like this are sufficient to show it false that, whenever a person believes unjustifiedly, his so believing is always also subject, all things considered, to unfavorable moral appraisal. They are not sufficient, however, to show it false that, whenever a person believes unjustifiedly, his so believing is always also subject to unfavorable moral appraisal *prima facie*. But if a subject is not always responsible for believing unjustifiedly, even a *prima facie* correlation thesis$_j$ is false.

Possible explanations of someone's believing unjustifiedly are: negligent incontinence[10]—he has been careless or perfunctory in inquiry, but, jumping to conclusions, has formed a belief anyway; self-deception—self-interest has skewed his perception of the weight or relevance of this or that evidence; *or* cognitive inadequacy—he has done his best, but on this matter his best cognitive effort isn't good enough, and has resulted in an unjustified belief. (The first two kinds of explanation are not really so distinct as this rather crude list makes them appear, since a sort of one-sided carelessness in inquiry is one of the forms in which self-deception manifests itself; but, though they may be, negligence in inquiry and incontinence in belief-formation need not be self-interested.)

One may distinguish two kinds of cognitive inadequacy: the personal—an individual's good-faith misjudgment of the weight of complex evidence—and the cultural. The latter arises because of the perspectival character of judgments of relevance, their dependence on background beliefs. Sometimes the explanation of someone's believing on skimpy evidence is that he doesn't realize that certain relevant evidence *is* relevant, because the background beliefs which determine what evidence he perceives as relevant are mistaken—background beliefs which are taken for known facts in his epistemic community, and which he may have no way of knowing are not so.

Where there has been no negligence and no covert operation of wishes or fears, where the explanation of the person's believing unjustifiedly is cognitive inadequacy, personal or cultural, unfavorable moral appraisal is inappropriate even if the belief is harmful.[11]

Perhaps it will be argued in defense of a *prima facie* correlation thesis, that, even in cases of unjustified believing explicable by cognitive inadequacy, the subject is still morally culpable in an indirect way; culpable, that is, not directly for believing unjustifiedly (*ex hypothesi*, that represents his best cognitive effort at the time), but indirectly, for not having cultivated better judgment. There are circumstances where this is appropriate—for example, in some cases where it is this person's (this doctor's, this lawyer's, this juror's, this academic's) particular responsibility to know about the matter at hand; but the correlation thesis, requires that it always be so. And this is not true. Even if one were morally required to cultivate one's capacity to judge evidence to the very best of which one is capable (a very demanding assumption), still, for any person, there would be some degree of finesse which he could not, by even the most strenuous mental discipline, surpass.

Or perhaps it will be argued in defense of the correlation thesis, that, even in cases of unjustified believing explicable by cognitive inadequacy, the subject is still morally culpable by omission: he morally-ought to be aware of his cognitive limitations. There are circumstances where this observation is appropriate too; but, again, the correlation thesis, requires that it always be so. And this is not true either. Even if one were morally required to be as aware as possible of one's cognitive limitations (again, a very demanding assumption), a complete grasp of those limitations may be beyond one's cognitive powers. If a person has done the best he can, not only to find out whether p, but also to determine that he is competent to find out whether p, he is not morally culpable even if his belief in his competence and his belief that p are, by reason of cognitive inadequacy, unjustified. If these arguments are correct, the correlation thesis, even in its weaker, *prima facie*, form, is false.

Unlike the correlation thesis, which requires that unjustified believing be always (at least *prima facie*) harmful and always something for which the subject may properly be held responsible, the overlap thesis, requires only that unjustified believing *sometimes* cause (at least *prima facie*) harm and *sometimes* be something for which the subject may properly be held responsible.

And this is so. Acting on false beliefs sometimes causes either actual harm, or, at least, unacceptable risk of harm. Justified beliefs may be false, and unjustified beliefs may be true; nevertheless if, as we hope and believe they are, our criteria of justification are indicative of truth, justified beliefs are likely to be true, and unjustified beliefs are likely to be false. And so, acting on unjustified beliefs is also (though less) likely to cause harm, or, at least, unacceptable risk of harm.

And when unjustified believing is the result either of negligence or of self-deception, though it is not belief at will, it *is* willful—it is, as we say, a kind of 'willful ignorance'. One might reasonably feel that a person who knowingly causes harm reveals himself to be a more hardened character than a person who induces himself to believe, unjustifiedly, that his action will not be harmful. Nevertheless, the quasi-voluntary nature of willful ignorance seems to suffice, at least sometimes, for the ascription of responsibility.

In other words, believing unjustifiedly is sometimes a form of morally culpable ignorance. It is not, of course, the only form. Ignorance comes in at least three varieties: one may fail to know because one has no belief on the matter at hand (agnosticism), or because the belief one has is false (mis-belief), or because the belief one has is unjustified (over-belief). Agnosticism, in turn, comes in at least three sub-varieties: one may have no belief because one hasn't investigated and has no evidence either way (plain agnosticism); because, though one has investigated, and has evidence, that evidence seems insufficient to settle the matter (can't-tell agnosticism); or because one has failed to draw a conclusion which the evidence would warrant (under-belief). There are epistemologically and psychologically interesting similarities between the phenomena of under-belief and over-belief;[12] but it is the latter that concerns me here. Over-belief, unjustified believing, constitutes culpable ignorance when, as it sometimes but not invariably is, it is both harmful and peccable.

If these arguments are correct, the overlap thesis$_j$ is true.[13]

* * *

The arguments thus far put the strategy of W. K. Clifford's celebrated paper, 'The Ethics of Belief',[14] in a new perspective. The main thesis of that paper is that 'it is wrong always, everywhere, and for anyone, to believe anything upon insufficient evidence'. Neither here nor elsewhere in the paper does Clifford ever distinguish 'it is epistemologically wrong' from 'it is morally wrong'.[15] But he offers no arguments for identifying the two, or even for the special-case thesis$_j$, that the former is a sub-species of the latter. Instead, extrapolating from a striking case where unjustified believing *is* culpable ignorance, he tries to persuade one that *all* cases of unjustified believing are, in some measure, both harmful and willful. He offers, in other words, only arguments that could, at most, establish the correlation thesis$_j$. It is illuminating, as a further test of the claim that the correlation thesis$_j$ is not true, although the overlap thesis$_j$ is, to show how Clifford's attempted extrapolation fails.

In the vivid case with which Clifford's paper opens, we are to imagine a ship-owner who 'knowingly and willingly' suppresses his doubts, doesn't check, manages sincerely to believe that his vessel is seaworthy, and allows the ship to depart. He *'had no right to believe on such evidence as was before him'*, Clifford observes; and he 'is verily guilty' of the deaths of passengers and crew when the ship goes down.[16] The description of the ship-owner's self-deception as 'knowing and willingly' undertaken[17] is a bit lacking in subtlety; and it would have been desirable that Clifford say explicitly that it is the element of willfulness that justifies an unfavorable moral appraisal in this case, as in more straightforward cases where harm is knowingly caused—for example, if the ship-owner knew full well that the vessel was unseaworthy and allowed it to depart anyway. Nevertheless, Clifford's judgment of this case seems correct: it is a case of morally culpable ignorance, of failure in a duty to know.

But the case has a number of features which are not invariably found whenever someone believes unjustifiedly, and some of which are essential to the unfavorable moral appraisal appropriate here. The unjustified belief is false; the proposition concerned is of great practical importance; the person concerned is in a position of special responsibility; the false belief leads to dramatically harmful consequences; and the belief is willfully self-induced. The correlation thesis$_1$ is false unless the ignorance would still be morally culpable even if all these features were absent.

Clifford is aware that a belief held on insufficient evidence may be true, and clear that it is the belief's being unjustified, not its being false, that matters. There are two points to consider here, only one of which Clifford raises. The first, which he does not mention, concerns cases of false but justified belief. If the ship-owner had investigated carefully and honestly, and had been justified in believing the vessel seaworthy, but his justified belief had been false, and the ship went down, the appropriate verdict from a moral point of view would surely be that he was not to blame for the false belief, nor, therefore, for what one would be inclined to describe as a tragic accident. The second point, which Clifford does discuss, concerns cases of unjustified but true belief. He first remarks that the ship-owner would still be morally responsible even if his belief that the vessel was seaworthy was true, because 'he had no right to believe on such evidence as was before him'. This trades on his failure to distinguish epistemic from ethical justification, and hence fails. Later, however,[18] Clifford comes up with a better argument: by failing to investigate properly, and inducing himself to believe on inadequate evidence, the ship-owner would have taken an unacceptable risk of causing harm. That seems correct. So far, so good, for Clifford and for the correlation thesis₁.

But what if the proposition concerned were not, as in the original case, a consequential one, or if the person with the unjustified belief were not the person responsible for deciding whether the ship is to be allowed to make the voyage? Where, then, is the harm, or, if the unjustified belief happens to be true, the risk of harm? Clifford offers what are in effect two kinds of answer to these questions about apparently harmless unjustified belief. The first is—urging that a belief must be connected to action somehow, however indirectly, to count as a belief at all—that no belief is really altogether inconsequential; there is always at least the potential that action might be based on it, and might prove harmful.[19] The second is to suggest that unjustified believing always discourages scrupulous inquiry and strengthens the habit of 'credulity'; it weakens the epistemic fiber, one might say, and hence carries, if not invariably a risk of harm, a risk of risk of harm.[20]

Clifford's responses depend on two false assumptions: that mere potential for harm, however remote, is sufficient for unfavorable moral appraisal (provided the subject is responsible for the unjustified belief); and that a subject is always responsible for unjustified believing. But remote potential for harm is *not* sufficient; if it were, not only drunken driving, but owning a car, would be morally culpable. And a subject is *not* always responsible for believing unjustifiedly; the cause, sometimes, is cognitive inadequacy.

Matters are confused by the way Clifford combines the two responses in the argument that unjustified believing encourages 'credulity', and *thereby* carries potential for harm or risk of harm. It is true that sloppy inquiry, jumping to conclusions, wishful thinking, manifest undesirable dispositions—dispositions to which, no doubt, some people are temperamentally more inclined than others, but dispositions which one can either check and discourage in oneself, or allow to operate unchecked, and, by unchecked indulgence, encourage. They are bad habits which may, if unchecked, become inveterate. (It is not clear, however, that Clifford is right to suggest that any individual's indulgence in such habits is bound to encourage them in others.) But it is not true that unjustified believing is always the result of self-deception or negligence; so Clifford's oblique argument that unjustified believing is always harmful also fails.

These disagreements with Clifford by no means imply agreement with his most famous critic, William James.[21] Clifford holds that it is always wrong to believe on insufficient evidence. I have pointed out that Clifford fails to distinguish 'epistemologically wrong' from 'morally wrong', and argued that his thesis is not true if interpreted as an ethical claim. James holds that it is *not* always wrong to believe on insufficient evidence. He would be correct, therefore, if by 'wrong' he meant 'morally wrong' only; but this is not what he means.

Like Clifford, James never distinguishes these two possible ways of taking 'ought', 'justified', 'our duty in the matter of opinion', etc. Some of the arguments in 'The Will to Believe' seem to be intended as epistemological: that knowing the truth is no less valuable than avoiding error,[22] that believing that p sometimes contributes to bringing it about that p is true.[23] But others seem to be of an ethical character: that we should not condemn those who have faith for believing without adequate evidence, but should 'respect one another's mental freedom';[24] and the quotation from Fitz-James Stephen at the close of the paper, urging that we have faith because '[i]f death ends all, we cannot meet death better'.[25] This suggests that the best way to read James is as holding that it is not always wrong *either* epistemologically *or* morally to believe on insufficient evidence.[26]

James' argument about respect for others' mental freedom deserves special comment. If, like James, one fails to distinguish epistemic from ethical justification, one can make room for (moral) tolerance of others' unjustified opinions only as James seems to, by weakening one's standards of epistemic justification. But if one distinguishes the two, one has no need of any such radical epistemological measures. In any case, one's judgment that another's belief is unjustified must, because of the perspectival character of judgments of justification, their dependence on one's background beliefs, be acknowledged to be thoroughly fallible. And, most to the present point, unjustified believing is not morally culpable if it results from cognitive inadequacy, whether personal or cultural.

Unlike both James and Clifford, I distinguish epistemological from ethical justification. Like James and unlike Clifford, I do not think it always morally wrong to believe on inadequate evidence. Clifford's position is over-demanding morally. Like Clifford and unlike James, however, I think it is always epistemologically wrong to believe on inadequate evidence—in the sense that believing on inadequate evidence is always epistemologically unjustified belief. James' position is over-permissive epistemologically.

Perhaps it will be objected that sometimes it is all to the good— *epistemologically* all to the good—that a person believe something even though his evidence is inadequate; for example, the scientist whose faith in an as yet inadequately supported theory motivates him to develop, articulate, and test it, and thus advances inquiry. This objection is focused, not on the concept of epistemic justification, but on questions about the conduct of inquiry.[27] It is *irrelevant* to the claim that believing on inadequate evidence is always believing unjustifiedly; it argues, rather, that believing unjustifiedly is not always damaging, and may even be helpful, to the progress of inquiry. This, I think, is true. Not that over-belief is ever an optimal condition for the conduct of inquiry; the ideal, I take it, would be, not for our hypothetical scientist to have faith in the theory's truth, but for him to recognize it as, though thus far unworthy of belief, nevertheless promising enough to be worthy of serious further investigation.[28] Still, given human inquirers' inevitable frailties, a scientific community in which some are disposed to over-belief and others to under-belief may, by virtue of individuals' epistemic imperfections serendipitously compensating for each other, be a reasonable *ersatz* of a community of inquirers who conform to the epistemological ideal. So, although over-belief is always epistemologically wrong both in the sense of 'epistemologically unjustified', and in the sense of 'not the ideal with respect to the conduct of inquiry', it is not always epistemologically wrong in the sense of 'damaging to the conduct of inquiry'.

So I do not mean to deny that, as James observes, 'science would be much less advanced than she is if the passionate desires of individuals to get their own faiths confirmed had been kept out of the game'.[29] The point is, rather, that because James fails to distinguish the question of whether believing on inadequate evidence is always unjustified belief from the question of whether believing on inadequate evidence is always damaging to the conduct of inquiry, he runs together a correct negative answer to the latter with an incorrect—over-permissive—negative answer to the former.[30]

Clifford and James simply fail to distinguish epistemic from ethical justification; Chisholm explicitly maintains that epistemic justification is a sub-species of ethical justification. James claims that it is sometimes legitimate to believe on insufficient evidence, suggesting that a man who has a moral duty to believe that p may thereby be epistemologically justified in so believing; Chisholm explicitly denies this, but he also protests that Clifford's 'rigid evidentialism' is epistemologically over-demanding, suggesting, instead, that a belief is epistemologically 'innocent until proven guilty'.[31]

So Chisholm's position is further from Clifford's and closer to James' than his borrowing Clifford's title for part I of *Perceiving* might have led one to expect. And my disagreement with Chisholm, like my disagreement with James, extends beyond the matter of the distinctness of epistemological from ethical justification to a more strictly epistemological issue. For, where the question of epistemic justification is concerned, my position is closer to Clifford's than to James'. Closer, but not identical: for I think it vital to acknowledge the gradational character of epistemic justification:[32] whether, or to what degree, a person is justified in a belief depends on how good—how supportive, how comprehensive, and how independently secure—his evidence with respect to that belief is.[33] Ideally, I should prefer to put this in terms which also acknowledge that belief, as well as justification, comes in degrees. But the point on which I am presently taking issue with Chisholm doesn't depend on these subtleties; it is that, by my lights, one believes that p unjustifiedly, even if one's evidence supports p over not-p, unless one's evidence includes enough of the relevant evidence.[34]

The goal of inquiry is substantial truth. When one focuses on guidelines for the conduct of inquiry, one must concern oneself with substance as well as truth. But when one focuses on criteria of justification, one is *ipso facto* restricting oneself to the dimension of truth; for truth-indicativeness is the characteristic virtue of criteria of justification. Noting, correctly, as James does, that 'playing it safe' is not always the most successful course in inquiry, Chisholm then suggests, incorrectly, as James does, that this motivates less demanding criteria of justification.[35]

***

Complex as this has been, it has been, thus far, focused quite narrowly, on the question of the relation of epistemic to ethical *justification* only—on which I find myself in disagreement with Chisholm. I want, by way of conclusion, to offer some more positive thoughts with regard to a different dimension of epistemic appraisal—the appraisal of a person *qua* inquirer or cognizer.[36]

Our vocabulary for epistemic appraisals of character is varied and subtle ('meticulous', 'sloppy', 'imaginative', 'closed-minded', 'brilliant', 'obtuse', ...). It is striking that a significant sub-class of this vocabulary is shared with ethics: 'honest', 'responsible', 'negligent', ... , come immediately to mind. And I am not sure but that here the relation of epistemic to ethical appraisal may be as intimate as the special-case thesis maintains; perhaps, at least without an 'otherwise', 'he is a good man but intellectually dishonest', really does have the authentic ring of oxymoron.

Recall that, if my earlier arguments are correct, it is precisely when a person's unjustified believing stems, not from cognitive inadequacy, but from self-deception or negligent incontinence—from a lack of intellectual integrity[37] on his part—that we hold him responsible for his belief. This suggests a friendly reinterpretation of what is most plausible in Clifford's condemnation of 'the habit of credulity', and Chisholm's defense of the special-case thesis, as pointing to the *moral* importance of *intellectual* integrity.

Which prompts the following concluding observation. At the price of a little over-simplification, one might say that, as courage is the soldier's virtue *par excellence*, so intellectual integrity is the academic's. (The over-simplification is that intellectual integrity itself requires a kind of courage, the hardihood called for in relinquishing dearly-held beliefs, or in resisting some conventional wisdom or fashionable shibboleth.) As C. I. Lewis writes, more eloquently than I could:

> Almost we may say that one who presents argument is worthy of confidence only if he be first a moral man, a man of integrity .... [W]e presume, on the part of those who follow any scientific vocation, ... a sort of tacit oath never to subordinate the motive of objective truth-seeking to any subjective preference or inclination or any expediency or opportunistic consideration.[38][†]

Notes

1. In principle, there are two other possibilities: that epistemic appraisal and ethical appraisal are identical; that ethical appraisal is a special case of epistemic appraisal. I shall not consider either here. The first seems too obviously false to consider; the latter, with its Platonic overtones, would require a paper of its own.
2. R. M. Chisholm (1991) 'Firth and the Ethics of Belief', *Philosophy and Phenomenological Research*, LI.1, pp. 119–28 (the quotation is from p. 119). See also R. M. Chisholm (1956) 'Epistemic Statements and the Ethics of Belief',

---

[†] Since writing this essay I have returned to the topic of intellectual integrity in several papers: see 'Confessions of an Old-Fashioned Prig' in S. Haack (1998), *Manifesto of a Passionate Moderate: Unfashionable Essays* (Chicago: University of Chicago Press), pp. 7–30; (2008 [2005]) 'The Ideal of Intellectual Integrity, in Life and Literature' in S. Haack, *Putting Philosophy to Work: Inquiry and Its Place in Culture* (Amherst, NY: Prometheus Books), pp. 195–208; and (2007) 'Engaging with the Engaged Inquirer: Response to Mark Migotti' in C. de Waal (ed.) *Susan Haack: A Lady of Distinctions* (Amherst, NY: Prometheus Books), pp. 277–80.

Philosophy and Phenomenological Research, XVI, pp. 447–60; R. M. Chisholm (1957) *Perceiving: A Philosophical Study* (Ithaca, NY: Cornell University Press); R. Firth (1959) 'Chisholm and the Ethics of Belief', *Philosophical Review*, 68, pp. 493–506; R. M. Chisholm (1956) '"Appear," "Take," and "Evident"', *Journal of Philosophy*, LIII.23, pp. 722–31; R. Firth (1956) 'Ultimate Evidence', *Journal of Philosophy*, LIII.23, pp. 732–9; R. M. Chisholm (1961) 'Evidence as Justification', *Journal of Philosophy*, 58, pp. 739–48; R. M. Chisholm (1966) *Theory of Knowledge* (Englewood Cliffs, NJ: Prentice Hall), 2nd edn, 1977, 3rd edn, 1989; R. M. Chisholm (1968) 'Lewis's Ethics of Belief' in P. A. Schilpp (ed.) *The Philosophy of C. I. Lewis* (La Salle, IL: Open Court), pp. 223–42; R. Firth (1978) 'Are Epistemic Concepts Reducible to Ethical Concepts?' in A. I. Goldman and J. Kim (eds.) *Values and Morals* (Dordrecht: Reidel), pp. 215–30; R. M. Chisholm (1986) 'Self-Profile' in R. J. Bogdan (ed.) *Roderick M. Chisholm* (Dordrecht: Reidel), pp. 3–77.

From time to time Chisholm writes of 'analogies' between ethics and epistemology: see, e.g., Chisholm, *Perceiving*, pp. 12, 13, 18, 30; Chisholm, '"Appear," "Take," and "Evident"', pp. 723ff.; Chisholm, *Theory of Knowledge*, p. 1 of the 1st, 1966, edn and pp. 57–8 of the 3rd, 1989 edn; R. M. Chisholm (1980) 'Epistemic Reasoning and the Logic of Epistemic Concepts' in G. H. Von Wright (ed.) *Logic and Philosophy* (The Hague: Nijhoff), pp. 71–8. If, as it seems, his point is that there are structural analogies between the overriding of a one moral requirement by another, and the inductive overriding of a certain body of evidence by further evidence, this is quite compatible with his commitment to the special-case thesis$_1$.

On p. 54 of his 'Self-Profile' Chisholm writes that 'epistemic concepts are not *moral* concepts'; by the final sentence of the section, however (p. 56), he writes that the concepts of epistemology are *reducible to* the concepts of ethics.

3. If, as I believe, the answer to the next-to-last of these questions is clearly 'yes', this is sufficient to show the special-case thesis false in its most general form.
4. Chisholm, 'Firth and the Ethics of Belief', pp. 125–7.
5. Chisholm, 'Lewis' Ethics of Belief', pp. 223–4.
6. A phrase of which F. C. S. Schiller reminds us in his commentary on James' 'The Will to Believe'. F. C. S. Schiller (n.d.) *Problems of Belief* (London: Hodder and Stoughton), p. 111. See, besides Chisholm's discussion of the quasi-voluntary nature of belief referred to above, H. H. Price (1954) 'Belief and the Will', *Proceedings of the Aristotelian Society*, Supplement, 28, pp. 1–27.
7. Chisholm, 'Firth and the Ethics of Belief', p. 127; cf. Chisholm, *Theory of Knowledge*, 3rd edn, pp. 58–9.
8. In his 'Self-Profile' Chisholm suggests two arguments for the general form of the special-case thesis. The concept of requirement, Chisholm says, is central to ethics, and the concept of epistemic preferability can be defined in terms of requirement; to reach the conclusion that the concept of epistemic preferability is reducible to ethical concepts, however, one needs the stronger premise that the concept of requirement is *uniquely* ethical. Knowledge, Chisholm says, is, as Aristotle thought, intrinsically valuable; to reach the conclusion that epistemic concepts are reducible to ethical concepts, however, one needs the stronger premise that knowledge is intrinsically *morally* valuable.

9. *Perhaps*, if surviving his illness enables him to continue his morally admirable work, or to meet his obligations to others, a favorable moral appraisal is in order; but that issue need not be decided here. In the case described, the person's believing that p makes it more likely that p will turn out true, but the point does not depend on that. Think of the kind of the case Peirce envisages when he observes that he could not condemn a man who, having lost his wife, induces himself to believe in an afterlife in which they will be reunited, even though the belief is unjustified, if, without it, 'his usefulness would be at an end.' C. S. Peirce (1931–58 [1898]) *Collected Papers*, ed. C. Hartshorne, P. Weiss, and A. Burks (Cambridge, MA: Harvard University Press), 5.583.
10. A phrase adapted from J. Heil (1984) 'Doxastic Incontinence', *Mind*, 93, pp. 56–70.
11. This comports with the attractive conjecture (proposed by J. Shelton (1983), 'Contextualism: A Right Answer to the Wrong Question', *Southwest Philosophical Studies*, 9.2, pp. 117–24), that the appeal of contextualist theories of epistemic justification may arise in part from a confusion of epistemological with ethical justification. The same conjecture might also serve to explain Goldman's claim that there are two concepts of epistemic justification, one objective and reliabilist, the other context-relative; see A. I. Goldman (1988), 'Strong and Weak Justification', in J. Tomberlin, ed., *Philosophical Perspectives, 2: Epistemology* (Ridgeview, Atascadero, CA), pp. 51–70.
12. See Chisholm, *Perceiving*, p. 14.
13. My arguments against the special-case thesis$_j$ and the correlation thesis$_j$ presuppose that harmfulness and responsibility are necessary for unfavorable moral appraisal; my arguments for the overlap thesis$_j$ presuppose that they are sufficient. These assumptions, though fairly weak, are of course not vacuous. For example, as the argument against the correlation thesis$_j$ revealed, someone who maintained that one has a moral obligation to develop one's capacities, generally, or one's capacity to judge evidence, specifically, would reject the former presupposition.
14. W. K. Clifford (1947 [1877]) 'The Ethics of Belief' in *The Ethics of Belief and Other Essays* (London: Watts and Co.), pp. 70–96.
15. Richard Gale ([1980] William James and the Ethics of Belief', *American Philosophical Quarterly*, 17.1, pp. 1–14) claims (p. 1) that Clifford has to be read as proposing the ethical thesis, that it is always morally wrong to believe on insufficient evidence; he observes in a footnote, however, that Clifford's words also bear another interpretation, that it is always epistemologically wrong to believe on insufficient evidence.
16. Clifford, 'The Ethics of Belief', p. 70.
17. Ibid., p. 71.
18. Ibid., p. 72.
19. Ibid., p. 73.
20. Ibid., p. 76.
21. W. James (1956 [1896]) 'The Will to Believe' in *The Will to Believe and Other Essays in Popular Philosophy* (New York: Dover), pp. 1–31.
22. Ibid., pp. 17ff.
23. Ibid., pp. 23–4.
24. Ibid., p. 30.
25. Ibid., p. 31.

26. Cf. J. W. Meiland (1980) 'What Ought we to Believe? or, the Ethics of Belief Revisited', *American Philosophical Quarterly*, 17.1, pp. 15–24, which precisely, but more explicitly, follows James in this regard.
27. The distinction is articulated in more detail in S. Haack (1993) *Evidence and Inquiry: Towards Reconstruction in Epistemology* (Oxford: Blackwell; 2nd edn, 2009, Amherst, NY: Prometheus Books, 2009), chapter 10.
28. 'The Will to Believe' is dedicated 'To My Old Friend, CHARLES SANDERS PEIRCE, to whose philosophic comradeship in old times I owe more incitement and help than I can express or repay'. In a letter of thanks, Peirce writes to James that in practical affairs, '"Faith," in the sense that one will adhere consistently to a given line of conduct, is highly necessary [...] But if it means that you are not going to be alert for indications that the moment has come to change your tactics, I think it ruinous in practice.' C. S. Peirce (1897), in *The Collected Papers of Charles Sanders Peirce*, 8.251. The next year one finds Peirce writing of the 'Will to Learn', (5.583), and commenting that, where science is concerned, *'[f]ull belief* is willingness to act upon [...] the proposition [...] [The] accepted propositions [of science] are but opinions at most; and the whole list is provisional' (1.635).
29. James, 'The Will to Believe', p. 21.
30. The argument here raises an awkward question about the intended scope of James' Will to Believe doctrine. His initial statement, that 'our passional nature lawfully may decide' any genuine option 'that cannot by its nature be decided on intellectual grounds', strongly suggests that the doctrine is to apply only to hypotheses, for example, of a religious nature, which are in principle undecidable by evidence. (Which, however, raises the further awkward question, whether such hypotheses would qualify as meaningful by the standards of the Pragmatic Maxim.) James' later reference to the role of 'faith' in scientific inquiry, however, suggests that the scope of the doctrine is intended to be much broader, applying also to hypotheses with respect to which we merely happen, thus far, to lack sufficient evidence.
31. Chisholm, *Perceiving*, pp. 9, 11, 100; Chisholm, *Theory of Knowledge*, pp. 18–19. (The reference to Clifford is, however, missing from the second and third editions of *Theory of Knowledge*.) Chisholm's disagreement with Clifford on this matter seems to have escaped the attention of some commentators; see, e.g., L. Pojman (1983) 'The Ethics of Belief', *Southwest Philosophical Studies*, 9.2, pp. 85–92, who describes Chisholm as subscribing to 'rigid evidentialism', according to which 'one ought to believe propositions if and only if they are backed by sufficient evidence'. Pojman attributes this account of Chisholm's position to Meiland, 'What Ought we to Believe?'; but the attribution is incorrect, since Meiland is careful to distinguish a stronger evidentialism (one has a right to believe that p only if the evidence is sufficient) from a weaker (one has a right to believe that p provided one does not have sufficient evidence for not-p), and does not say which, if either, he takes Chisholm to hold.
32. Chisholm, too, seems to acknowledge the gradational character of epistemic justification, most clearly in the third edition of *Theory of Knowledge*. But the fact that epistemic justification comes in degrees, whereas (I take it) ethical justification does not, suggests a further argument against the special-case thesis$_J$.

33. It is because I take comprehensiveness to be only one of three determinants of degree of justification that I shifted, above, from Clifford's favored expression, 'insufficient evidence', to writing of 'inadequate evidence', which is, I hope, less likely to suggest failure of comprehensiveness alone.
34. My account of the determinants of degree of epistemic justification—one of which is, how much of the relevant evidence the subject's evidence includes—is spelled out in detail in *Evidence and Inquiry*, chapter 4.

    My comprehensiveness requirement is motivated in part by an analogy between the structure of empirical justification and a crossword puzzle; as the reasonableness of one's confidence that a crossword entry is correct depends in part on how many of the intersecting entries one has completed, so one's degree of justification in a belief depends in part on how much of the relevant evidence one's evidence includes. So my neglect of the analogy thesis$_1$ does not stem from any prejudice against analogies, nor, I should add, from the belief that there are no interesting analogies between meta-epistemology and meta-ethics. For explorations of such analogies, see (besides Firth's papers referred to above) R. B. Brandt (1967) 'Epistemology and Ethics, Parallels Between' in the *Encyclopedia of Philosophy*, ed. Paul Edwards (New York: Collier Macmillan); R. B. Brandt (1985) 'The Concept of Rational Belief', *The Monist*, 68.1, pp. 3–23; and W. P. Alston (1978) 'Meta-Ethics and Meta-Epistemology' in Goldman and Kim (eds.), *Values and Morals*, pp. 275–98.
35. Chisholm, *Perceiving*, p. 22; Chisholm, *Theory of Knowledge*, 3rd edn, pp. 13–14.
36. There remain, of course, many other important questions which I shall have to put aside: for example, whether Chisholm and Firth are correct in supposing that justification is as central a concept in ethics as, I agree, it is in epistemology.
37. An expression which comports with the plausible idea that thinking is well-construed as inner dialogue, and self-deception as involving distracting one's own attention from inconvenient evidence, as the deception of another involves distracting his attention. Cf. Peirce, *Collected Papers*, 5.421, 1905.
38. C. I. Lewis (1955) *The Ground and Nature of the Right* (New York: Columbia University Press) p. 34. Of course, Lewis is using 'scientific' in a broad sense, equivalent to 'intellectual'. The reference to a 'tacit oath', by the way, suggests that the special-case thesis$_1$ may seem more plausible than it really is to those who are bound by such an oath, and thus have a special moral duty to objective truth-seeking.

6
Sensitive Truths and Sceptical Doubt

Henrik Rydenfelt

1 Introduction

For an essay of about 30 pages, William James' 'The Will to Believe' (1897) has resulted in much debate. Discussion on the exact nature of James' argument continues to occupy the pages of philosophical journals, and no consensus has been achieved about its merits. In what follows, I will first sketch a reading of James' 'will to believe' argument which maintains that James attempts to defend a passional decision to believe on *epistemic* (as opposed to either prudential or moral) grounds. Central to this reading is a premise of James' which maintains that there are claims the truth of or evidence for which is sensitive to our believing attitude towards those claims, and where a 'passional' decision to believe is thus required. I will then proceed to argue that James' examples of such 'sensitive truths' are problematic and insufficient for the purposes of his argument. Instead, as I will propose, the 'will to believe' argument is largely vulnerable to an objection first raised by Charles S. Peirce, who pointed out that the testing of a hypothesis does not require a believing attitude towards it.

While James' argument as such is not successful, as I will then attempt to show, there is an interesting case of belief where a passional decision such as that recommended by James appears to be called for: the belief that there is a reality independent of our thoughts, beliefs, wishes, and the like. In practice, this belief underlies the scientific project of experimentation itself. Thus doubt—such as that exhibited by the traditional epistemological sceptic—concerning it will render the project of (scientific) inquiry practically futile. Moreover, this issue bears an interesting analogy to the discussion of moral beliefs in 'The Will to Believe'. In James' view, there is a practical difference between the 'moralist' who believes that there is a moral order to the world independent of our ethical preferences and ideals—a notion which James connects with the 'religious hypothesis'—and the moral *sceptic* who doubts the reality of such an order. This difference lies, I will argue, in that the moral sceptic will not—analogously to his epistemological counterpart—engage in the project of improving his moral preferences, as he doubts the very possibility of their development. While not sensitive truths in the sense required for James' argument, the belief in an independent reality and the belief in the moral order of the world remain special cases of belief of central importance, where a 'passional' decision instead of any intellectual argument is our only response to sceptical doubt.

2 A Reading of James' Argument

The topic of James' essay is the relationship between belief and evidence. James sets out to contest the (evidentialist) view of W. K. Clifford, who in his 'Ethics of Belief' of 1879 argued that it is 'wrong always, everywhere, and for every one, to believe anything upon insufficient evidence'.[1] James does not intend to argue that our beliefs should not primarily be based on and conform to available evidence; instead, he wishes to question the universality of Clifford's position. The main thesis of James' essay is that in *some* cases, it is *not* wrong to believe without sufficient evidence, but quite the converse, we *should* do so: '*Our passional nature not only lawfully may, but must, decide an option between propositions, whenever it is a genuine option that cannot by its nature be decided on intellectual grounds.*'[2] This thesis is by its nature normative: it maintains that when faced by what James calls a 'genuine' option we have both the right *and* the duty to make our choice between belief and doubt without sufficient evidence. While James defends the entitlement to *choose* between doubt and belief, as doubt is our default condition, his argument in effect intends to show that in some cases we *may and should believe* without sufficient intellectual grounds, or evidence.

In addition to his requirement that passional decisions to believe can only be made when evidence is unavailable, James poses three further conditions to an option that may be considered 'genuine' and open to the application of the 'will to believe' strategy.[3] Firstly, the choice between doubt and belief must be *live*: both alternatives have to be appealing and possible to entertain. It has to be *forced*: there cannot be a third alternative. And it must be *momentous*: unique and important consequences must result from it. In such cases, James argues that neither doubting nor believing is unequivocally recommendable but, rather, both are expressions of our passional nature, the former simply placing the 'fear of [the hypothesis's] being in error' before the 'hope that it may be true'.[4]

An obvious criticism of James' position is that, even when faced with a genuine option, it is dubious whether and how we can *choose* to believe rather than doubt. We cannot, as many have pointed out, believe 'at will'. However, James' argument does not require that our choice is one involving a momentary decision to believe or doubt. In his view, the passional decision to believe can be made only when one is already inclined to believe; and such a decision is by its nature a process: it is to set aside doubts about a live option which one is already prone to believe.

Assuming, then, that the choice between the two passional attitudes is at least to an extent available to us, how are we to make that choice? It is important to notice that—contrary to widespread assumptions—James' argument in 'The Will to Believe' does not include much reference to the usefulness of religious belief. The popular view that James thinks we should believe in God without evidence because such belief is advantageous is not completely unfounded: suggestions of an argument of this sort can be found both in *The Varieties of Religious Belief* (1902) and, more explicitly, in *Pragmatism* (1907).[5] Even in 'The Will to Believe', James does point out that religious belief entails a promise of a 'vital good' that will be lost unless one believes.[6] However, this is far from the gist of James' argument. His defence of his normative claim does not rest on *prudential* considerations: he does not argue that we should believe rather than doubt because of the practical advantages of belief. Also, while James like Clifford before him does not draw a clear distinction between ethical and epistemic normativity, James does not argue that belief without sufficient evidence is recommendable because such belief, in some cases, leads to the ethically right, or morally more acceptable conduct (at least in any straightforward fashion).

Rather, James' argument is based on *epistemic* considerations. He argues for the justification of believing without evidence on the grounds that without initial belief, we may be forever severed from attaining a number of truths. In our intellectual life, James holds, we are faced with a choice between two maxims. Either we follow the rule '*We must know the truth*' or another, substantially different maxim, '*We must avoid error.*'[7] This may be called the first premise of his argument, which on the whole centres on the choice between these two maxims.

As James points out, in many cases, the two maxims will have the same results: 'believing truth' and 'shunning error' often coincide. However, the 'will to believe' argument requires that there is a practical difference resulting from our choice of maxim. And indeed, James holds that sometimes by following the second maxim we end up shunning truth quite like by following the first we end up believing falsehoods. If we believe only what we have gathered evidence for, some truths will be left out; if we believe more, we are prone to believe what is not true.[8]

But so far, the maxims are at best on a par. Why should we in some cases follow the first rather than the second? James' second premise is that '*a rule of thinking which would absolutely prevent me from acknowledging certain kinds of truth if those kinds of truth were really there, would be an irrational rule*'.[9] That is, if it can be shown that following some intellectual rule will result in our *not* attaining all truths attainable, it is reasonable to abandon that rule at least when it would be detrimental to our search for truth about some issue. Again, the rationality—and hence the normative consideration—in question is epistemic rather than ethical or moral in nature. James wishes to show that we are *intellectually* better off by following the first maxim, at times giving our passional nature the chance of adding to our inventories of belief. James' conclusion should hence be read as the expression of an *epistemic right and duty* to believe without sufficient evidence when truths would otherwise be lost.

The most central problem with James' second premise is that there appears to be no relevant asymmetry between the two intellectual rules. Namely, an opponent could easily formulate a *converse* premise: an intellectual rule which would lead to believing certain kinds of *falsehoods* without sufficient evidence would be an irrational rule. There is, one might argue, a similar right and duty to *doubt* in cases where falsehoods would otherwise continue to be believed. Accepting James' premise thus already entails an inclination towards one of the two choices of our 'passional nature', that of the hope of gaining a truth rather than the fear of believing a falsehood. For James' argument to be successful, we will already need to be prepared to risk believing falsehoods, if that enables us to (potentially) believe all truths, rather than the converse. Here James appears to have no choice but to rely on the reader's willingness to take such a risk.

Finally, the third premise of James' argument is, as one might expect, that there indeed are cases where following the second maxim would prevent us from attaining some truths. This premise maintains that there are claims the truth of or evidence for which is in some way sensitive to initial belief in them. In some cases, James holds, beliefs cannot be true without being believed: as he puts this idea elsewhere, 'our faith beforehand in an uncertified result *is the only thing that makes the result come true*'.[10] In other cases, he refers to the possibility that 'evidence might be forever withheld from us unless we met the hypothesis half-way'.[11] Hence, doubting, according to James, can in some cases result in a permanent loss of truth. For this reason we should, at times, believe without evidence, or let our 'passional' nature decide for the believing attitude as the epistemically rational alternative. Rather than further contesting James' two other premises, as constructed here, it is this idea that the following criticism will concentrate on.

3 Sensitive Truths

For James' third premise to hold sway, it must be shown that, in some cases, belief is prerequisite for the truth of that belief itself, or that believing is prerequisite for the possibility of gathering evidence for the belief. That is, in some cases, belief has to be a *necessary* condition for making a claim true *or* obtaining evidence that supports it. Such truths sensitive to our attitudes ('sensitive truths' or henceforth STs) will thus need to fulfil either of the following two conditions:

(1) p is sensitive if believing that p is a necessary condition for the truth of p, or
(2) p is sensitive if believing that p is a necessary condition for obtaining evidence that shows the truth of p.

In addition to serving James' argument, this idea is naturally of broader interest. If STs of the first sense exist, and we have the capacity of believing these STs, we are at times forced to *decide* whether one or another belief is true. If our belief can 'create the fact', as James holds, in many cases we will even face a choice of what to 'make true'.[12] And if STs of the second sense exist, our success in finding out truths may to a surprisingly large measure depend on what we are prone to believe without sufficient evidence, or what sort of ideas and hypotheses naturally suggest themselves to us as believing agents.

But are there such 'sensitive truths'? James' examples of what he claims to be STs include beliefs about the following:

(A) First-person capacities
(B) Cooperation with others
(C) Moral value

All of these examples rest heavily on the pragmatist idea that belief are habits or rules of action, each contributing differently to the way we will act at least in some conceivable circumstances. James does not equate the practical consequences of doubt (or the lack of belief) with *disbelief*: doubting *p* does not necessarily result in acting as if *p* were untrue, while disbelieving *p* (or the belief that not-*p*) does. However, he points out that doubting *p* will in many situations lead to action (or lack thereof) similar to that which results from disbelief. For example, doubting a religious hypothesis will lead us to act 'more or less as if religion were *not* true',[13] or, as James puts this point elsewhere, 'it is often practically impossible to distinguish doubt from dogmatic negation'.[14] On these grounds, James then argues that without the sort of *conduct* that results from believing *p*, we will be in some cases prevented from learning the truth of *p*.

Of cases of the first type, James' patent example is the belief of a mountain climber that she can leap over a wide gulf to save her own life. If she believes that she has the ability to make the jump, James argues, she will act unhesitatingly and succeed, in effect bringing about the truth of her belief. But if she doubts whether she can make it, she hesitates at the decisive moment, and fails—or she may even decide not to try the jump at all.[15] Now, it is evidently the case that if we doubt whether we are capable of some action, and success in performing that action is of great importance, we will not even attempt it. And as James points out, doubt and hesitation may turn out fatal, while a more trusting attitude can be of considerable aid.

Still, it is highly contentious whether such cases are STs in the first sense. Facts concerning one's capacities, after all, are not dependent on their *actualization* in some circumstances. Although doubt about one's ability to jump may at times result in one's not even trying a leap, the ability itself does not depend on whether one ever attempts. In other words, the *truth* about one's capacities does not hinge on one's beliefs about those capacities, despite the fact that some particular actions in particular situations may remain unperformed without such beliefs. Even if a lack of hesitation may turn out to be beneficial for one's purposes, it is not true that such a lack is invariably prerequisite to one's success, or even that doubt necessarily results in possibly fatal second-guessing.

In a similar vein, neither is the *belief* in one's capacity to jump over a cliff necessary for acquiring evidence for that capacity itself. In various conceivable scenarios (including ones with careful security measures in place) one may attempt the jump despite the fact one doubts whether one will succeed. Doubt itself—unlike utter disbelief—does not *necessarily* result in a lack of serious attempt, even at great personal risk. The first type of cases then fail to be STs also in the second sense.

The second set of examples James considers, beliefs concerning social relations and cooperation, faces similar problems. James holds that in some cases, belief or 'faith' in the beliefs, actions or emotions of others is prerequisite for the truth of those beliefs. In 'The Will to Believe', he presents two (different) scenarios of this sort. In the first example, a person's belief in the amicability and liking of another may ultimately bring about the truth of that belief by modifying the first person's actions so that they are prone to result in such liking.[16] But it is evident that this example fails to serve James' purposes: believing is certainly not a necessary condition for such a belief to be true. Another example concerns cooperation: a train full of passengers ends up being robbed 'because the [passengers] cannot count on one another, while each passenger fears that if he makes a movement of resistance, he will be shot before anyone else backs him up'.[17] While such situations would allow for a variety of analyses in terms of action and belief, for the purposes of James' argument it would be needed to show that beliefs about actions or beliefs of others are necessary for such action or belief to occur. In this example, again, at least the belief of any *individual* does not seem to be a necessary condition for its truth in the required sense. As in the first type of cases, even doubt about what others believe or how they are likely to act does not preclude spontaneous—albeit perhaps unusually courageous—cooperation. For this reason, such beliefs fail to be STs in the second sense, too: doubt over the attitudes, beliefs, and cooperation of others does not prevent one from acting. Rather, especially in cases such as that of the train robbery, doubt is an element of the bravery of the acting individual.

The reason for James' troubles is that, with both the first and the second set of examples, he appears to confound doubt—which as such does not exclude attempt, or experimentation—with disbelief, which would render *trying* practically unlikely to occur. Already in 1897, a criticism along these lines was proposed by Charles S. Peirce, to whom James dedicated his volume *The Will to Believe and Other Essays* that year. After having read 'The Will to Believe', Peirce made the following remark to James in a letter:

> If an opportunity occurs to do business with a man; and the success of it depends on his integrity, then if I decide to go into the transaction, I must go on the hypothesis he is an honest man, and there is no sense at all in halting between two lines of conduct. But that

won't prevent my collecting further evidence with haste and energy, because it may show me it is time to change my plan. That is the sort of 'faith' that seems useful. The hypothesis to be taken up is not necessarily a probable one. [...] You must have a consistent plan of procedure, and the hypothesis you try is the one which comes next in turn to be tried according to that plan.[18]

In effect, Peirce here describes a practical experiment on the hypothesis that the business partner is honest. As the example shows, such experimentation requires no belief in the truth of the hypothesis itself. We may be doubtful about the truth of a claim while nevertheless consider proceeding along the line of conduct that it suggests the most rational course of action. Peirce, as no contrary evidence is available, decides to act as if the business partner were honest, as that course of action is the most reasonable one in light of his (other) beliefs concerning his circumstances. But the fact he does not fully *believe* in the businessman's integrity is shown by Peirce's being simultaneously engaged in gathering further evidence. In practical situations, genuine belief would rather render such inquiry futile: we do not waste time and effort investigating what we already do believe.

This is the case also in a more clearly *scientific* setting, where the testing of a hypothesis does not require belief in *that* hypothesis. Indeed, on the contrary, Peirce famously exclaimed that belief has no place in science.[19] To be sure, taken as such this claim is something of an exaggeration: proving or disproving of a hypothesis is itself done with reliance on other theories—the beliefs which form the bedrock of that scientific practice at that time. But the point Peirce intends to make is that the pure scientist, seeking truth merely, does not believe in the hypothesis he is trying to prove; far rather, he often attempts to accumulate evidence against it.

The general problem of James' examples so far results from the problematic idea that belief is *necessary* for some course of action ever to take place. As Peirce's example shows, no *particular* belief is a necessary condition for any *particular* action. As differing beliefs may result in similar actions in similar circumstances, doubt over a claim cannot bar us from testing and attempting, from finding out whether it is true. In a practical, everyday setting, our other beliefs may recommend a course of action despite our uncertainty and indeed doubt about the chances of that action attaining our aims. In scientific inquiry, this is even more pronouncedly the case: experimentation requires no belief in the hypothesis to be tested; if anything, the converse is usually the case.

4 Moral Beliefs and the 'Religious Hypothesis'

The third set of examples James discusses—moral beliefs, or beliefs about value—is more complex and also of more interest. Here James addresses questions of wider philosophical import, and his most general examples approach central issues in philosophy of religion, including those of the existence and nature of the divine. Understanding James' intricate position here, however, requires some attention to the details of his overall position. Firstly, there is James' account of moral claims. In 'The Will to Believe', James draws a clear distinction between moral beliefs and beliefs concerning facts. Moral questions are not 'questions of what sensibly exists, but what is good', and as such, they do not allow for 'sensible proof'.[20] This account receives its clearest statement in his earlier address, 'The Moral Philosopher and the Moral Life' (1891), where James—anticipating the contemporary expressivist position in meta-ethics—maintains that our moral claims do not refer to properties in the world but are expressions of the desires or demands of 'sentient beings' such as ourselves. Secondly, James (in 'The Will to Believe') also draws a distinction between the 'moralist' and the moral sceptic. The former maintains that his moral claims (as expressions of his own desires and demands) can be further *met* by a moral order that exists in the world itself. It is due to this belief that the moralist, unlike the moral sceptic, who doubts such a view, thinks that our moral claims may be true.

James' examples of the third type of STs, exhibit James arguing that some moral claims are *made true* by our belief in them. In his other presentations and writings of the time he wrote 'The Will to Believe', James is particularly interested in showing how the *belief* that 'life is worth living' *makes* life worth living.[21] 'Our own reactions on the world', James holds, is what may make life and the world *'from the moral point of view* [...] a success'.[22] This claim is, however, immediately dubious. Naturally, our reactions to the world, motivated by *our* moral point of view, may make life and the world better *from* that point of view. But from the fact that we have strived for and even achieved a certain moral order in our world and society it does not follow that we *should* have done so in the first place—that there is anything in the world that would meet *those* exact demands. Any moral claim—however suspicious—might otherwise be 'made true' in this manner.

James also presents moral beliefs as the slightly more complex, second type of STs: he argues that our gaining evidence for moral claims is (at least sometimes) dependent on initial belief. In his early writings, he appears to maintain that moral beliefs may be verified via the action that ensues of them, as moral conduct can ultimately lead to such results that he considers evidence for their truth. In the early piece, 'The Sentiment of Rationality' (1879, 1882), James describes this process of verification as follows:

> [T]he verification of the theory which you may hold as to the objectively moral character of the world can consist only in this—that if you proceed to act upon your theory it will be reversed by nothing that later turns up as your action's fruit; it will harmonize so well with the entire drift of experience that the latter will, as it were, adopt it, or at most give it an ampler interpretation, without obliging you in any way to change the essence of its formulation.[23]

But how are we to understand such 'verification'? A simplistic reading would have James here proposing that a moral view is 'verified' by being met by rewards of a kind. Such a view would obviously be both philosophically and practically dubious. It is hardly the case that morally correct action leads to beneficial results (at least of any immediate sort). Quite the converse, moral action and its 'fruits' are notoriously often out of accord, with the best of intentions leading into the worst of results for the acting individual.

Surely, this is not the interpretation James intended. Rather, the gist of the matter for James does not concern the 'verification' of a particular moral view, but goes back to the more profound issue between the 'moralist' and the moral sceptic: whether or not there is a moral order to reality, which our moral preferences may (imperfectly) reflect, in the first place. Throughout his writings, James' defence of the 'moralist' position oscillates between the idea that such an order may be actualized in the course of history as known to us and the notion that belief in such an order forces us to assume a further dimension to reality, our conduct 'terminating and eventuating and bearing fruit somewhere in an unseen spiritual world'.[24] It is here that moral belief approaches religious belief, especially James' formulation of the *essence of religion* in 'The Will to Believe'—the pair of affirmations that 'the best things are the more eternal things' and that 'we are better off even now if we believe [the] first affirmation to be true'.[25]

This essence of religion is the foundation of the pluralistic world-view that permeates James' later writings. Against the absolute idealist, James maintains that the world is not a ready-made, rational whole: instead, our particular strivings can make a difference as to its future. Against the materialistic, scientific world-view, James argues that the world is not one without any rational order such that our actions may advance. God, in the pluralistic scheme, is perhaps a finite but powerful being, an important ally in our strivings, whose reality secures that the ideal and the 'eternal' moral order in some way remains, whatever turn actual history may take. From the perspective of the pluralistic thinker, their mutual differences aside, the absolutist and the materialist rather side with the moral *sceptic* by undermining the importance of our active participation in this development. For the pluralist, we may make a genuine difference: through our actions, the world *may* develop so that it reflects a higher moral order.

The exact connection between (the belief in) the reality of the moral order and (the belief in) the existence of a divine thinker is a formidable issue on its own right, and cannot be considered in any detail here. One question concerns whether James simply assimilates the moral order with the divine thinker itself: whether God, in this picture of things, simply *is* the moral order of the world. A more naturalistic interpretation of the order itself may be suggested in an evolutionary vein, setting the two ideas more clearly apart. But when these two ideas are separated, another question concerns the fashion in which the moral order of the world itself entails (or implies) the existence of a divine thinker. For example, in his much debated piece, 'A Neglected Argument for the Reality of God' (1908) Peirce argued—among other things—that the order and growth of the universe *suggests* (but does not necessarily entail) the hypothesis of God's reality.[26]

A problem for James' position, more relevant for the discussion at hand, ensues of the very distinction he draws between the moral sceptic, materialist and absolutist, on the one hand, and the pluralistic 'moralist' of his own vision, on the other. The former three, in their different ways, reject the pluralistic view that our strivings may make a difference as to the (moral) course of the world. But they all are similar to the Jamesian pluralist in that they *act* in accordance with their moral views (whatever those views may be). Importantly, James nowhere maintains that that the moral sceptic is refuted, or guilty of contradicting himself, by *acting* with moral intentions: it is merely a differing interpretation of how such action may be reflected in the order of the world that distinguishes the sceptic and the moralist. But what, then, is the genuine *practical* difference between accepting the pluralistic moralist view that James proposes and its alternatives?

The centrality of this issue is forcefully emphasized by James himself in connection with religious belief. On pragmatist grounds, if 'such action required or inspired by the religious hypothesis is in no way different from that dictated by the naturalistic hypothesis', religious belief remains a 'superfluity' and the quarrel one of words merely.[27] At many points, however, it remains unclear what the relevant difference in conduct is supposed to amount to. James often suggests that the view he proposes, especially in contrast to that of the sceptic and the materialist, leads to a *strenuous mood*, which is a more serious attitude towards our strivings and their relevance to the course the world may take. But this change in mood or attitude, or emotional adjustment, while perhaps central to our view of life, appears to inspire no relevant change in conduct itself.

James' difficulties in spelling out the practical consequences of moral and religious belief has important consequences on our original question: whether moral beliefs can be STs in the second sense, or presuppose initial belief in order for us to ever gain evidence for them. As James does not supply a view of what would count as evidence for a moral belief, it remains unclear what sort of conduct, on part of the believer, would be required to gain such evidence. In the absence of such an account, moral beliefs are not plausible cases of STs in the second sense. Moreover, this is the case even with the belief far more central to James' discussion—the belief that there *is* moral order to the world and the related 'religious hypothesis'. If the moral sceptic (as well as the absolutist and the materialist) and the Jamesian pluralist all engage in moral action, it remains open how this belief could be of any (necessary) aid in gaining evidence for the reality of the moral order. Indeed, in what follows, I will suggest that there *is* a salient practical difference between the moralist and the moral sceptic, but this difference will not have implications as to our gaining evidence for the 'moralist' position (or the 'religious hypothesis') itself.

5 Scepticism and (Moral) Science

The third premise of James' argument in 'The Will to Believe', as construed here, requires that some truths are sensitive to our attitudes: either the truth of a claim, or our learning its truth, requires belief in that claim as its necessary condition. As we have seen, none of James' examples of such beliefs holds sway; indeed, it appears dubious that any truths are 'sensitive' in this manner. For this reason, James' argument as such falters: it does not succeed in showing that sometimes the believing attitude is recommendable on solid epistemic grounds. As we have noted, especially in connection with the examples James presents as cases of the second type of sensitive truths, the underlying reason for this problem is that doubt over a hypothesis—unlike, at least in most practical scenarios, straightforward disbelief—does not prevent us from testing and attempting. What, then, remains of the 'will to believe'?

In what follows I will argue that there is an interesting case of belief which, while not a 'sensitive truth' in the sense James' argument would require, is set apart from most others. This is the belief that there is a reality independent of us, which is prerequisite for the (scientific) practice of experimentation itself. As such, this belief plays a special and crucial role in our intellectual lives. While the testing of particular scientific hypotheses or practical beliefs does not require any particular belief, my suggestion here goes, a strategy akin to James' 'will to believe' may be our only response to overarching, *sceptical* doubt. Moreover, as I hope to show, this belief bears an important analogy to the case James considered, the belief that the world has a moral order.

Consider the pragmatist account of truth especially as presented by Peirce. In his famous pieces of 1877 and 1878, 'The Fixation of Belief' and 'How to Make Our Ideas Clear', Peirce argued that there is only one method of the settlement of opinion that we will ultimately find satisfactory. Instead of rendering our beliefs dependent on subjective changes of view, this *scientific method* attempts to fix belief so that it accords with a reality independent of our opinions, hopes, wishes and the like. In practice, Peirce maintained, truth is the opinion that inquirers into the nature of such a reality would ultimately agree upon, and that further investigation would not bring into doubt.[28] This scientific method is the 'empiricist' attitude that James describes and assimilates his own view with in 'The Will to Believe': it gives up the notion of (immediately) achievable objective certitude, while retaining the belief that there is a truth which a systematic inquiry may approach. The realistic hypothesis that underlies the scientific method implies that there *is* truth (conceived of in the scientific fashion) attainable by inquiry.

The distinctive feature of the realistic hypothesis is that belief in it appears to play a special role in our intellectual lives, one which mere doubt is enough to undermine. Consider the case of the *epistemological sceptic*, who doubts that his beliefs reflect anything in an independent reality. By analogy with the Jamesian moral sceptic's view of moral preferences, he considers his beliefs as merely (a part of) the habits of action his conduct is based upon. (In the view I am ascribing to them here, neither kind of sceptic thus *denies* that our beliefs or moral preferences can be met by something in the world; they merely doubt that this is the case.) As we have seen, doubt over any particular hypothesis does not prevent us from obtaining evidence for or against it: when in doubt, we may always experiment. However—and this is the crucial point—the sceptic's doubt over whether there is a reality that would respond to such experimentation would make the whole *point* of such experimentation practically dubious or futile. Why experiment at all, if one does not *believe* that experimentation may yield evidence for or against the hypothesis?

To be more precise, there is a relevant disanalogy between doubting a particular hypothesis and doubting the whole idea of experimenting itself. Doubt over a particular hypothesis leaves open the *possibility* of that hypothesis being true and, hence, allows for experimentation. However, doubt about whether there is an independent reality—in effect, doubt about truth itself, conceived of in the scientific fashion— makes such experimentation practically pointless. Obviously nothing prevents the sceptic from engaging in something analogous to scientific inquiry. But unlike the scientist in doubt over the truth of a hypothesis, the sceptic who doubts the feasibility of the acquisition of evidence (or the 'existence' of truth) itself has no real incentive to engage in experimentation of any kind. Viewed from the perspective of the scientific method, the belief in an independent reality is required for experimental inquiry to concretely take place.

Importantly, in the moral case, an analogous consideration presents itself. As we have seen, the moral sceptic, in doubting that our moral preferences can be met by reality, is not prevented from acting in accordance with his moral views. This was the reason why the belief in a moral order of the world does not appear to be a 'sensitive truth' in either of the senses required for James' argument. However, moral scepticism appears to prevent the attempt of *revising* one's moral preferences in accordance with an independent moral order. And for this reason, there indeed turns out to be a practical difference between (also) the *moral* sceptic and the Jamesian moralist.

James' own writings include at least a suggestion of such a difference between the moralist (or those who are taken by the 'strenuous mood') and those doubtful of whether there is more to morality than our subjective preferences merely. In 'The Moral Philosopher and the Moral Life', James considers three fundamental questions of ethics, of which the last and the most difficult concerns the measure of our different demands, moral preferences, or ideals. We should first note that James' main answer to this *casuistic* question is that in optimal circumstances, all our ideals are satisfied with the least harm done to the development of others. This Jamesian *Republic of Ends*, as we could call it, is a rather problematic response. For one thing, its measure of ideals is itself questionable from the point of view of other ideals of measurement itself; for another, it is dubious that we could consistently maintain that any ideal or demand is as worthy of satisfaction as any other. Perhaps for reasons related to such problems, in his later writings, James never appears to repeat this 'republican' suggestion.

However, James' discussion of the casuistic question includes another strand of thought, which is more relevant to the issue at hand: his comparison of the development of ethics to that of physics. Here it is worth quoting James at length:

> [E]thical science is just like physical science, and instead of being deducible all at once from abstract principles, must simply bide its time, and be ready to revise its conclusions from day to day. The presumption of course, in both sciences, always is that the vulgarly accepted opinions are true, and the right casuistic order that which public opinion believes in; and surely it would be folly quite as great, in most of us, to strike out independently and to aim at originality in ethics as in physics. Every now and then, however, some one is born with the right to be original, and his revolutionary thought or action may bear prosperous fruit. He may replace old 'laws of nature' by better ones; he may, by breaking old moral rules in a certain place, bring in a total condition of things more ideal than would have followed had the rules been kept.[29]

The moral philosopher, in James' view, has to accept that moral thought itself is in development. While it is mostly recommendable to rest content with the received ethical vision, or our moral common sense, the unearthing of new moral rules is possible in a manner analogous to the discovery of new natural laws. As I have argued, the sceptical position, by contrast, would disclose the notion of such development of moral preferences, or the casuistic scale itself: it would render *moral inquiry* practically pointless. (The extent to which the moral order itself implies a divine thinker is, as already noted, another complicated issue.)

This last point can be made differently by distinguishing two different understandings of the central pragmatist concept of *meliorism*. By that concept, James usually means the (pluralistic) idea that our actions may make the world a better place in accordance with our moral beliefs and preferences. But based on his idea of moral science, meliorism could also be understood to imply that it is possible to *improve* our moral preferences themselves in light of the world's moral order. Aside of our conduct improving the world merely, here it is the world that improves our conduct. It is this second notion of meliorism that complete scepticism about such a moral order undermines; just like physical science, moral science requires initial belief in its core 'hypothesis'. Conceived of in the Jamesian fashion, our acceptance of this belief is dependent on a passional decision rather than a proof of an intellectual nature.

6 Conclusion

By the epistemic reading of James' argument in 'The Will to Believe' presented here, James maintains that the passional attitude of believing without sufficient evidence must sometimes be followed in order for us to gain access to some truths. The success of the argument crucially depends on the claim that there are truths sensitive to our attitudes: such claims either the truth of which or evidence for which necessarily requires initial belief. But the three kinds of cases concerning first-person abilities, cooperation, and moral beliefs that James presents as examples fail to be 'sensitive' in either of these senses. Truth itself is hardly sensitive to our attitudes of belief and doubt; and evidence may be acquired without any belief in a scientific hypothesis or a practical course of action to be tested and attempted. This, in a nutshell, is why the 'will to believe' argument is ultimately unsuccessful.

However, as I have suggested, there are special cases of belief where an analogue of James' 'will to believe' strategy is called for. These cases are not particular scientific hypotheses or practical beliefs, but rather the sort of beliefs that contest a globalized, *sceptical* doubt: the belief that there is an independent reality which may be the object of inquiries, and the belief that there is a moral order to the world. These beliefs are required for the meaningfulness of the project of inquiry, or the improvement of our beliefs and moral stances themselves. The sceptic—whether epistemological or moral—may obviously act on the *possibility* that there is an independent reality: as his view has been phrased here, this is something he does not *deny* but merely consistently *doubts*. In practice, however, without such belief, inquiry—whether scientific or moral, to the extent that these can be separated—does not get off the ground. As the epistemological or moral sceptic cannot, as James himself maintained, be shown to be wrong on intellectual grounds, in practice, recommending a 'passional decision' of the sort he envisioned remains our only response to such sceptical doubt.

Notes

1. W. K. Clifford (1879) 'The Ethics of Belief' in *Lectures and Essays*, Vol. 2 (London: Macmillan), p. 186.
2. W. James (1979) *The Will to Believe and Other Essays in Popular Philosophy* (Cambridge, MA: Harvard University Press), p. 20.
3. Ibid., pp. 14–15.
4. Ibid., p. 30.
5. W. James (1985) *The Varieties of Religious Experience* (Cambridge, MA: Harvard University Press); W. James (1975) *Pragmatism* (Cambridge, MA: Harvard University Press), chapter 8.
6. Ibid., p. 30.
7. Ibid., p. 24.
8. Ibid., pp. 24–5, 30–1.
9. Ibid., pp. 31–2.
10. Ibid., p. 53; cf. p. 29.
11. Ibid., p. 31.
12. Ibid., p. 29.
13. Ibid., p. 32.
14. Ibid., p. 88.
15. Ibid., pp. 53–4, 80.
16. Ibid., pp. 28, 31.
17. Ibid., p. 29.
18. Letter from Peirce to James, March 13, 1897 (MS L 224).
19. C. S. Peirce (1998) 'Philosophy and the Conduct of Life' in *The Essential Peirce*, Vol. 2, ed. Peirce Edition Project (Bloomington and Indianapolis: Indiana University Press), p. 33.
20. James, *The Will to Believe*, p. 27.
21. Ibid., pp. 52–6, 83–4.
22. Ibid., pp. 54–5.
23. Ibid., p. 86.
24. Ibid., p. 52; cf. p. 161.
25. Ibid., pp. 29–30.
26. C. S. Peirce (1998) 'A Neglected Argument for the Reality of God' in *The Essential Peirce*, Vol. 2, pp. 434–50.
27. James, *The Will to Believe*, p. 32 footnote 4. Cf. James, *Varieties*, pp. 407–8.
28. C. S. Peirce 'The Fixation of Belief' and 'How to Make Our Ideas Clear' in *The Essential Peirce*, Vol. 1 (C. Kloesel and N. Houser, eds., Bloomington and Indianapolis: Indiana University Press, 1992), pp. 109–23 and 124–41, respectively.
29. James, *The Will to Believe*, p. 156.

7
Reconceptualizing Evidentialism and the Evidentialist Critique of Religion

Dirk-Martin Grube

In the following, I will provide a close reading of William James' famous article 'The Will to Believe'[1] (henceforth TWTB). I will identify two philosophical issues which have a prominent place in it, viz. the issues of evidentialism and the evidentialist critique of religion (sections 1–5). In sections 6–9 I will embed James' contribution to those issues into the current discussion on them; in section 6–7 I will show the relevance of James' argument for the discussion of evidentialism; in sections 8–9 I will show its relevance for the discussion on the evidentialist critique of religion.

TWTB's basic point is deconstructive: it does not provide a *positive* theory on religion but seeks to undermine the *opinio communis* on the issue that prevailed at the turn to the twentieth century. It thus belongs to the same *genre* as the other famous piece of early-twentieth-century deconstructive work, the second edition of Karl Barth's famous Commentary on the Letter to the Romans: Barth goes at great length to undermine a dominant strand in theology, Liberal Theology.[2] Similarly, TWTB undermines a dominant strand in philosophy or, rather, a dominant strand in culture at large. The characteristics of both pieces, above all, their polemical style, can be explained to a good extent with this genre: both attack an opponent that has a deep impact on the surrounding culture and, being the underdog, both overreact at times in the heat of the fight.

What does the dominant cultural strand at the turn to the twentieth century consist of to which James reacts? It consists of the sort of evidentialism which is captured in William Clifford's famous maxim 'it it wrong always, everywhere, and for anyone, to believe anything upon insufficient evidence'.[3] It thus consists of a certain form of evidentialism which, in addition, insists on the relevant evidence being of an 'intellectual' sort. The upshot of this intellectualist evidentialism for religion is a skeptical one: evidentialists of this sort criticize religion. In short, TWTB is a reaction to the dominance of the intellectualist evidentialism and the critique of religion which is based upon it. This is the background to which James reacts.

My intention to read TWTB closely has a particular hermeneutical corollary: rather than attempting to embed it within the greater whole of James' oeuvre, I will embed it in the cultural context in which it emerged. In the same sense in which it is worth the while to read Barth's Commentary on Romans as a reaction to the environment in which it emerged, it is worth the while to read TWTB as a reaction to the environment in which *it* emerged. This will be shown in the following sections.

1 The Basic Features of TWTB

James' defense of religion in TWTB is among the most ferociously attacked arguments there are. James is charged with promoting intellectual laziness, wishful thinking, and the like. Not only notorious critics of religion, such as Russell,[4] are highly critical of James but also people who are generally sympathetic to religion, such as John Hick.[5]

There are several reasons for the ferociousness of that critique. Among others, James' provocative style in TWTB contributes to it.[6] But what fuels the resentments most is probably the assumption that James tries to provide an argument to the effect that the will can make religious claims true. His critics take James to argue that we can use the will or, worse, passion to make us believe that religious claims are true, whereas truth is understood more or less along the lines of a classical correspondence theory of truth.

In line with many current James-interpreters, I think that this critique is mistaken. The reason is that, at least, in this article, James does not target the issue of truth. TWTB can and should thus be read as *not* contributing to the discussion on truth proper.

But then the question rises to what discussion it *does* make a contribution. On this point, opinions differ. It has to be acknowledged that answering positively what James' contribution consists of is more difficult than ruling out the mistaken assumption that his arguments are meant to contribute to the theory of truth. The reason is that this loosely woven article can be read in different ways. For example, Sami Pihlström suggests that James' point is that it is 'impossible to distinguish sharply between intellectual and non-intellectual reasons in the practice of human decision-making' since both are 'reciprocally contained in one another'.[7]

In this chapter, I will follow this hint and interpret TWTB as being directed against the ideal that our reasoning should be purely intellectualist. In particular, I will interpret it as being directed against the evidentialist ideal that beliefs should be formed only on the basis of intellectual evidence.

James' critique of the evidentialist ideal is a methodological point. Yet, this methodological point is closely interwoven with a substantial point. This point consists in rejecting the evidentialist critique of religion that Clifford and like-minded evidentialists make. James argues that it is not the case that we are entitled to hold beliefs only on the basis of sufficient intellectual evidence. Thus, critics of religion arguing that religious beliefs should be abandoned since there is not enough intellectual evidence for them got it wrong. In *this* context, James introduces the notions of will and passion and suggests that they can be also invoked for the purposes of justifying religious beliefs.

Thus, in the interpretation suggested here, the argument in *TWTB is concerned with questions of belief-acquisition*. James is out to provide criteria for the justification of beliefs. He is out to answer the question under what circumstances the subject is entitled to her beliefs.

Frankly, this point should be quite obvious to an unbiased reading of TWTB. Yet, given the history of the interpretations of TWTB, it is not. Thus, it should be emphasized here. Probably due to the associations that crop up when considering James' name, such as 'truth as expediency', TWTB has over and again been read as contributing to the theory of truth. Yet, no matter what James says about truth elsewhere, in TWTB he is clearly *not* concerned with providing a theory of truth but, rather, with providing a *theory of justification*. Both theories and the discussion on them should be strictly demarcated in order to understand TWTB properly.

2 The Function of the 'Logical Intellect'

In TWTB, James wants to provide 'a defence of our right to adopt a believing attitude in religious matters, in spite of the fact that our merely logical intellect may not have been coerced'.[8] Here, James criticizes the universal pretensions of people arguing that the 'logical intellect' is the only true judge in religious and related matters. Against them, James contends that it can be legitimate to invoke 'non-intellectual' resources, such as will or passion, when it comes to judging religious beliefs.

What is the point of introducing the notion of 'intellectualism' at this point? James does not explicitly answer this question and our reconstruction of his intentions should thus go beyond what he explicitly says. I think that the introduction of intellectualism cannot be accounted for if we do not assume that it is linked with evidentialism. Put more straightforwardly, *James understands evidentialism to consist of an insistence on nothing but intellectualist resources*. When evidentialists, such as Clifford, insist on the provision of evidence, they have only intellectual evidence in mind. For the evidentialist, there is no such thing as non-intellectual evidence. The use of will, passion, and the like as justificatory resources are thus excluded from the beginning on.

But what if there is not enough intellectual evidence in a given case, asks James. In some cases, we can leave it at that and walk away from the issue. But in other cases, this is impossible. And religion is one of those cases. What is at stake in the decision to believe or not to believe is of such importance that remaining neutral is out of the question. The evidentialist suggestion that if there is insufficient evidence for religious belief we should simply walk away from it is not convincing. Above all, the evidentialist making such a suggestion has no right to occupy the epistemic 'high-grounds' regarding belief-acquisition. Her suggestion is not based upon purely intellectual, 'rational', considerations but upon a sort of passion as well, viz. *upon the passionate fear of being mistaken*. Thus, from a meta-epistemological perspective, the person invoking passion to the effect of hoping that religious belief is true is no worse off than the evidentialist skeptic.

Thus, contrary to what is often assumed, James does not advocate a general hostility towards 'intellectualist' reason. Nor does he provide an all-out legitimation for abrogating intellectual reason in favor of emotions or the will. Rather, he argues with the special characteristics of the situation at hand, in this case the religious beliefs at hand. Only in situations such as the one of religious belief are we entitled to invoke non-intellectual resources, such as will[9] or passion, when being intellectually uncertain. And the evidentialist denying this possibility deprives us unwarrantedly of valuable justificatory resources. This complex set of conditions should be kept in mind when evaluating the strength of James' argument.

3 Religion as a 'Genuine Option'

Let us look more closely at James' notion of a 'genuine option' which is crucial for assessing his argument in TWTB. He defines an 'option' as a decision between two hypotheses. A *'genuine option'* is an umbrella-notion that embraces three different sorts of decision-situations: only if the decisions involved in it are 'live' rather than 'dead', 'forced' rather than 'avoidable', and 'momentous' rather than 'trivial', is an option a genuine one.[10]

The point of those specifications can be summarized for our purposes here as follows: a 'genuine option' is a situation in which making a decision is of crucial importance while *not deciding is not an option*. That is to say, a 'genuine option' is a decision-situation in which the stakes involved are very high but from which you cannot walk away; rather, you *have to* decide one way or the other.

What is the function of introducing the notion of 'genuine options' into the argument? This notion functions as a restraint on the use of the justificatory strategy employed in TWTB. James argues that the strategy employed is not open to being applied to all sorts of beliefs but works only in cases where 'genuine options' are at stake. Since the religious beliefs he has in mind *are* genuine options, this particular strategy works in this case. But it does not work in other cases. In short, within the overall strategy of the argument, *invoking the notion of a genuine option has the function to exclude an arbitrary usage of the justificatory strategy employed in TWTB.*

James concedes that in certain realms of inquiry, e.g. in the natural sciences, a decision between two options can often be avoided. He provides the example of the Röntgen rays.[11] But in religion, the situation is different. Here, 'we cannot escape the issue by remaining sceptical and waiting for more light, because, although we do avoid error in that way *if religion be untrue*, we lose the good, *if it be true*, just as certainly as we positively chose to disbelieve'.[12] Given what is at stake in religion, it is not possible to avoid the issue and walk away from it (as it is in the Röntgen case). Walking away from it would be tantamount to unbelief:

> It is as if a man should hesitate indefinitely to ask a certain woman to marry him because he was not perfectly sure that she would prove an angel after he brought her home. Would he not cut himself off from that particular angel-possibility as decisively as if he went and married someone else?[13]

In certain cases, refraining from making a decision comes down to *having made a decision already*. Religion belongs to those cases: concerning the question of religious belief, refraining from making a decision comes down to *having made a decision already*, viz. in favor of unbelief. Having implicitly made a decision against religion, the skeptic deprives herself of the benefits that religion has to offer.

4 Summary of the Crucial Ingredients of the Argument in TWTB

From the considerations provided thus far, James proceeds to attack the skeptical critic of religion. He does so by criticizing what he now calls skepticism, i.e. the evidentialist prohibition to believe anything upon insufficient evidence. To that end, he uses the following, much-quoted words:

> Scepticism, then, is not avoidance of option; it is option of a particular kind of risk. Better risk loss of truth than chance of error—that is your faith-vetoer's exact position...To preach scepticism to us as a duty until 'sufficient evidence' for religion be found, is tantamount therefore to telling us, when in presence of the religious hypothesis, that to yield to our fear of its being error is wiser and better than to yield to our hope that it may be true. It is not intellect against all passions, then; it is only intellect with one passion laying down its law. And by what, forsooth, is the supreme wisdom of this passion warranted? Dupery for dupery, what proof is there that dupery through hope is so much worse than dupery through fear?[14]

Here you have the ingredients of James' argument in a nutshell:

- The evidentialist critic of religious belief is betraying herself when she thinks that her refusal to make a decision on the question of religious belief can really avoid the issue. In truth, she has taken sides already, she has opted for the side of unbelief. Having taken sides she has, intentionally or not, implicitly decided to accept the risks that come with such a decision, chiefly among them the risk of losing truth.
- She is also betraying herself when she thinks that she has a right to occupy the epistemic 'high grounds' by relying only on intellectual resources and avoiding non-intellectual ones, such as the passions. In truth, she is relying on passion or some other pre-rational emotion in the same way as her religious opponent is. It is just a different kind of passion, viz. the passionate fear of being mistaken.
- Finally, there is no reason to think that the passion based upon the fear of being mistaken is in any way epistemically superior to

the passionate hope that religious belief may be true. Thinking differently is simply an act of intellectual imperialism, 'intellect with one passion laying down its laws' (see above).

5 James Does Not Support 'Wishful Thinking'

What about the common charges that James promotes wishful thinking, intellectual laziness, and the like, as mentioned above (see section 1)? Does he lightheartedly abandon the necessity to search for evidence? Does he thus suggest a whole-scale reconstruction of our common justificatory practices to the effect that non-intellectual resources can substitute intellectual evidence whenever it serves our purposes?

Given the reconstruction of the argument in TWTB provided above, those charges can be rejected. On pain of repeating myself, let me summarize why: the introduction of non-intellectual resources into our justificatory practices is restricted to certain very specific cases. Only in as far as a decision is a 'genuine option' in the sense specified is TWTB's justificatory strategy applicable. Only if we cannot avoid the necessity to decide either way are we entitled to reject the necessity to search for intellectual evidence. If, however, we *can* avoid deciding, it may be wiser to wait until sufficient intellectual evidence is found.

Concerning religious beliefs, James does not license 'wishful thinking'—at least, not in the way in which this charge is usually meant. We are justified in believing religious claims only if the requirements laid down by the notion of a 'genuine option' are met. And 'believing', it will be remembered, is not tantamount to 'holding to be true' but, rather, to *'being legitimately entitled to hope'*. We are thus legitimately entitled to hope that religious beliefs are true provided they are cases of 'genuine options'.

In other cases, however, we are not justified to believe in this fashion. Thus, the justificatory strategy implied in James' argument works in the case of certain religious claims (and related cases) but is *not a blank check for invoking hope in the place of evidence as a general rule.*

There is one further presupposition implied in this line of argument to which James does not pay much attention in TWTB but which is crucial for appreciating its success: *this line of argument presupposes that the evidence for and against a given religious belief is equal or roughly equal.* If and only if this is the case can the justificatory strategy implied in TWTB be applied.

Therefore, we are entitled to rely on non-intellectual resources, such as will or passion, only in cases in which we are uncertain on intellectual grounds. We can we justify religious beliefs along the lines suggested in TWTB only in those cases. In cases, however, in which we *are* 'intellectually' certain, i.e. in which we have overwhelming evidence either way, we do not need to resort to non-intellectual resources. In those cases, we possess more straightforward means of adjudicating our beliefs: we should simply believe that for which there is overwhelming evidence.

That the TWTB-argument presupposes that there is no overwhelming evidence for or against religion is important for judging its merits. James' critics (see above, section 1) frequently overlook it when they charge him with licensing wishful thinking, intellectual laziness, and the like. They think that he wants to *substitute* will or passion for evidence. But in TWTB this is clearly *not* his intention. He does not suggest that non-intellectual resources, such as will or passion, should take over the role of intellectual ones as a matter of principle. Rather, he suggests that we are justified in looking for non-intellectual resources in cases in which our intellectual resources are exhausted *and* in which we are confronted with 'genuine options', i.e. cannot afford to walk away from an issue but have to make a decision.

In summary, our right[15] to invoke the justificatory strategy implied in TWTB is not a blank check for all sorts of irrationalism but works only in cases in which both of the following requirements are met: *a decision must be a 'genuine option' and the evidence for and against a belief must be roughly equal*. Those requirements must be met for us to legitimately invoke the justificatory strategy implied in TWTB.

However, if those requirements *are* met, then there is no reason to give priority to the skeptical rule over the 'rule of hope', to say things in Jamesian parlance. On the contrary, under those circumstances, it would be imprudent or even irrational to refrain from believing a claim unless sufficient evidence for it can be found. For those religious claims that meet those requirements and the evidence for and against them is roughly equal, the skeptical rule does not apply. In those cases, the principle to refrain from hoping religious claims to be true on evidentialist grounds is imprudent or irrational.

6 Why Evidentialist Maxims such as Clifford's Should Be Abandoned

James' contributions to the issues of evidentialism and to the evidentialist critique of religion are not only relevant as a *Zeitzeugnis* but are also relevant today. I will show that in the rest of this chapter by embedding them into their context, i.e. into the current discussions on both issues.

As indicated, James targets in TWTB evidentialist maxims such as Clifford's 'it is wrong always, everywhere, and for anyone, to believe anything upon insufficient evidence' (see above, Introduction). Although Clifford himself does not explicitly attack religion, it is clear that his point in suggesting this maxim is to criticize religion implicitly: he targets the mechanisms upon which religious people come to acquire their beliefs.[16] He is thus one of those who, in James' words, 'preach skepticism to us as a duty until sufficient evidence for religion be found' (see above).

Crucial for understanding Clifford's critique of religion is to comprehend the fashion in which his evidentialist maxim functions. I will thus delve into its functioning as well as James' critique of it more deeply.

This maxim functions as a general principle. It means literally what it says, viz. that we should refrain from forming beliefs in the face of insufficient evidence under all circumstances. The evidentialist ideal it implies is thus connected to universal applicability claims. It is meant to be applicable in all realms of inquiry, in the theoretical realm as well as in the practical realm.

This maxim is thus supposed to regulate not only the acquisition of knowledge proper. That is, it is not geared only towards the acquisition of truth in the strict sense of the word. Rather, it functions as a general principle which is applicable in the realm of practical decision-making as well: forming beliefs upon insufficient evidence is never permitted, not even in the practical realm.

This connection of the evidentialist ideal with universal applicability claims is James' prime target in TWTB. And his critique of this connection is entirely convincing in my view. Applied as principles without exceptions in the realm of practical decision-making, evidentialist maxims such as Clifford's lead to absurd consequences.

This is plain from some practical examples. Take e.g. the burning question whether the world-wide changes of the weather, in particular, global warming, are to be accounted for by 'natural' factors. Is it just one more of those changes of the weather pattern which occur from time to time? Or is it 'human-made', i.e. caused by the human pollution of the environment? Does e.g. the immense increase of carbon dioxide exhaustion contribute to it significantly?

As far as I know, there is no convincing evidence available for either side. Yet, it would be highly imprudent to refrain from forming beliefs on the issue and wait until sufficient evidence will be available. The reason is simply that it might then be too late. Because if it were true that the global warming is 'human-made', then we are probably on the way to seriously damaging our home-planet. If that is the case, however, then it would be extremely unwise to sit back and do nothing but wait for more evidence to become available. If evidentialist maxims imply that that is what we should do, they prevent us from taking action which is necessary to secure the well-being or even survival of our species. Since that would be very imprudent, evidentialist maxims à la Clifford should not be used.

Obviously, this example does not show that it is indeed the case that global warming is 'human-made'. Yet, it shows that a principled use of evidentialist maxims is not helpful in cases such as this one. Using them in the practical realm as principles without exception would be very unwise because in this realm decisions often have to be made in the face of insufficient evidence.

Or take the case of the accident at Chernobyl in 1986: the nuclear power plant there had a melt-down and radioactive fall-out was released on a large scale, spreading to other parts of Europe. I remember that the consequences of that fall-out for everyday life were discussed intensively in Germany back then. For example, there was a discussion as to whether it would still be safe to consume products which are particularly susceptible to being contaminated from the fall-out, such as dairy products and wild-grown mushrooms. In that situation, some experts invoked evidentialist principles: they argued that, since there is not enough evidence available on the issue, there are not enough reasons to believe that consuming dairy products and wild grown-mushrooms will have detrimental consequences for our health.

The result of this invocation of evidentialist principles can be interpreted in two ways, both of which are unsatisfying: either it can be interpreted as an advice on forming beliefs without any practical impact, or, else as implying practical consequences. In the first case, it is not at all helpful, in the second, potentially harmful. Let me explain.

Either, suggesting that there is not enough evidence for believing that eating contaminated dairy products is harmful for the consumers' health is meant to be restricted to the theoretical realm proper. That is, it is meant to be an advice that we should refrain from forming beliefs on the subject. Depending on what is meant by 'belief', this may be true. Yet, it is irrelevant to the issue at stake. The consumer is not interested in the theoretical question whether she has a right to form beliefs in the strictly theoretical sense of the word. Rather, she is interested in the practical question whether it is wise to continue consuming contaminated food. The answer that she has no right to form theoretical beliefs on the issue will thus not help her because she has to make a decision on the issue. In short, restricting the pay-off of the information that there is not enough evidence on the issue to the purely theoretical realm is not helpful at all.[17] It does not help the consumer who has to make a practical decision between stopping the consumption of dairy products and continuing to consume them.

Or, else, practical consequences can be drawn from the invocation of evidentialist maxims. An evidentialist à la Clifford can argue in the following fashion: there is not enough evidence that eating contaminated dairy products will have seriously harmful consequences for the consumers' health and—since we should never believe anything upon insufficient evidence—we should not believe that eating dairy products will have seriously harmful consequences for the consumers' health. Since we should not believe that, we have no reason to act upon it. That is, we have no reason to change our eating habits.

Absurd as it may sound, it follows from a certain interpretation of evidentialist maxims such as Clifford's (from what I remember, some experts did indeed draw practical conclusions of this sort from invoking evidentialist maxims). But drawing this practical consequence from the invocation of evidentialist maxims is obviously highly questionable: it risks jeopardizing the health of the consumers. If it is the case that continuing to consume dairy products has detrimental effects for consumers' health, the expert suggesting that there is no reason to refrain from consuming them has obviously given wrong advice. In this case, her evidentialist maxim has lead her astray by giving advice which is harmful to consumers.

In sum, applying evidentialist maxims as universal principles can lead to undesirable consequences: if applied as rules in the practical realm, they can lead to very imprudent actions (sitting back in the face of the possible global warming), be of no help at all for practical decision-making (if restricted to belief-forming as a purely theoretical endeavor), or can even lead to harmful consequences (suggesting continuing to consume possibly contaminated food). Evidentialist maxims should thus not be applied as universal principles.

The reason that maxims such as 'it wrong always, everywhere, and for anyone, to believe anything upon insufficient evidence' do not work in the practical realm is that this realm exerts certain practical demands upon us: as humans, we are situated in a particular life-world in which we often cannot afford to postpone decisions or to walk away from them, even if there is not enough evidence available. If, being responsible agents, we want to ground those decisions upon reasonable beliefs, we cannot but have to form them upon insufficient evidence.

This is the point James—arguing in a good pragmatist spirit—raises against Clifford and the likes: his notion of a 'genuine option' is meant to point to our being embedded in a particular life-world which exerts practical demands upon us. Being embedded in such a fashion, we often have to make decisions in spite of the fact that there is not enough evidence available.

James' arguments are entirely successful in my view: evidentialist ideals should not be understood as general principles. Since Clifford and like-minded evidentialists do this,[18] they should be stopped right in their tracks. Evidentialist maxims to the effect that we should always refrain from forming beliefs in the face of insufficient evidence can lead to very imprudent or even harmful consequences and should thus be abandoned.

7 Reconstructing Evidentialism

Does the suggestion to abandon evidentialist maxims such as Clifford's imply to abandon evidentialism as an epistemic ideal altogether? Does acknowledging the success of James' critique of Clifford and like-minded evidentialists thus imply an all-out rejection of evidentialism? Do people endorsing the TWTB-argument, such as myself, thus commit themselves to rejecting evidentialism as en epistemic ideal?

Before answering that question, let me first point out that rejecting evidentialism as such would be a high price for adopting James' arguments. After all, evidentialism has emerged as the very form of reasoning in our intellectual culture since the rise of modernity. It came to substitute the pre-modern reliance on tradition and authority and went hand in hand with an emphasis upon autonomy and responsibility (for belief-acquisition). If we do not wish to be pre-modern, we all rely automatically on evidence (last, but not least, James does). We do so without even thinking about it. The search for evidence has become the standard justificatory practice in modernity. Rejecting it would be a very high price indeed for accepting the argument in TWTB.

Fortunately, it does not have to be rejected if this argument is accepted. James does thus not necessarily have to be read as suggesting that all forms of evidentialism should be abandoned. Although he rejects forms of evidentialism based upon maxims as crude as Clifford's, his contentions can be reconciled with more refined forms of evidentialism.

For the purposes of reconciling James' contentions with some form of evidentialism, let us look more closely at his argumentative strategy: in TWTB, he does not attack evidentialism head-on. Rather, he chooses examples from the practical realm in order to show that evidentialist maxims such as Clifford's do not work (remember e.g. the case of the man waiting indefinitely before proposing to a woman because he has not enough evidence that she is an angel). Thus, James targets primarily the application of evidentialist maxims to certain practical cases, not the evidentialist ideal implied in them.

As indicated, this works against Clifford and like-minded evidentialists who connect universal pretensions to their evidentialist maxims. Yet, if we reconstruct evidentialist maxims without those pretensions, we can acknowledge the force of James' critique without having to abandon all forms of evidentialism.

The key to doing so is to distinguish between different realms of application of evidentialist maxims and make the fashion in which they are applied dependent upon that realm. Used as a general principle, i.e. as being applicable without exception, maxims of this sort pertain solely to the theoretical realm: when dealing with knowledge proper, the maxim to refrain from forming beliefs in the face of insufficient evidence is a prudent advice. The reason is that, for all we know, evidence is the best guide to arrive at truth proper.

And if life were an (epistemic) paradise, we could leave it at that. Yet, life isn't. As human beings, we are embedded in a particular life-world which exerts its practical demands on us. Often, we do not have enough evidence nor the time to wait for it to become available. Yet, we still have to decide one way or the other and, being responsible agents, have to form beliefs upon which our decisions can be rationally based. In situations like that, we should not use evidentialist principles in Clifford's heavy-handed fashion, i.e. as universal principles without exception (see above, section 6). Yet, nothing speaks against using them in a more refined fashion.

Let me explain. Evidentialist criteria should be used as 'rules of preference' rather than as principles without exception. The prudent evidentialist will use evidentialist principles whenever possible, yet, not insist on their applicability without exception à la Clifford. She will admit that there are occasions in which evidentialist principles have to be overruled by non-evidentialist ones.

To put my point in current epistemic parlance: evidentialist maxims which suggest that we should never believe anything upon insufficient evidence are valuable when dealing with epistemic justification in the strict sense of the word. That is, regarding knowledge proper, only evidence will do.

Yet, we should distinguish justifications to be applied in the practical realm from those strictly epistemic justifications. The former contain all those justificatory practices which have to be made under 'real-life' constraints, such as time-constraints. I will call the justificatory practices under 'real-life' constraints practical justifications.

When dealing with practical justifications, we should allow for the possibility that prudential, moral or other concerns can overrule evidentialist ones. To be sure, there is no need to throw the requirement to search for evidence overboard lightheartedly in the practical realm. Whenever possible, let's go by the evidence. Yet, let us not make a principle out of it à la Clifford: under 'real-life' constraints, we are often better off overruling the search for evidence with other, non-evidentialist criteria.[19]

This suggestion ties in with what many current evidentialists propose. Take e.g. the influential current defense of evidentialism by Conee and Feldman: they insist that the evidentialism they propose does not make a judgment on the morality of belief—different from what Clifford suggests.[20] They restrict the realm of applicability of evidentialist principles explicitly to the epistemic domain proper: 'the *epistemic* justification of belief is a function of evidence'.[21] They thus allow for the possibility that epistemic justification is overruled by non-epistemic concerns. For example, they allow explicitly for the possibility that 'moral, or prudential, factors favor believing a proposition for which one has little or no evidence'.[22]

If construed in this fashion, evidentialism is not necessarily incompatible with the argument in TWTB. There are thus possibilities to reconcile James' argument with evidentialist concerns. For that purpose, evidentialism has to be construed in a more refined and more moderate fashion than hard-nosed evidentialists, such as Clifford, suggest. The application of the maxim that one should refrain from believing in the face of insufficient evidence should be restricted to the theoretical realm, i.e. when knowledge proper is at stake.[23]

From this realm, the practical realm should be distinguished. Here, the negatively formulated maxim to refrain from believing should not be applied but be substituted by a positively formulated maxim, viz.: 'Look for evidence, whenever possible. However, don't insist on evidence stubbornly but be ready to invoke non-evidentialist criteria, whenever necessary.'

If evidentialism is formulated in this fashion, the person subscribing to the argument of TWTB can embrace it.

8 The Evidentialist Critic of Religion Has No Reason to Claim the Epistemic 'High Grounds'

James' goal in TWTB is to criticize those 'who preach skepticism to us as a duty until sufficient evidence for religion be found' (see above). In other words, he wants to criticize those evidentialists who reject religion on the grounds that there is not enough evidence for it. Let us call this position *'evidentialist atheism'*.[24]

The question to be raised is then how the critique of evidentialism reconstructed above contributes to criticizing 'evidentialist atheism'. This question will be addressed in this and the following section.

An important contribution is that James shows that evidentialist atheists have no reason to claim the epistemic 'high grounds'. The above reconstruction of his argument shows that insisting on evidentialist principles does not imply the right to claim any epistemic privileges. Contrary to what most evidence-based atheists assume, the fact that they rely on nothing but evidence does not mean that they are particularly rational or 'scientific'—or, if so, being rational or being 'scientific' is not particularly meritorious. The above reconstruction has demonstrated that it is imprudent or even morally harmful to use Clifford-like maxims as universal principles. Insisting on such a use signals a certain inflexibility of the mind more so than any positive epistemic values.

Rather than indicating rationality, it indicates an unawareness of the limits of one's methodology. Thus, it signifies the lack of the self-critical attitude which distinguishes the critical 'scientist' or critical thinker from the closed-minded one.

This is apparent in Bertrand Russell's famous answer to the question how he would explain his unbelief when being brought into the presence of God after his death. His answer was: 'I'd say "Not enough evidence God! Not enough evidence!".'[25]

If taken seriously, this answer reveals the lack of the ability to be self-critical which characterizes hard-nosed evidentialists. Every realist—and Russell surely is one—would admit that he had made a mistake when using a methodology which manifestly leads him to misinterpret reality. Although his evidentialist methodology leads him manifestly astray— viz. to deny the existence of God although, following this example, God exists—Russell is not prepared to admit that. Rather, he insists stubbornly on using his evidentialist methodology without exception. Apart from being very imprudent in the face of a God who presumably has the power to determine the fate of the deceased, this indicates a lack of the awareness of the limits of one's methodology. It indicates the lack of the ability to be self-critical that indicates closed-mindedness.

The reconstruction of the TWTB-argument provided above thus helps to unmask this feature of evidentialism: hard-nosed evidentialists are closed-minded thinkers who stubbornly insist on the use of a particular methodology without the willingness or capability to relativize its use. Rather than being particularly rational, they are particularly uncritical of the limits of their favorite methodological ideal.

This is the reason why James mocks the evidentialist critics of religion so harshly in TWTB. The reason is not that he opposes evidentialism on principled grounds. As indicated, his arguments can be reconciled with evidentialism (provided that it is construed in a refined fashion: see above, section 7). The reason why he lashes out that strongly to them is, rather, that he senses a certain degree of self-righteousness in their claims to be 'purely intellectualist' when remaining skeptical. He holds that this self-righteousness is unwarranted because they have no right to claim the epistemic 'high grounds'. They are not as rational as they themselves think. Their motivation is not purely intellectual but, on closer scrutiny, turns out to be shot through with emotions, viz. 'the passionate fear of being mistaken' (see above). Their self-righteousness is thus based upon their closed-mindedness, viz. upon being incapable of self-critically acknowledging the limits of their methodology.

9 The Pay-off of the TWTB-Argument for the Discussion on Atheism

Another upshot of James' argument is that he points to the insufficiency of the basic evidentialist argument against religion: holding that there is not enough evidence for religion is not sufficient for successfully rejecting it. It would be if the maxim would hold that we should always refrain from believing anything upon insufficient evidence. Yet, as the above reconstruction of James' critique of Clifford has demonstrated, this maxim is mistaken. Although we do not have enough evidence to hold that the global warming is 'human-made', it may still be wise to assume it is.[26] Thus, in addition to holding that there is not enough evidence for religion, the evidentialist atheist needs an additional premise ruling out that religions belong into the set of cases in which we have to form beliefs in the absence of sufficient evidence.

James thus succeeds in raising a second hurdle to evidentialist atheism—a hurdle which, in my view, cannot be cleared that easily. That is to say, I think that there are good reasons to assume that religion—at least, some versions of it—belong indeed into the set of cases in which we have to form beliefs upon insufficient evidence.[27]

However, given the complexities of the current discussion on evidentialist atheism, we must be careful not to overemphasize the value of James' point. It is successful in raising doubts about forms of atheism which are based upon methodological scruples à la Clifford. It shows the deficiency of the argument that there is not enough evidence for religion. Yet, it does not contribute to the discussion of forms of evidentialist atheism which attempt to provide *positive* evidence for atheism.

Examples of the latter are the 'New Atheists'.[28] Most of them do not only rely on the negative argument that there is not enough evidence for religion but attempt also to provide positive evidence why religion should be abandoned. They attempt to provide sociobiological evidence, evidence taken from the 'science of religion', and similar sorts of 'scientific' evidence. For example, Dawkins argues that religions are unnecessary because the relevant features of our cultural life can be sufficiently accounted for by evolutionary theory, because they imply wasting valuable resources, lead to morally harmful consequences, etc.[29]

There may be other reasons why this evidence is to be discarded—above all, arguments in the neighborhood of the charge of over-interpreting the scientific findings the 'New Atheists' base their claims on.[30] Yet, from the point of view of my concern in this chapter, viz. to assess the strength of James' arguments in TWTB, it must be concluded that his arguments do not work against this sort of atheism. Atheist arguments to the effect that positive evidence exists why religion should be discarded are not affected by James' critique.

In sum, James' arguments in TWTB are successful in raising doubts about certain forms of evidentialist atheism: they are successful against forms of this atheism which presuppose methodological maxims of Clifford's sort. They show that those evidentialist atheists presuppose more than they admit. They do not only presuppose the general evidentialist maxim to refrain from believing in the face of insufficient evidence plus the assumption that there is not enough evidence for religion. In addition, they assume that religion belongs to the set of those cases in which we can afford to refrain from forming beliefs upon insufficient evidence. That is, they assume that religion does not belong into the set of cases in which the example of the changes of the weather-pattern or that of eating dairy products after Chernobyl belong. They presuppose it without, however, arguing for it. They thus suppress a premise which is necessary to make their argument succeed. Their arguments are thus flawed.

The conceptual pay-off of James' argument in TWTB is to be distinguished from classical *positive* arguments for religion. It is to be distinguished from the pay-off of, say, the physico-teleological argument for the existence of God.[31] Rather, James provides a negative argument to the effect that a prominent critique of religion is flawed.

The point of TWTB is thus not to justify religion but the *possibility of religion*. James wants to create conceptual space for the possibility of pursuing religion. The point of his argument is thus to be appreciated before the background of a predominantly atheist culture: in an intellectual culture in which atheism has become the dominant position, James challenges this dominance. TWTB is thus to be read as a piece of deconstructive work, undermining the then—and still—dominant position atheism has in our Western culture.

Notes

1. W. James (1896) 'The Will to Believe' in W. James (1979) *The Will to Believe and Other Essays in Popular Philosophy* (Cambridge, MA: Harvard University Press), pp. 13–33.
2. See e.g. D.-M. Grube (2008) 'Reconstructing the Dialectics in Karl Barth's "Epistle to the Romans": The Role of Transcendental Arguments in Theological Theorizing', *Bijdragen—International Journal in Philosophy and Theology*, 69(2), pp. 127–46.
3. W. Clifford (2007) 'The Ethics of Belief' in M. Peterson, W. Hasker, B. Reichenbach, and D. Basinger (eds.) *Philosophy of Religion. Selected Readings* (reprinted from W. Clifford (1974) *Lectures and Essays* (New York: Macmillan), p. 109 (see also Henrik Rydenfelt's reconstruction of James' arguments against evidentialism in this volume).
4. See B. Russell (1966) *Philosophical Essays* (London: Allen and Unwin), in particular 'William James' Conception of Truth', pp. 112–30, and 'Pragmatism', pp. 49–111.
5. See J. Hick (1988) *Faith and Knowledge*, 2nd edn (Basingstoke: Macmillan), pp. 35–44; and J. Hick (1990) *Philosophy of Religion*, 4th edn (Englewood Cliffs: Prentice Hall), pp. 59–60.
6. TWTB grew out of an address delivered originally to the Yale and Brown University Clubs. It is written to be presented orally, often paying more attention to the effect of the argument rather than to its systematic analysis.
7. S. Pihlström (1998) *Pragmatism and Philosophical Anthropology: Understanding our Human Life in a Human World* (New York and Bern: Peter Lang), p. 122.
8. James, 'The Will to Believe', p. 13.
9. See M. Gail Hamner (2003) *American Pragmatism* (Oxford: Oxford University Press), pp. 126ff. for how James' emphasis upon the will emerges from his engagement with the German and Scottish psychology of the day.

10. For the further specifications of those decision-situations, see TWTB (see n 1), pp. 14–15.
11. C.f. James, 'The Will to Believe', p. 26.
12. Ibid., p. 30.
13. Ibid.
14. Ibid.
15. Following a clue James provides in one of his letters (see the discussion in J. Hick, *Faith and Knowledge*, p. 40n19), some James researchers call this line of argument 'right to believe' and distinguish it from the 'will to believe' doctrine according to which acting in accordance with a particular belief can help to make that belief true (see G. Kennedy (1958) 'Pragmatism, Pragmaticism, and the Will to Believe: A Reconsideration', *The Journal of Philosophy*, 55, pp. 578–88). I am interested here only in the first doctrine. However, I will not discuss it under the heading 'right to believe' but follow the standard usage and discuss it under the heading 'will to believe'.
16. The examples Clifford provides, e.g. that of the shipowner who fails to inquire thoroughly into the seaworthiness of his ship because he is guided by certain interests (see Clifford, 'The Ethics of Belief', pp. 104–7), are examples of 'wishful thinking'. Clifford's (thinly disguised) point is that he regards the religious person to acquire her beliefs along similar lines.
17. This point may be quite obvious. Yet, I go into it here because in the English-speaking realm, 'belief' is sometimes understood in such a strictly theoretical fashion. Yet, *if* 'belief' is restricted in this sense, its use is very limited.
18. In the context of criticizing James, Russell suggests the following maxim as a 'true precept of veracity, which includes both the pursuit of truth and the avoidance of error': 'We ought to give to every proposition which we consider as nearly as possible that degree of credence which is warranted by the probability it acquires from the evidence known to us' (Russell, 'Pragmatism', p. 86).
19. Let me add that the occasions in which evidentialist criteria will not do are numerous and will probably increase even more: to the extent that our life-world and its technological and comparable advancements and their consequences become more complex, the occasions in which we will have to form beliefs upon insufficient evidence will increase.
20. Clifford has it over *moral* requirements and uses thus strong evaluative language ('it is *wrong*...'; see above).
21. E. Conee and R. Feldman (2004) *Evidentialism* (Oxford: Oxford University Press), p. 2 (emphasis mine).
22. Ibid., p. 2.
23. It should also be acknowledged that achieving knowledge proper is primarily a goal for epistemologists. For 'real life' purposes, however, knowledge proper is often too high an ideal.
24. Evidentialist atheism is to be distinguished from other sorts of atheism, say that of Freud or Feuerbach. The latter base their atheism upon substantive assumptions, mostly of a metaphysical nature (e.g. on the 'essence of human beings'), whereas the evidence-based atheist can stay clear from such presuppositions.
25. From W. Salmon (1978) 'Religion & Science: A New Look at Hume's Dialogues', *Philosophical Studies*, 33, p. 176.

26. To repeat: my point here is not to emphasize that it is indeed wise but to argue that evidentialist maxims of the above sort are mistaken. Whether or not it is indeed wise depends upon a number of further considerations which go beyond the argument of this chapter. Whether or not it is wise belongs to the set of problems of making decisions under uncertainty and implies the considerations which are characteristic for them (e.g. weighing the seriousness of the consequences of deciding for a particular option against the probability of its outcome).
27. On this point, see e.g. D.-M. Grube (2005) 'Justification rather than Truth: Gotthold Ephraim Lessing's Defence of Positive Religion in the Ring-Parable', *Bijdragen—International Journal in Philosophy and Theology*, 4, pp. 357–78, 373–8.
28. I think of the atheist movement which currently receives much attention in popular culture in the USA and England, consisting of writers such as Richard Dawkins, Daniel C. Dennett, Christopher Hitchens, and Sam Harris.
29. R. Dawkins (2006) *The God Delusion* (London and Toronto: Bantam Press).
30. For example, the evolution theory becomes in the hands of Dawkins and the like a sort of *'Welterklärungstheorie'* which pretends to explain all basic features of our world, ranging from the emergence of intelligence and morality to making moral judgments itself (see e.g. Dawkins, *The God Delusion*, pp. 209–34). This pretension, however, hardly follows from the scientific findings they have made.
31. Cf. Henry Jackman's contention that James' argument '... is not intended to convince an atheist that she would be better off believing in God. Rather, it is intended to convince someone already inclined to believe in God that there is nothing wrong with such a belief in spite of its lack of conclusive evidence for it'. H. Jackman (1999) 'Prudential Arguments. Naturalized Epistemology, and the Will to Believe', *Transactions of the Charles Sanders Peirce Society*, 35(1), p. 8.

8
Possibility and Permission? Intellectual Character, Inquiry, and the Ethics of Belief

Guy Axtell

> In detail all the religious beliefs are illusory or absurd. How hold the dignity of the general function upright in this state of things? ... It is a question of *life*, of living in these gifts or not living, etc. There is a chance to do something strong here, but it is extremely difficult.
> —James, *Manuscript and Essay Notes*[1]

David Hollinger points out that

> [C]laims about the continuity between [William] James' 'The Will to Believe' [1896] and *Varieties of Religious Experience* [1902] ... are rarely engaged critically because many of the philosophers who address 'The Will to Believe' are not much interested in *Varieties*, and many of the religious studies scholars for whom *Varieties* is a vital text have relatively little invested in the agendas that drive philosophers' interpretation of 'The Will to Believe'.[2]

This already serious problem is compounded if we are specifically trying to understand and evaluate James' ethics of belief, for as Gregory Pappas rightly notes, 'the difficulty in reconstructing James' position in the ethics of belief stems from the fact that there is no place where he explicitly presents it in a comprehensive and systematic way. Rather, it seems, a significant portion of his extensive writing is relevant to its unraveling.'[3]

These points about James' interpreters and James' own writings warn us of some major roadblocks to delineating a self-consistent and viable Jamesian ethics of belief. In order to overcome these impediments the first half of this chapter investigates claims that have been made about the 'trajectory' of James' philosophy of religion from his early 'subjective method' through his post-1900 writings, including *Varieties* and his several 'faith-ladder' papers. It will attempt to clarify James' transition towards sounder strategies for defending what he called religious 'faith ventures', or 'overbeliefs', which John Stuart Mill earlier called *experiments of living*.[4]

It is obvious enough that James was a conflicted thinker in numerous ways, always struggling with issues of religious diversity, science and faith, intellectualism and fideism, etc. These remain difficult but important issues, and James' own discussions of the 'divided self' of the 'twice-born' character shows his awareness of discordancy in himself as well as others. But I want to allege that there is also hidden unity or deeper internal consistency in James' approach to the ethics of belief, a unity which I believe other commentators have missed for the reasons that Hollinger and Pappas point out to us. To make good on this thesis we will relate James' multiple defenses of the right to believe to later developments in the science/religion literature and in philosophy of science proper, developments that I see James perceptively anticipating, yet providing a less-than clear exposition of. The constructive second part of the chapter will sketch ways to capitalize on this hidden unity in the construction of our virtue theoretic but also neo-Jamesian account of doxastic responsibility. The *Hidden Unity Thesis* (hereafter *HUT*) consists of two claims:

(a) William James develops his philosophical defense of an individual's ethical and intellectual right to their responsibly-held religious faith ventures in terms of what the contemporary religion/science literature refers to as the *Dialogue Model* of the relationship between science and religion, *and*
(b) James' writings support what is common to and what is most advantageous in the *Dialogue Model*; but at the same time his writings reflect the substantial *tensions* between its two distinct versions, due to their diverging fideistic/intellectualistic orientation.

The terminology we have just used is drawn from Ian Barbour's influential taxonomy of views about the relationship between science and religion, which is also employed in much of the best theoretical work in the science/religion literature. It may be possible to surpass Barbour's taxonomy of *Conflict, Independence, Dialogue* and *Integration* Models, but this straightforward and easily-applicable model is developed in Barbour's writings in ways that support our project by explicitly recognizing how divergent motivations can nevertheless lead to adoption of the same model.

Two sub-versions of the *Dialogue Model* as Barbour describes them are:

I. Presuppositions and Limit-Questions (hereafter *LQ*)
II. Conceptual and Methodological Parallels (hereafter *MP*)

'Limit questions' (*LQ*) and 'methodological parallels' (*MP*) are distinct ways of arguing for a potential if not yet actual two-way conversation where there are things to be learned on both sides. Their connections with the ethics of belief are likely to appear vague to readers at first, but will be our direct focus later, after we properly explicate them. James was constantly debating faith ventures (fideism, moderate and radical) and intellectualism (including what contemporary literature refers to as religious and skeptical rationalism or intellectualism). It is significant that those who find *LQ* appealing typically do not find *MP* appealing, and vice versa. I will show that James was arguing for and continuing to develop *both* versions of *Dialogue* concurrently even in his last works, despite the evident tensions between them. That he should do so allows us to straightforwardly explain many surface tensions between things he says both about and in defense of religious 'overbeliefs'.

James, most of whose books of philosophy derive directly from high-profile public lecture series, was well aware of the need to address distinct audiences when speaking on issues of religion and science, reason and faith, etc. This strategic or audience-specific approach is all the more useful when the audiences see little merit in the dialogue one is proposing. Models of faith and of faith's relationship with secular reasoning are plural, and *Dialogue* requires listening to all of these voices. So although it may indeed seem odd that James should want to develop both an *LQ* and a *MP* defense, I argue that there is no logical inconsistency in trying to give both versions, one more fideistic, the other more intellectualistic, its best articulation. It was the pragmatic thing to do. If this is correct *and* we can show textual evidence of our interpretation then we should accept *HUT*, acknowledging a significant degree of previously unrecognized unity to James' account.

On the one hand, both allegations of tensions and certain claims about the 'trajectory' of James' thinking about the ethics of belief can be shown to be as much a matter of one-sidedness in our interpretations, as of James himself. On the other hand it will be argued that our own contentions have implications for how we understand the self-consistency and viability of the Jamesian ethics of belief. Our contention will be that what connects LQ an MP to issues of doxastic responsibility and the ethics of belief is what Gregory Pappas, in 'William James' Virtuous Religious Believer', calls 'the character issue' in James' thought.

1 Motivating the Dialogue Model

Thus far the thesis has been rather 'thin' and formal: we can find substantially greater coherence, strength and contemporary relevance in James' thought if we read him as supporting not a single but rather two distinct versions of *Dialogue* that sometimes run in tension with one another. But let us put a little more meat on these bones in order to clarify exactly what this claim amounts to. Then we can move to identify those threads in James' writings that may plausibly be interpreted as intending to develop philosophical arguments along the lines of LQ or MP. Here is Barbour's introduction to the *Dialogue Model* and its sub-versions:

> *Dialogue* portrays more constructive relationships between science and religion than does either the *Conflict* or the *Independence* view, but it does not offer the degree of conceptual unity claimed by advocates of *Integration*. *Dialogue* may arise from considering the *presuppositions* of the scientific enterprise, or from exploring similarities between the *methods* of science and those of religion, or from analyzing *concepts* in one field that are analogous to those in another. In comparing science and religion, *Dialogue* emphasizes similarities in presuppositions, methods, and concepts, whereas *Independence* emphasizes differences.[5]

An LQ defense needs to be developed as befits the *Dialogue* model, and will be weaker otherwise. But in his early works James refers to 'a certain class of truths' in regard to which 'faith' is appropriate, being underdetermined by or outside the purview of scientific evidence. Hollinger interprets WTB as reflecting an early *Independence* or 'separate spheres' response to the science and religion relationship, and he reads *Varieties* 'as a product of the particular phase in James' career when he was shifting from one strategy to another' in his multi-edged fight against moral evidentialism and aggressive secularizers on the one hand, and religious dogmatism and intolerance on the other. James was showing himself less enamored with his earlier exception-case approach that depended upon trans-empirical concepts and the underdetermination-based argument with respect especially to them. This came in response to critics of his earlier approach, including some of his more scientifically oriented friends like C. S. Peirce. But James wasn't yet confident in this strategy of submitting religious beliefs to the tribunal of reason, and also wasn't quite sure what he wanted to vindicate scientifically under the sign of 'religion'. James' *Pragmatism*[6] places a greater emphasis on holistic desiderata of theory choice *across* disciplines, as against what Hollinger and numerous others view as WTB's 'very unpragmatic' distinction of a class of questions—the exception case:[7]

> *Pragmatism* was the point in James's career at which he consolidated his defense of religious belief so that it could more easily operate within, rather than outside of, scientific inquiry. He downplayed the distinction [between spheres or between decidable and undecidable] that had been central to *The Will to Believe*. In *Pragmatism*, religious beliefs were to be put at risk in conscientious investigation, the better to maximize the chances of their being proven true.[8]

In comparison with WTB which is often criticized from both sides for confusing faith-based commitments and hypotheses, Hollinger views James' last works as more internally-consistent expressions of the pragmatic perspective.[9] The fideistic line is thus the earlier of James' two basic lines of argumentation, and it certainly gets greatly qualified and reworked. But there are no good textual grounds for reading James as giving up or moving 'away from' *LQ* or *MP*. I want to show that James' later writings show that both *LQ*- and *MP*-based defenses of religious overbeliefs are concurrently developed through to the end of his life.

1.1 Presuppositions and Limit Questions

Hollinger's reading of James is largely amenable to our own in that he articulates James' growing concern to develop an *MP* version of the *Dialogue Model*. But his reading of James' uni-directional trajectory cannot explain his continued interest in the more fideistic defense of the faith-ladder and his concurrent development of the *LQ* version. Questions that arise at the horizons, borders, or natural limits of empirical evidence and scientific reasoning are 'limit questions'. The fideistic side of James' thinking stemmed from concern with the personal value of religious commitments and the social benefits of what John Stuart Mill called a marketplace of ideas. This active advocacy was also supported by his empirical and comparative study of religious experience, and by what we'll later develop as his *descriptive* fideism. Two of the abiding philosophical views of James, from very early to very late, were the need for recognition of the imprint of character and personality over our whole cognitive ecology, and the subsequent demand for toleration and respect for what Mill called *experiments of living*:

> [T]here should be different experiments of living; that free scope should be given to varieties of character, short of injury to others; and that the worth of different modes of life should be proved practically, when anyone thinks fit to try them.[10]

One of the earliest and most radical examples of James' fideism is the 'subjective method' of his first published philosophical essays. This was a method of affirming or rejecting metaphysical and spiritual claims on 'subjective' grounds, e.g. our desires and preferences. Perhaps the most radical statement of the subjective method is this:

> If a certain formula for expressing the nature of the world violates my moral demand, I shall feel as free to throw it overboard, or at least to doubt it, as if it disappointed my demand for uniformity of sequence, for example; the one demand being, so far as I can see, quite as subjective and emotional as the other is.

Here, in the early (1884) paper 'The Dilemma of Determinism', James even claims about overbeliefs, religious or over perennial philosophical divides like free will and determinism, that 'facts practically have hardly anything to do' with their justification.[11] James is too willing here, as in 'The Sentiment of Rationality', to treat theoretical claims of various sorts as fairing equally well in regards to empirical adequacy or ability to capture shared facts. This undermines the sense in which they are supposed to be intellectual competitors, or else reduces 'competition' to personal standards. The language of 'hypothesis' also seems ill-fitted with 'formulas for expressing the nature of the world', and what it means to accept or affirm them. No wonder, then, that despite James' reference to the scientific language of 'hypotheses', Hollinger takes the subjective method to manifest an *Independence* model.

The subjective method reflects a pretty radical fideism and seems committed to an *Independence* rather than a *Dialogue* model. This seems to hold through the writing of his *Will to Believe* lecture, where he argues that while Clifford's evidentialist norm of belief should be adhered to for truths of an everyday kind, 'it is utterly worthless, it is absurd indeed, in the search for truth of a different kind'.[12]

This appeal to different kinds of truth appears a doubtful strategy to both Hollinger and Pappas; the individual is not the *only*, although she may be the primary and the 'default' chooser of her risk. Pragmatists today are generally critical of the exception-case strategy and this division in WTB of intellectually undecided and undecidable options, which runs in tension with and tends to obscure his psychological, descriptive claim that preferences are always operative, and don't come into play just when intellectually underdetermined 'options' for belief arise. It appears to be both an inconsistency and a mistake for the pragmatist to leave 'epistemic rationality' entirely to their evidentialist opponents and argue simply that prudential rationality in some cases effects what one ought to believe, all things considered.

There are, to be sure, some interesting interpretations comparing James' subjective method and Kierkegaard's notion of truth as subjectivity. Both clearly hold faith to be the kind of commitment one can subjectively have in the face of a situation recognized as objectively uncertain. By the time he writes the 'Preface' for *The Will to Believe and Other Essays*, James already has critics believing that his right to believe would run cover for religious extremism. There he responds directly to the concern that he is 'preaching reckless faith' and opening the floodgates to wishful thinking. While his 'tests' of overbeliefs are still largely subjective or personal, his response involves an explicitly Darwinian image of robust competition, adaptation, and survival only of the fittest: 'Meanwhile the freest competition of the various faiths with one another, and their openest application to life by their several champions, are the most favorable conditions under which the survival of the fittest can proceed.'[13]

Wernham points out that the term 'faith-ladder' does not occur in James' work before 1906, but that there are multiple instances of it between then and his death in 1910. In 'Faith and the Right to Believe' James defines faith tendencies, for the purposes of his empirical method, as 'extremely active psychological forces, constantly outstripping evidence'.[14] Let's call this James' *descriptive fideism*; it is his claim that the psychological dynamics of religious faith as studied through its 'characters' and 'varieties' integrally involve the will or the passional nature of human agents. This descriptive fideism is best illustrated in what James termed the 'faith-ladder' and its progressive rungs or steps:

1. There is nothing absurd in a certain view of the world being true, nothing self-contradictory;
2. It *might* have been true under certain conditions;
3. It *may* be true, even now;
4. It is *fit* to be true;

5. It *ought* to be true;
6. It *must* be true;
7. It *shall* be true, at any rate true for *me*.

Descriptive fideism should be distinguished from any religious apologetic strategy or philosophical thesis; a skeptic could accept it as well as a theist. Evangelical Protestant religious apologetics often try to 'sink' the fideistic character or their own tradition. But how could James, a forger of the fields of empirical psychology and of East/West comparative philosophy of religion, not acknowledge religious characters habitually living upon the faith-ladder? It was quite evident to James that faith tendencies are value-charged schemes of thought. The faith-ladder is obviously 'no intellectual chain of inferences', but rather reveals 'leaps' from ought-to-be to is, and from might be true to is true. 'These faith tendencies in turn are but expressions of our good-will towards certain forms of result';[15] they constitute a 'slope of good-will on which in the larger questions of life men habitually live'. One can't properly address the question of one's 'right' to believe (or the limits to that right), without accepting something like the faith-ladder's psychological descriptions of how the believer typically reasons.[16]

James' *LQ*-type defense of the right to believe is still present but far more qualified where it appears in the 'Philosophy' and 'Conclusions' sections of *Varieties*. So to return to our main line of argument, it is supportive of *HUT* that at the very end of his life James is still utilizing the 'faith-ladder' and detailed descriptions of the religious character-types studied in *Varieties*, to support his philosophical *LQ*-type defense of the right to indulge in religious overbeliefs. James' philosophical response to psychological fideism is complex, but is plausibly interpreted as a defense of overbeliefs as personal answers to one's own demands for intelligibility and meaning: 'the greeting of our whole nature to a kind of world conceived as well adapted to that nature'. The *LQ* argument as a *philosophic* defense of a faith venture is supported by, but distinct from, *psychological fideism*.

Barbour thinks the Methodological Parallels version of *Dialogue* is the strongest, but he also argues that unless we are biased by scientism we will recognize 'limit situations' of human experience, and questions that science may itself suggest but are not science's or science's alone to answer:

> Advocates of Dialogue hold that science has presuppositions and raises limit-questions that science itself cannot answer. Religious

traditions can suggest possible answers to such questions, these thinkers assert, without violating the integrity of science. The distinction between the disciplines is maintained, but thoughtful dialogue can occur.[17]

Even in *Varieties* James maintains that reason's role is to 'indicate the opening', allowing faith to 'jump in'. Any proponent of *Dialogue* should have an account of what distinguishes them from crass forms of god-of-the-gaps reasoning. But arguably, only scientistic thinking would prevent recognition of meaningful questions and propositions of a philosophical, theological, esthetic, ethical, etc. nature that aren't directly amenable to scientific method. But the *kinds* of beliefs defendable in this way will vary in their epistemic status. To be deemed socially and ethically reasonable, they must not be intolerant, and to be personally valuable they must show their personal fruits.

While *Dialogue* holds that scientists should recognize the limits of science and avoid confusing scientific practices with metaphysical or philosophic interpretations of science, it also holds that religionists should recognize the mood of faith in their own search for 'ultimate explanations' and acknowledge as well that the riskiness of, and disagreement over, such answers that we give ourselves calls for intellectual humility. Religious traditions and personal experiences often 'suggest possible answers', but the proponent of the *LQ* sub-version of *Dialogue* demands that responsible overbeliefs avoid conflating 'God may be the answer' (for me, at any rate)—a value-charged step up the faith-ladder—with 'Science *needs* God as the answer.' A 'God-hypothesis' framed as the latter kind of claim seems to me patently fallacious, but it should not be confused with the Jamesian use of the religious hypothesis, which is geared towards the former idea—to possibilities and permissions.

Speculative personal and communal answers to boundary situations/ limit questions is one (but as we'll see, only one) way of understanding why James so often notes the tenuous evidential status of overbeliefs. Their 'grounds' are only partly found in 'evidence', especially evidence of a kind apt for empirical or naturalistic study. The answer our total experience suggests to us is typically of great personal value, unless it cuts off inquiry. Social psychology shows us that group and individual identity are often associated with risk-taking, including cognitive risk-taking. At any rate our diverse experiments of living, whether we acknowledge it or not, are, in more and less healthy ways, 'congruous with our personal susceptibilities' and passional needs; they are also a reflection of the intellectual strategies a person uses to counter-balance the two ways we constantly risk losing the truth: by believing too much or too little; too brashly or too cautiously; by unwisely issuing an 'unhedged license' or a general 'faith veto'.

James held that overbeliefs are for all of these reasons to be tolerated as normal functions so long as they are not intolerant themselves. 'Ultimate explanations' in terms of answers we give ourselves or that a religious tradition typically supplies are, as overbeliefs to James, largely matters of *possibility and permission*, and not of intellectual necessity. James writes, '[L]et it be distinctly recognized for what it is—the mood of Faith, not Science'.[18] In what I see as the penultimate conclusion of *Varieties*, the defense of the psychological 'indispensability' of religious overbeliefs for many people is crucially limited in James' claim, 'It may be that possibility and permission of this sort are all that the religious consciousness requires to live on ... No fact of human nature is more characteristic than its willingness to live on a chance.'[19]

1.2 Conceptual and Methodological Parallels

HUT describes James as developing not only a moderately fideistic *LQ* version of *Dialogue*, but also a more intellectualistic *MP* version. So let's see how Barbour describes the *MP* version, and then look at the concluding sections of *Varieties* as a place where James gives such an approach its fullest development.

Barbour writes that for proponents of the Conceptual and Methodological Parallels (*MP*) sub-version of the *Dialogue* model, 'science is not as objective nor religion as subjective as had been assumed ... Scientific data are theory-laden, not theory-free. Theoretical assumptions enter the selection, reporting, and interpretation of what are taken to be data ... analogies and models often play a role'.[20] Dialogue, however, does not hide the fact that science is clearly more objective than religion, or that the kinds of evidence religion draws from are sometimes radically different from those in science, that adjustments are often far more ad hoc, and that the possibility of testing is much more limited. Proponents of *Dialogue* are fully aware that 'religion is more than an intellectual system, because its goal is personal transformation and a way of life'.[21]

As we saw Hollinger argue, James' late work extends WTB's earlier but vaguer analogies between naturalistically and religiously-oriented research programs, and shows a greater concern with doxastic responsibility by placing the shared religious hypothesis and a person's doxastic and sub-doxastic ventures 'more at risk in conscientious investigation'. In the Preface to *The Will to Believe and Other Essays*, when trying to respond to critics, especially those who say James confuses faith and hypothesis, James expounds his distinction between commitment to a generic or inter-faith religious hypothesis and particular 'active faith' commitments: 'If religious hypotheses about the universe be in order at all, then the active faiths of individuals in them, freely expressing themselves in life, are the experimental tests by which they are verified, and the only means by which their truth or falsehood can be brought out.'[22]

This distinction gets further development in the final chapters of *Varieties*, where 'overbeliefs' are presented as different, sometime idiosyncratic ways of 'building out' a more generic but also more rationally-defensible religious hypothesis. In *Varieties* James still holds that focusing on intellectual constructions, including theologies and creeds, is an inversion of the natural order of religious life, where feelings and conduct are the primary and constant elements. He asserts again that 'the theories which Religion generates, being thus variable, are secondary'.

There is no contradiction between taking intellectual constructions as secondary to feelings in action, and still finding important roles for philosophy, especially where a mediator and moderator of cultural politics is so obviously need. But it does lead James to substantially qualify his long-standing anti-intellectualism. In writings prior to 1900 James had often been a severe critic of intellectualism. It marks an important qualification in James' thought that in *Varieties* he makes a distinction between two *kinds* of intellectualism: the one kind is still that of his older targets (philosophical and theological), and the other kind the intellectualism that studies religion scientifically and phenomenologically, applying 'constructive or comparative and critical' reason to them. This latter is his so-called 'science of religions'.[23] Hollinger says James wasn't quite sure what he wanted to vindicate scientifically under the sign of science of religions but that as 'criticism and induction', he still marks its off sharply from the 'metaphysics and deduction' of the idealist metaphysicians including Royce, Caird, and Cardinal Newman.[24]

The 'Philosophy' and 'Conclusion' sections of *Varieties* 'were meant to deal with the theoretical dimension of religion'.[25] There James calls for 'pass[ing] beyond the view of merely subjective utility, and mak[ing] inquiry into the intellectual content itself'.[26] Experiences are private, but hypotheses are public. Comparative religious studies invites the formulation of hypotheses that may be realist or anti-realist, supernaturalistic or realist, etc. James (controversially) described a 'science of religions' that sought to formulate hypotheses by 'discriminat[ing] the common and essential form the individual and local elements of religious belief'.[27] What had been the 'religious hypothesis' in WTB is now the 'common nucleus' of an inter-faith research program. It is still confined to what is 'common and generic' but overbeliefs 'build out' this cognitive core in one or another way by associating it with other beliefs, values, and practices.

James sums up what we he calls the 'nucleus' of the religious life (and what Lakatos calls the 'core' of a research program), at the beginning of the 'Conclusions' section (Lecture XX). James allows that 'the faith-state may hold a very minimum of intellectual content', but he is also more careful than in WTB to frame what he takes to be the three claims at the core of religious life as assertions and without resort to metaphor, the better to establish the initial plausibility of the religious believer's realist understanding of their own use of language. He says he has tried to 'reduce religion to its lowest admissible terms, to that minimum, free from individualistic excrescences, which all religions contain as their nucleus, and which it may be hoped that all religious persons may agree'. A few pages later he transitions into speaking about what he calls overbeliefs, or 'buildings-out' of such a hypothesis (or what on Lakatos' understanding of research programs is called the 'belt', with its positive heuristic):

> [R]ound it [the nucleus or hard core] the ruddier additional beliefs in which the different individuals make their venture might be grafted, and flourishing as richly as you please ... And we shall soon be in the varied world of concrete religious constructions once more.[28]

> If we follow any one of them, or if we follow philosophical theory and embrace monistic pantheism on non-mystical grounds, we do so in the exercise of our individual freedom, and build out our religion in the way most congruous with our personal susceptibilities.[29]

While it is these overbeliefs as enablers of a religious life that excite James and that he primarily sought to defend, it is noteworthy that he excuses himself to his audience 'to let me dryly pursue the analytic part of the task'. James has made his amends with the form of 'intellectualism' he endorses through the positive roles he assigns to psychology, philosophy, and a science of religions. Much of what was prescriptive in the subjective method of his early writings is now presented (as it should be) as descriptive psychology of religious character-types; the advocacy of the right to one's overbeliefs is premised pragmatically on their fruits in vitalizing a religious life (as in *LQ*), but also intellectually on this now-clearer development of the philosophical work performed by a core/overbelief distinction within an interfaith religious research program.

Many interpreters have noticed and built upon the anticipations James seems to be making in his *MP* version of *Dialogue*, of developments in post-positivist philosophy of science, and more specifically of Imre Lakatos' MSRP, or 'methodology of scientific research programs'. Some other contemporary philosophies of religion, including John Hick's argument for religious pluralism, are substantially similar to the approach James pioneered in *Varieties* (a point often obscured by Hick's almost vehement rejection of James for the fideistic strategy of WTB). Lakatos' work has been influential across multiple fields through its plausible description of theoretical research programs as composed of a thin but fact-asserting 'core', and a more varied and readily revisable group of auxiliary or 'belt' assumptions that might include axiological and methodological assumptions.

The holistic relationship between theories and their grounds is one important further connection to Lakatos, who describes research programs as needing to be assessed historically rather than synchronically, a 'progressive' or 'degenerative' program distinguishing itself by the manner in which it responds to problems with the phenomena it studies and the explanations it offers.[30] Lakatos insists that the refutability of a scientific research program's 'core' claim or claims must in principle be acknowledged; but within the program in which it is embedded, it is tenaciously protected from refutation by a vast 'protective belt' of auxiliary hypotheses.[31] The belt, being more directly exposed to empirical problems and potential refutation, 'is constantly modified, increased, complicated, while the hard core remains intact'[32]; this clearly matches much of the argument in *Varieties* for the lower epistemic status James assigns to overbeliefs *vis-à-vis* the formal hypothesis or 'common nucleus' of the program.

Our comparisons between James and Lakatos' MSRP are by no means perfect, but neither do we need them to be perfect in order to support *Dialogue*. That there should be such clear connections between James' *MP* version of *Dialogue* in *Varieties* and Lakatos' MSRP is unsurprising, given the holistic character of reasoning that both authors assert in their respective fields. Nor was James unfamiliar with the work of his French contemporary Pierre Duhem, whose philosophy of science

Lakatos and other post-positivists drew upon.[33] While both Duhem and Lakatos wrote directly only about science, the applicability of MSRP to non-scientific theories is clearly supported in a footnote: 'The concepts of "progressive" and "degenerating" problem-shifts, [and] the idea of proliferation of theories can be generalized to any sort of rational discussion and thus serve as tools for a general theory of criticism.'[34]

1.3 Conclusion of Part 1

It is clear that James was working towards making his defense of religious overbelief more intellectually acceptable, and we have seen how shifting away from his earlier *Independence* model to a *Dialogue* model serves this purpose. The development of the *LQ* sub-version of *Dialogue* brings only some qualifications to the fideistic tenor of his thought, but the development of the MP sub-version drove his newly dubbed science of religions, with its crucial distinction between the epistemic merits of the 'nucleus' of a religious hypothesis and the (still 'indispensable' but) easily criticizable overbeliefs. But while our *Hidden Unity Thesis* (*HUT*) allows us to acknowledge such a 'trajectory' in James' thinking, it still runs counter-point to the many interpretations that take James' trajectory to be *uni-directional* (possibly including Hollinger's own claim that James was 'shifting from *one* strategy to another' (emphasis added)). For *HUT* maintains a *bi-directional* trajectory in James' philosophical maturity, where two distinctly different (which is not of course to say unconnected) defenses of religious overbelief are mounted.

For one group of James' interpreters, 'science of religions' sounds far too intellectualist to be 'in character' for James or a realistic possibility. For another group, James' 'faith-ladder' immediately sets off fears of being intellectually irresponsible and irrational. So Richard Rorty, as an example of the first group, in 'Religious Faith, Intellectual Responsibility and Romance' argues both that James erred gravely in pursuing his intellectual defense of overbeliefs in *Varieties*, but also that so long as they remain private beliefs and admirably 'fuzzy' in content, one is perfectly entitled and the kinds of 'irrationality' that might be pointed out in such beliefs are nothing unusual or to get worked up about. So James' should have stayed with his early *Independence Model*, and supported it simply on liberal political principles to the extent that theists and atheists can both respect 'the priority of democracy to philosophy': 'James should have rested content with the argument of *The Will to Believe*, and never pressed the question of "the religious hypothesis".'[35] The other group thinks like Barbour that an *MP* defense is in many cases possible, and where it is, also much to be preferred.

Possibility and Permission 179

John Hick is most unsympathetic in his comments on the argument of WTB, happy to saddle James with the crassest interpretation of a 'pragmatic defense' of religious belief and to dismiss it quickly on this basis. Yet his own philosophy of religion, like *Varieties'* MP strain, is based upon a 'realistically' interpreted core religious 'hypothesis' and a secondary tier of further beliefs recognized a culturally conditioned intellectual constructs. Any major tradition provides a potentially valid way of approaching Godhead so long as it is taken with an appropriate measure of epistemic humility.

Both groups of James' interpreters are right in a way, but Hollinger's thesis seems confirmed: their own preferences for how the relationship between reason and faith should be understood shape what they think James' argument *was*, and what they think James' argument *should have been*. What the one-sided or uni-directional interpretations never admit is that James made both these points explicitly himself. He said let's talk about the ethically and intellectually proper weight of caution and how that may constrain theistic commitments and related risk-taking; let's find out about how criticism proceeds once religion is tied to a 'some characteristic realm of fact'[36] such that science and serious thought-experiments can bear upon it. Let's find out whether neuroscience, etc. may support or be adverse to the claim that the essence of religion is true.[37] The truth of the matter, *HUT* maintains, is that these challenging questions are among those that promote the deeper and more inter-disciplinary study of religion that James want to see, and that a deeper unity in James' philosophy of religion is that he was developing both *LQ* and *MP* arguments concurrently. He was trying to promote dialogue to different audiences or readerships, and so found it appealing to argumentatively support *all* of the ways we have seen associated with *Dialogue*, and despite, but certainly not in a manner oblivious to, the tensions between them.

2   A Neo-Jamesian Ethics of Belief

What are the sources of the normativity we attach to this odd phrase, 'ethics of belief'? What doxastic norms and what account of intellectual responsibility and culpability are most suiting? These are difficult questions. James' ethics of belief is often taken to be primarily negative, in the sense of resisting the rigorously universalizing account of doxastic norms as represented through William Clifford. It is true, of course, that James' writings are overwhelmingly balanced on the side of defending a right to believe rather than articulating proper *limits* of the right. But as Pappas argues in 'William James' Virtuous Religious Believer', 'James does have a more positive position ... an answer to the question of how we ought to lead our doxastic life, i.e., the character issue'.[38]

Proper motivations and good intellectual habits are central to how James intended to handle questions about ethical and doxastic responsibility. Indeed, Pappas shows Dewey and the broader pragmatist tradition to be sympathetic to a character-based approach in the ethics of belief, especially as it brings critical intelligence to bear on these questions. 'What is intriguing is that neither James nor Dewey in their extensive works have provided a comparable pragmatic analysis and defense of those traits of character which are assumed in their conception of a good believer.' To complete this task, Pappas thinks, 'would be to fully provide a pragmatist ethics of belief'.[39]

This part of the chapter will try to push forward the project Pappas describes, by sketching a neo-Jamesian ethics of belief along virtue-theoretic lines. What classical American pragmatism and my character epistemology have primarily in common is the centrality of *inquiry* and of *practices/norms* of communities of inquiry to the evaluation of agents and their beliefs. Inquiry-centered and agent-focused epistemology contrasts with cognitive-state-centered and belief-focused approaches. Myself and others have argued for its advantages over much mainstream epistemological internalism and externalism. As Roger Pouivet aptly notes: 'Virtue epistemologists generally agree that, more than anything, good intellectual habits ground our pretensions to warranted beliefs, and to knowledge. And habits are properties of persons, not of beliefs.'[40] Stephen Napier puts it this way:

> One theoretical fallout of [virtue] responsibilism is that it marks a shift away from analyzing epistemic concepts (e.g. knowledge) in terms of other epistemic concepts (e.g., justification) to analyzing epistemic concepts with reference to kinds of human *activity* ... Much of analytic epistemology focuses on epistemic *concepts*, whereas the responsibilist focus is on epistemic *activity*.[41]

The proposed approach to the ethics of belief through contemporary character (or virtue) epistemology I want to show responds more powerfully to internalist evidentialism, undercutting on sensible epistemic grounds the account of knowledge and justification that for the 'epistemic evidentialist' is supposed to provide rules of epistemic rationality. It also responds more powerfully to moral evidentialism by providing a principled account of how we restrict the proper scope of the 'ethics of belief'.[42] More constructively, I want to show that it supports the possibility of reasonable disagreement (as epistemic evidentialism arguably cannot), and therefore also the Rawlsian conception of reasonable pluralism that goes together with the epistemology of democracy. Its effect is to offer an account of the ethics of belief more permissive than that of self-described evidentialists (moral or epistemological) from William Clifford to Sam Harris and Richard Feldman—yet an account better suited to explain what it means to take responsibility for how one acquires and modifies their beliefs. Invitations to 'indulge in private over-beliefs' are shown to be normal aspects of a person's identity, but the account should also be normative in a sense not just of *allowing*, but of *enabling* self- and peer-criticism and the belief maintenance or revision that ensues from it.[43] Let us simply organize our approach by first tying it further with Pappas' thesis and his supporting research on 'the character issue' as it pertains to James' ethics of belief; we can then extend this study to include what some other contemporary pragmatists and character epistemologists have written that we can use to support our task. We will look especially at Robert Audi's and Susan Haack's work on the ethics of belief. This should put us into position to say how the proposed neo-Jamesian ethics of belief supports but also sets constraints upon *LQ*- and *MP*-based defenses of religious belief.

2.1 Gregory Pappas

The concern for rules in the ethics of belief, Pappas suggests, arises out of thinking that if we do not fix rules, then we allow open doors to credulousness and self-deception. Pappas asserts that for James 'the remedy is not a rule but the cultivation of character in the right direction'.[44] For James, 'the problem for the man is less what act he shall now resolve to do than what being he shall now choose to become'.[45] Pappas thinks that

> to remain faithful to the pragmatist spirit one cannot ground or even describe an ideal or virtues on such things as fixed ends, human nature, or *a priori* ground. Only by first providing the pragmatist analysis of these important terms can one construct an ethics of belief consistent with the pragmatist view.

Yet neither James nor Dewey, he rightly points out, have provided such a detailed pragmatic analysis of 'character-traits manifested by reasonable inquirers'.

Pappas argues more specifically that for James the 'character question' about how we ought to conduct our 'doxastic life' (i.e. that part of our life that has to do with the acquiring, holding, development, and revising of our beliefs)[46] is intimately connected both philosophically and in James' own thinking with a situational approach. 'James' situational approach assumes the importance of virtue in the ethics of belief.'[47]

The tools Pappas interprets James as saying best serve a sound ethics of belief are 'qualities of a good believer such as a willingness to be open to refutation, a generous attitude towards experience, and a willingness to work out a compromise between different demands'.[48] The Jamesian virtuous religious believer 'is a believer that in general is willing to be faithful to experience and faces the risks and responsibilities that this involves'.[49]

Holistic reasoning is something that is very strong in James, and in pragmatist philosophy more generally. We will need to look at various aspects of holism, since it is important to our view that holistic and ampliative (non-deductive) reasoning are central to both *LQ* and *MP* defenses of faith ventures, but apply in somewhat different ways. Pappas' main focus is on the way in which James presents the balancing work performed by holistic *character*. He shows us how James follows Mill in attributing philosophical differences to character types and in wanting to provide useful taxonomies in terms of character types. In *Varieties* James organizes several lectures around thick descriptions of 'divided selves', 'healthy' and 'sick' souled, 'once' and 'twice-born', etc. He writes that 'strong affections need a strong will; strong active powers need a strong intellect; strong intellect need strong sympathies, to keep life steady. If the balance exists, no one faculty can possibly be too strong—we only get the stronger all-around character.'[50] This is what Pappas describes as James' norm of *balanced-holistic* character.

2.2 Robert Audi

Pappas is approaching our topic by way of his reading of James, but tying it to the development of an account of balanced holistic character. Several others who have written as virtue theorists on the ethics of belief bring up other connections that we can relate back to James. Robert Audi holds that 'intellectual character is properly evaluated both on the basis of how well grounded a person's beliefs are and on the basis of what the person does to see to it that they are well grounded'.[51] Doxastic responsibility is primarily a liability to criticism, and criticism may bear upon either largely synchronic or largely diachronic concerns. Of course one needn't suppose in either case that people have direct doxastic control—direct control over beliefs. 'For understanding the ethics of belief, however, it is important to see that indirect control of belief formation and revision, even just indirect *negative* control, is enough to ground *doxastic responsibility.*'[52] We can have some degree of indirect control of belief formation and belief elimination through what Audi calls *evidential conduct*, or what I have elsewhere called *zetetic* activities (motivations, habits, and strategies). 'Intellectual responsibility often requires our seeking evidence, or further evidence.'[53] As Clifford and James agreed, forward-looking doxastic norms are altogether central to the functions we expect an ethics of belief to serve. Contemporary epistemic evidentialism, ironically, allows no epistemic significance to norms other than synchronic fit. Their arguments that the evidentialist norm is simply 'belief's own ethics' are thus easily undercut when one rejects their internalist and deontological account of epistemic value maximization that reduces what matters epistemologically to a wholly synchronic affair.[54]

Pragmatists and character epistemologists do not presuppose a fact/value dichotomy or an always sharp distinction between intellectual and ethical evaluation. Indeed, both groups are likely to understand practical reason as significantly analogous to theoretical reason. But they do see doxastic norms as *diachronic* and not merely synchronic, and therefore recognize *prospective* evidential conduct as an important aspect of intellectual responsibility. Audi helpfully articulates five distinct kinds of standards governing prospective intellectual responsibility: 'They call for seeking evidence, for attempting to achieve a kind of reflective equilibrium, for focusing in a certain way on grounds of our beliefs, for making interpersonal comparisons in grounds and cognitions, and for rectifying certain disproportions in our own cognitive systems.'[55] Audi connects the ethics of belief directly with the epistemology of disagreement in arguing that 'intellectually responsible persons may justifiably avoid responding to disagreement with an apparent epistemic peer without skepticism that undermines their own convictions', but also that 'epistemic virtue embodies a kind of humility as an element in intellectual responsibility and tolerance as an element in moral character'.[56]

2.3 Rose Ann Christian and Susan Haack

Two other pragmatist philosophers besides Pappas whose reconstructions of the ethics of belief support our project are Rose Ann Christian and Susan Haack. As Christian envisions pragmatist ethics of belief, it functions such that James' ideal of an intellectually tolerant society may be furthered, while Clifford's worries about an intellectually vicious or degenerate society may be respected but also assuaged.[57] A key to the first task is to clarify and restrict the proper scope of the 'ethics of belief', and to properly acknowledge the 'impurities' of epistemic agency and the many significant 'overlaps' or 'entanglements' between epistemic and ethical evaluation. This serves to contextualize the issue of intellectual rights and censure, and to make responsible inquiry (a diachronic concern) rather than an internalist conception of propositional epistemic *justification* (conceived as a wholly synchronic concern) the proper locus of praise and blame. It also allows, as evidentialism cannot, for some permissions or *invitations* to believe that are not merely reducible to obligations to either believe, disbelieve, or suspend belief in a target proposition based on fit with present evidence. It insists that not just 'fit' but how the evidence is got (or ill-got) can make a difference to the epistemic standing of a belief. James' model of faith rests on a *permissibility* thesis, under which varied and conflicting faith-commitments may equally have a place in the 'intellectual republic'.[58] 'Possibility and permission' (not 'compulsion' or coercive argument), James believed, are the touchstones of religious overbelief, and 'all that it requires to live on'. A key to the second task is for people to *take* responsibility for their doxastic habits and accept culpability for harmful treatment of others based upon religious beliefs.

Christian describes how she and Susan Haack both understand the complex interrelationships between ethical and intellectual evaluation:

> Whereas Clifford seeks to establish that everyone always has an inalienable, moral responsibility to adhere to the most exacting of epistemic standards, Haack aims to identify the limits of such responsibility. She does this by restricting the domain in which instances of believing may be judged on ethical as well as epistemic grounds: by distinguishing role-specific responsibilities from those that are more generally appropriate; and by identifying circumstances that serve to exonerate individuals from unfortunate epistemic failures.[59]

Character epistemologists generally think that focusing on epistemic *agency* rather than just belief states problematizes any very sharp distinction between epistemic and intellectual evaluation. But Haack also argues that an ethics of belief can have more normative force when it maintains a distinction, and that a shared failure to distinguish doxastic from ethical responsibility on the part of Clifford and James continues to confound progress in the ethics of belief.

Haack however also provides a helpful taxonomy of five models of the relationship between ethical and epistemic evaluation. She argues against the fact/value dichotomy and in favor of the *Overlap Thesis*: 'According to the position she advocates there is, not an invariable correlation, but partial overlap, where positive/negative epistemic appraisal is associated with positive/negative ethical appraisal.'[60] We can now develop some of these authors' ideas further as we turn to how our neo-Jamesian account allied with Haack's Overlap model will understand the *LQ* and *MP* defenses of religious faith ventures.

2.4 LQ: Pragmatic Defense of Moderate Fideism

While taking issue with James on numerous points, I want to sketch an account supportive of Mill's and James' shared theme of the social epistemic benefits of cognitive diversity and the personal value of *experiments of living*. Mill famously argued in *On Liberty*, 'Mankind are greater gainers by suffering each other to live as seem good to themselves than by compelling each to live as seems good to the rest.'[61] Our account should make it easy to connect a defense of permissible faith venture to the epistemology of liberal democracy, as well as to questions about how serious peer disagreement should weigh upon the rational confidence a person can have in different kinds of belief. Yet while being substantially more permissive of faith ventures than pragmatism's evidentialist opponents allow for, our fusion of these two inquiry-focused approaches, pragmatism and character epistemology, should also offer a positive account of what individual and collective intellectual responsibility consists in, and how this relates to the *limits* of responsible faith ventures. We now have a character epistemology that can restrict, as Haack wants, the 'proper scope' of the ethics of belief, but we also want it to provide real normative force—to have 'real teeth', enabling the kinds of criticisms and 'eliminations' James speaks of, which could be for reasons of severe evidential, ethical or psychological inadequacy. The way that I want to suggest is a *stratified* defense, where beliefs with few evidential merits receive a 'pragmatic' defense as ventures tolerated so long as they are tolerant themselves (*LQ* defense), but where greater respect is due to agents whose overbeliefs are defendable as idiosyncronically and/or culturally conditioned 'buildings out' of the 'core' of a (James might say, 'live') interfaith research program (*MP* defense, à la *Varieties*).

To turn to our *LQ* argument first, since faith tendencies as Jamesian descriptive fideism has it 'constantly outstrip evidence', the censure that we should expect an ethics of belief to provide is primarily sociopolitical and ethical. One obvious reason is that *ethically-motivated* curtailment of a right-to-believe, or a social harm argument, is among the only kinds of argument likely to be persuasive where tenets of faith might otherwise be taken as grounds for intolerance against those who aren't adherents of the 'home religion'. Rorty describes this as liberal society's tolerance towards personal beliefs that acknowledge 'the priority of democracy to philosophy'.

What character epistemology adds to this pragmatic and social approach is a (hopefully) sophisticated account of agency and responsibility in inquiry. Character epistemology as we have presented it ties fairly directly into the LQ defense through the support that it provides to the kind of normative account of public reason and associated 'deliberative virtues' that is appropriate in liberal society. It directly supports the Rawlsian 'burdens of reason' (or 'judgment'), which he defined as 'the sources of reasonable disagreement among reasonable persons, [that] are the many hazards involved in the correct (and conscientious) exercise of our powers of reason and judgment in the ordinary course of political life'.[62]

By refocusing the norms of doxastic responsibility that should inform an ethics of belief on diachronic, backwards, and forwards-looking norms and agent-focused assessments I think we can also provide a fuller account of the *limits* of responsible faith ventures. Like James and Rawls, the present account is holistic concerning the grounds that people actually appeal to in grounding those commitments Rawls identifies as 'comprehensive conceptions of the good'. Besides focusing on intellectual habits that make us good at inquiry, pragmatism also locates the type of reasoning most pertinent to comprehension conceptions of the good as holistic, rather than atomistic. Contextualism and holistic evidence are directly pertinent to the epistemic arguments John Rawls calls the 'burdens of judgment' with respect to comprehensive conceptions of the good. Both are directly pertinent to the grounds he offers for *reasonable pluralism*, which is also a central tenet of the contemporary theory of deliberative democracy: '[O]ur total experience, our whole course of life up to now, shapes the way we assess evidence and weigh moral and political values, and our total experiences surely differ'.[63] Philip Clayton further supports our view in arguing that *limit questions* draw attention to a 'crucial interplay between explanation and the broader quest for conceptual coherence—coherence within theories, among theories, and between theories and other nonscientific areas of experience'.[64]

Confirmation holism 'loosens up' the concept of an epistemic peer in a way that reflects the impurities of epistemic agency, and it better accommodates the possibility of reasonable disagreement among evidence-sharing peers, with all its advantages for the epistemology of liberal democracy. It helps us describe 'sources of the difficulties in arriving at agreement in judgment, sources that are compatible with the full reasonableness of those judging'.[65]

James speaks often of risk and responsibility going together; of self-awareness and ownership of the 'riskiness' of faith ventures, whether secular or religious. His early work focuses defense of overbeliefs partly on the cognitive risk of losing the truth by accepting a set of norms that do not allow a realistic and satisfying balance between intellectual courage and caution. His later work on my ('post-9/11') view still inadequately acknowledges the ethical risks of intolerant and other kinds of potentially harmful overbeliefs, but does take significant steps in that direction.

Still, the kind of defense of permissible faith ventures that draws from social epistemology and from Mill's thesis of the social and epistemic benefits of diversity is the right kind to make where beliefs are generally non-culpable, tolerant and personally fruitful, yet lack positive epistemic status (evidential justification; reliable etiology or causal history). James is thoroughly familiar with Mill, and wrote that '[T]he singular moderation which now distinguishes social, political, and religious discussion in England, and contrasts so strongly with the bigotry and dogmatism of sixty years ago, is largely due to J. S. Mill's example.'[66] Holistic reasoning ties directly into the ethics of belief because, according to Rawls, 'if we are reasonable, we should conduct ourselves in view of the plain facts about the burdens of reason'. Citizens need toleration of ambiguity, and higher-level skills for assessing evidence comparatively, contextually and holistically, for 'as reasonable persons, we are fully aware of these burdens, and try to take them into account ... We expect deep differences of opinion, and accept this diversity as the normal state of the public culture of a democratic society.'[67] For Rawls, reasonable pluralism is, indeed, the expected outcome of free expression in a democracy!

Haack's direct use of her *Overlap Thesis* to help restrict conditions for proper ethical censure of religious belief also supports our *LQ* defense. She writes: 'Investigation will be motivated not by theoretical questions as to the rationality of religious believing or the integrity of religious believers, but by concerns about the threat, if not the reality, of recognizable harm.'[68] The implications Haack draws from her ethics of belief further support our *LQ* or Millian/Rawlsian defense of what James called the 'the spirit of inner toleration, which is empiricism's glory' is summed up in three points:

1. First and foremost, in distinguishing epistemic from ethical appraisal, she discourages moral prohibition of others' unjustified opinions.

2. Second, in recognizing that assessments of the grounds for belief vary with cognitive ability and cultural location, she encourages healthy respect for differing epistemic perspectives.
3. Finally, in attending to 'the perspectival character of judgments of justification, and their dependence on background beliefs', she reminds us that our own judgments regarding the beliefs of others are 'thoroughly fallible'.[69] Epistemic appraisal of what others believe is not to be conducted with a heavy hand, therefore, but is to be leavened with a good measure of humility.[70]

So holistic reasoning is central to the defense of reasonable pluralism in Rawls' political theory, and should also be so for us in the *LQ* defense.

Perhaps this Millian/Rawlsian approach is all the defense they need (or can plausibly be given, as Rorty thought). But there are still important epistemological concerns this doesn't address. We can move towards identifying them by shifting from the *LQ*- to *MP*-based arguments in defense of overbeliefs. But in summary of the *LQ* argument, it highlights the 'mood of faith' and the speculative nature of Swinburnean 'ultimate explanations' and other personal answers to limit questions beyond the purview of science. An *LQ* defense of moderate fideism of this sort—what John Bishop refers to as Jamesian 'modest *supra-evidential fideism*'—is far stronger than simple tolerance of beliefs that are tolerant themselves, and so our ethics of belief is already more permissive than evidentialism's to that extent. But what are its limits, short of a right to believe whatever is not self-contradictory, which would surely be a lax standard? Certainly inter and intra-religious diversity have implications for the ethics of belief. When are or aren't we justified all-things-considered in maintaining a standing belief, philosophical, political, or religious, in the face of disagreement? This is a complex and, according to the pragmatists, a contextual issue. While epistemological evidentialism fails on epistemological grounds, *moral* evidentialism remains a perennial concern, even if Clifford overstated the collective demands on individual doxastic responsibility. There are certainly moral concerns to be addressed and pragmatists are themselves prone to take them seriously since they see doxastic norms as constituted on a partly social basis. But the moral evidentialist's arguments simply cannot lead us to anything as rigorous and austere (or as neat and tidy) as Clifford's dictum that 'It is wrong, always, anywhere, and for anyone, to believe anything on insufficient evidence.' Nor can they lead us, to use a contemporary example, to Sam Harris' prescription for secular intolerance of all that smacks of supernatural religious faith.[71]

2.5 MP: Intellectual Defenses of Permissible Faith Ventures

The higher gradation recognized in our *stratified* ethics of belief is belief that is candidate for an *MP* defense. Our *MP* defense of religious overbeliefs engages with *intellectual* demands and with virtue-relevant concerns of reliability and intellectually responsible inquiry. Few people are intellectually satisfied with overbeliefs simply described as 'basic', and for which they can give no non-question-begging account of grounds. Religious faith would not be faith without some kind of fideistic minimum. But most religious people see a complementarity of faith and reason, and desire to meet a properly understood 'Enlightenment challenge' to the reasonableness of belief. Neither a 'subjective method' nor personal answer to desire for ultimate explanation will do; they want to appeal to evidence and argument, even if to defend ideas to which their passions originally drew them. Our *stratified* account holds that these cases lead from *LQ* defenses to ones based more squarely on epistemic values and virtues.

Intellectually virtuous inquirers open their beliefs to criticism and thus to potential further confirmation or revision; they recognize failed experiments when they see them or live them. But they are also entitled to 'build out' a thin 'core' belief of a religious nature into a broader world-view in a manner consistent with their own sensibilities and notions of intelligibility. Lakatos' MSRP with its core/belt distinction helps us model not just 'research programs' and not just religious 'comprehensive conceptions of the good', but also contested philosophical 'isms'. It draws from his study of scientific theory-choice proceeding under conditions of evidential ambiguity, where evidential adequacy does not tell the difference and scientists have recourse to their own *bon sens* or at least to ampliative epistemic virtues or 'cognitive values'. So let us use the Millian expression *experiments of living* to describe what James calls overbeliefs, and *living experiments* to describe the cognitive risk-taking involved in holding to a particular political philosophy, view about human nature, or a naturalistic or supernatural world-view, etc. An ethics of belief will need to address responsibility with respect to both *living experiments* and *experiments of living*. A successful *MP* defense of religious belief offers a way to do this.

When we turn from James' science of religions in light of the later Lakatosian MSRP to matters of how the religious hypothesis and the naturalistic hypothesis might be *evaluated*, the first and most essential point to recognize is the keen *normativity* of this model. James writes: 'By confronting the spontaneous religious constructions with the results of natural science, philosophy can also eliminate doctrines that are now known to be scientifically absurd or incongruous.'[72] When James in *Varieties* discusses overbeliefs in the context of his MP version of *Dialogue*, he indicates that the types of satisfactions by which they are motivated may be different than those for a core religious hypothesis: 'Among the buildings-out of religion which the mind spontaneously indulges in, the aesthetic motive must never be forgotten.' In 'Religious Imagination and Virtue Epistemology' Roger Pouivet makes a closely related point, writing that 'In philosophical or natural theology, imagination has no place. But in everyday religious life, it may be useful and good. The idea is that, with respect to the imagination, we may adapt our epistemic requirements to the kind of intellectual domain we are in.'[73] Later on he writes:

> Unlike classical foundationalism, virtue epistemology is not bound to a negative account of imagination, especially religious imagination. It can even explain how religious imagination can be made *virtuous*. Generally considered, virtue is a disposition to act or to judge appropriately, according to one's situation. It is not an *a priori* rule. Moral virtue is the ability to perceive what must be done; intellectual virtue the ability to perceive what is to be thought. About religious imagination we can similarly say that it is not good or bad in itself but that its quality is to be measured against the standard of what is appropriate for a certain person in a particular epistemic situation. For Aquinas, it is not when we are trying to explain the nature of incorporeal entities that imagination is appropriate, but in practical religious life—for instance in recalling episodes from the lives of Jesus or the saints or for the purposes of devotion. At certain junctures in a religious life it would simply go against common sense to reject all appeal to images and the imagination in order to preserve a rigorist dogma about rationality.[74]

From a rhetorical perspective, James' invoking of his Darwinian image of a survival of the fittest among religious hypotheses and overbeliefs served to bring his account more in line with Mill's stated view in *On Liberty*, the view that 'Complete liberty of contradicting and disproving our opinion is the very condition which justifies us in assuming its truth for the purposes of action.'[75] But according to Marc Moffett this condition of reasonable acceptance when combined with certain assumptions employed by Feldman in his work on an evidentialist epistemology of disagreement is likely to lead to a generalized skepticism about theoretical beliefs. So if (extrinsicalist) evidentialists like Adler cannot square their account of belief with doubt, (intrinsicalist) evidentialists like Conee and Feldman it appears cannot square their account of epistemic obligation with the holistic nature of evidence for propositions such as that God exists, etc. 'According to Feldman, once we acknowledge that there is no rational way of choosing between two or more distinct theories, the only rational course of action is to suspend judgment since we will then recognize our starting point as epistemically arbitrary.'[76] Moffett's argument is that a combination of recognition of underdetermination ('religious ambiguity') and conservativism avoids this worry about the Millian account; it underlines epistemic humility while avoiding (as we'll see) any principled agnosticism that makes recognition of serious peer disagreement on shared evidence directly imply a universal duty of suspending belief.

So James seems to have the combination that Moffett argues independently is the best answer. James' post-1900 works reflect a deep rethinking about how underdetermination problems impact not just upon the reasonable acceptance of personal beliefs, but of shared strategies and theoretical programs of research. The result of this rethinking is indeed something close to Moffett's combination of (1) moderate holism about the relation between theory and evidence, and (2) 'epistemic conservativism', the claim that awareness of underdetermination does not automatically constitute a defeater for one's theoretical belief. This is especially clear when grounding for the belief flows from a broader live research program of which it is seen as an aspect or part. James' holism as a response to his concerns about the underdetermination of theory by evidence, and of the evidential ambiguity of our highest-order framing principles (hard cores) ties directly into the MSRP. James and Duhem were both sorting through an important problem of theory choice, one that would later take on the name of the underdetermination problem and play a role in the downfall of the 'logicist' account of metascience advocated by logical empiricists. As one philosopher of religion put it who has developed the *Dialogue Model* in this way, 'The emergence of holism and its consequences in philosophy of science have drastically changed what it means to supply evidence for a hypothesis.'[77]

Contextualists reject the shared assumptions of the 'Equal Weight' and 'No Defeater' responses to peer disagreement that predominate in evidentialist approaches to the epistemology of disagreement. Contextualists try more constructively to articulate middle paths in the avoidance of such false dichotomies. Let's try to articulate one ourselves; let's call the contextualism that Pappas and others claim is needed a 'dynamic response', in order to contrast it with the equal weight and no-defeater responses. Then,

> the 'dynamic' response holds that disagreement facts such as peerhood sometimes reliably indicate symmetry and sometimes do not;

and this often depends on other epistemically relevant facts about the circumstances of the disagreement. Thus, it turns out that on the dynamic view, some cases of disagreement yielded a defeater, others need not result in a defeater, and ... still others are sufficient to yield a partial defeater.[78]

James' conservativism and moderate confirmation holism answer to epistemological evidentialism and its associated work on the epistemology of disagreement. When James thinks about the 'public duty' demand that moral evidentialists like Clifford make, he counters it with an individual's 'private right' claim. As Pappas writes: 'James thinks it is not the legitimate task of a philosopher to determine the relative weights that should be given to the different demands that are made upon an individual in a situation. Instead it is up to the individual in interaction with the particular situation.'[79] John Dewey, he reminds us, wrote that 'what is most distasteful to James is a skepticism which brings with it nothing that can contribute constructively to investigation'.[80] We have now seen how not just Clifford's moral evidentialism but also contemporary epistemic evidentialism (or at least the 'equal weight view' of Richard Feldman) fits the description of such a skepticism. And we have seen how some contemporary work on epistemology of disagreement like Moffett's provides an effective counter to it by developing the 'Jamesian' combination of confirmation holism and epistemic conservativism.

But while conservativism has its place in the MP defense of religious belief, what is under-recognized even among many of those who have sought to develop methodological parallels between theistic and other sorts of research projects is how well it fosters reflection and reconstruction on the part of religious believers. Moderate fideism, through both limit questions and pursuit of methodological parallels with science, we have now seen, have the potential to constrain religious beliefs, especially when connected with education in critical thinking and development of the deliberative virtues.

Gary Gutting, one of the first to apply MSRP in philosophy of religion, makes this argument very clearly, with respect to the MP defense in particular. Gutting writes:

> The core of religious faith has only a very minimal propositional content, and consists primarily of living with an awareness of and an openness to the power and goodness of a divinity that remains essentially mysterious to us. The greatest cognitive failure of religions throughout history has been their confusion, due to fundamental self-misunderstanding,

of the core and the outer belt of their commitment. The separation of a core of belief from the outer belt of overbelief provides the basis for a rehabilitation of the cognitive claims of religion.[81]

3 Conclusion

Pappas's claim is that 'what James provides is a situational ethics of belief that relies on cultivating our characters in a certain direction'.[82] Like Pappas, I also see fulfilling this as demanding that we go well beyond the usual limited discussion of the *Will to Believe*.[83] MP is a more promising way to both defend and hedge the license to indulge in religious overbeliefs. Those too quick to dismiss interfaith dialogue and pronounce religious research programs as standing refuted, at the very least surrender the moderating potential of enticing religious believers to try to meet the Enlightenment challenge by considering carefully the deliberative virtues and the similarities and differences between scientific reasoning and value-charged religious faith. However, it strikes me that the reason why Gutting's bold claim about the *MP* model's strong normative force has never been realized may be the distinct characteristics of the 'historical religions' predominant in Western societies. When historical claims, such as a virgin birth or a resurrection event, are identified as defining tenets of a faith tradition, the model seems not to apply.

Perhaps then Rorty was right, and intellectual defense along the lines of the *MP* or core/belt model produces a Godhead that only a philosopher could love? Even if so Gutting's point nevertheless is illuminating about what Hollinger calls James' defense of the liberal Protestantism of his day. For however progressive that tradition was, as witnessed again in James' crediting of Mill for the new-found spirit of 'inner tolerance' of his own time, many of the liberal Protestants around him remained doctrinally conflicted, and James himself infatuated with defending 'beliefs' in some rather full-blooded sense. Even in our own time, the rehabilitation Gutting speaks of appears difficult to mainstream liberal Protestantism, and altogether foreign to orthodox Judaism and Islam, as well as to Christian evangelicals of the sort Clayton describes as 'the two Calvinisms', that with a Christian evidentialist apologetic (creation science, etc.) and that with an anti-rationalist 'basic belief' apologetic. Yet the peculiarities of the Middle Eastern religions, and the tendencies towards religious exclusivism and rivalry among these 'sons of Abraham' are not Gutting's, or James', or anyone else's fault. They are the realities that frame the difficult challenge for philosophy in serving the mediating and moderating role in cultural politics that James hoped it could serve.

To conclude then, the modesty of 'possibility and permission' still characterizes the Jamesian ethic of belief in *both* its *LQ* and *MP* defenses of religious faith ventures. Our approach has made it easy to see how James can both 'attack' the epistemic credentials of overbeliefs, as Richard Gale puts it, and yet maintain his judgment that one's overbeliefs are often among the most interesting and valuable things about a person. James' approach is therefore not so self-divided as some interpreters have supposed. Against the evidentialist ethic of belief, our neo-Jamesian account[84] affirms that faith ventures that pass a pragmatic test are *'certainly a lawful and possibly an indispensable thing'*. But it has also provided a more positive account of doxastic responsibility, and shown us how balanced character must be able to hold this permission together with epistemic humility in the face of serious peer disagreement. *'It may be that possibility and permission ... are all that the religious consciousness requires to live on'*.[85]

Notes

1. W. James (1988) *Manuscript Essays and Notes* (Cambridge, MA: Harvard University Press), #4476, p. 311.
2. D. Hollinger (2006) 'Damned for God's Glory: William James and the Scientific Vindication of Protestant Culture' in W. Proudfoot (ed.) *William James and a Science of Religions* (New York: Columbia University Press), p. 11.
3. G. Pappas (1994) 'William James' Virtuous Believer', *Transactions of the Charles S. Peirce Society*, 30(1), p. 77.
4. James dedicated *Pragmatism* to Mill, 'from whom I first learned the pragmatic openness of mind and whom my fancy likes to picture as our leader were he alive today'. W. James (1975 [1907]) *Pragmatism* (Cambridge, MA: Harvard University Press), p. 18.
5. I. Barbour (2000) *When Science Meets Religion: Enemies, Strangers, or Partners?* (San Francisco: HarperSanFrancisco), p. 23.
6. James, *Pragmatism*.
7. See also H. Jackman (1999) 'Prudential Arguments, Naturalized Epistemology, and the Will to Believe', *Transactions of the Charles S. Peirce Society*, 35(1), pp. 1–37.
8. D. Hollinger (1997) 'James, Clifford, and the Scientific Conscience' in R. A. Putnam (ed.) *The Cambridge Companion to William James* (Cambridge: Cambridge University Press), p. 80.
9. A conflation of faith and hypothesis was thus charged against James for his WTB argument, by those who want no truck with dialogue. But what strange bedfellows were these?
10. J. S. Mill (1859) *On Liberty*, chapter 3, URL: http://www.utilitarianism.com/ol/three.html (accessed 11 September, 2012).
11. W. James, 'The Dilemma of Determinism' (1979) in F. Burkhardt, F. Bowers, and I. K. Skrupselis (eds.) *The Will to Believe and Other Essays in Popular*

Philosophy (Cambridge, MA: Harvard University Press), pp. 117–18. This is quite a contrast to *Varieties* and still later works like 'Reason and Faith', which asserts that 'the religious question, we agreed, is a question about facts'. W. James (1927) 'Reason and Faith', *Journal of Philosophy*, 24(8), p. 199.
12. Gregory Fernando Pappas (1996) 'Open-mindedness and Courage: Complementary Virtues of Pragmatism', p. 78, *Transactions of the Charles S. Peirce Society*, 32(2), pp. 316–35. Pappas here quotes W. James (1978) *Essays in Philosophy* (Cambridge, MA: Harvard University Press), p. 332.
13. W. James (1979 [1896]) *The Will to Believe* (Cambridge, MA: Harvard University Press), p. xii.
14. Wernham writes that 'The ladder is not advocacy but description ... If one compares James' will-to-believe doctrine and the ladder, one finds differences between them and similarities too. The will-to-believe doctrine is advocacy.' J. C. S. Wernham (1987) *James's Will-To-Believe Doctrine: A Heretical View* (Montreal: McGill-Queens University Press; 1st edn).
15. W. James (19179 [1910]) 'Faith and the Right to Believe' in *Some Problems of Philosophy* (Cambridge, MA: Harvard University Press), p. 223.
16. On descriptive fideism and philosophical disputes about it, see also L. Pojman (1986) *Religious Belief and the Will* (London: Routledge and Kegan Paul), chapter 9.
17. Barbour, *When Science Meets Religion*, p. 52. Barbour puts this by saying that *Dialogue* resists what Nagle calls 'the illusion of a 'metaphysical wisdom' superior to 'mere science' (p. 363), but can allow the negative claim of the Vatican Observatory Study Group participants that science leaves open questions of 'the *origin* of ... laws and regularities—why they exist at all, or what meaning or significance they might have' (p. 167). This would be a kind of speculative belief that as James puts it, is consistent with known facts and can be put 'in terms to which physical science need not object' (p. 510).
18. W. James (1987) *Essays, Comments, Reviews* (Cambridge, MA: Harvard University Press), p. 115.
19. W. James (2002 [1902]) *The Varieties of Religious Experience* (New York: Dover Publications), p. 526.
20. Barbour, *When Science Meets Religion*, p. 25.
21. Ibid., p. 27.
22. James, *The Will to Believe*, p. xii.
23. It is able to form 'hypotheses', but with the restriction that such operations of the intellect 'presuppose immediate experiences as their subject matter', and so are 'consequent upon religious feeling', the true source of belief, 'not co-ordinate with it, not independent of what it ascertains' (James, *Varieties*, p. 342).
24. That James was so individualist (rather than communitarian) and anti-theological are apparent biases in James' view and, and for Hollinger, part of the evidence of how ensconced he was in the liberal Protestantism of his day.
25. J. E. Smith (1985) 'Introduction' in W. James, *The Varieties of Religious Experience* (Cambridge, MA: Harvard University Press), p. xlii.
26. James, *Varieties*, p. 399.
27. Ibid., p. 252.
28. Ibid., p. 504.
29. Ibid., p. 514.

30. See I. Lakatos (1978) *The Methodology of Scientific Research Programmes* (Cambridge: Cambridge University Press).
31. Lakatos, *The Methodology of Scientific Research Programmes*, p. 4.
32. Ibid., p. 179.
33. The connections between James and Duhem are historical as well as logical, as Isaac Nevo points out. See Isaac Nevo, 'Continuing Empiricist Epistemology: Holistic Aspects of William James's Pragmatism', *The Monist* 75 (1992), pp. 458–76. Given the basic correctness of Duhemian confirmation holism, Lakatos concludes that evaluation in science is comparative and historical: 'But, of course, if falsification depends on the emergence of better theories ... then falsification is *not* simply a relation between a theory and the empirical basis, but a multiple relation between competing theories, the original "empirical basis", and the empirical growth resulting from the competition' (ibid., p. 35).
34. Lakatos, *The Methodology of Scientific Research Programmes*, p. 92n3.
35. Other proponents of this sort of moderate fideism might be J. Welchman (2006) 'William James's "The Will to Believe" and the Ethics of Self-Experimentation', *Transactions of the Charles S. Peirce Society*, 42(2), 229–41; J. Bishop (2007) *Belief by Faith: An Essay in the Epistemology and Ethics of Religious Belief* (Oxford: Oxford University Press); and E. Suckiel (1997) *Heaven's Champion: William James's Philosophy of Religion* (Notre Dame: University of Notre Dame Press).
36. James, *Varieties*, p. 519.
37. Ibid., p. 490.
38. Pappas, 'William James' Virtuous Believer', p. 87.
39. Ibid., p. 101.
40. R. Pouivet (2010) 'Moral and Epistemic Virtues: A Thomistic and Analytical Perspective', *Forum Philosophicum: International Journal for Philosophy*, 15(1), p. 2.
41. S. Napier (2009) *Virtue Epistemology: Motivation and Knowledge* (London: Continuum), p. 144.
42. S. Haack (1997) 'The Ethics of Belief Reconsidered' in L. Hahn (ed.) *The Philosophy of Roderick M. Chisholm* (LaSalle, IL: Open Court), p. 130.
43. James, *The Will to Believe*, p. 8. Compare how close the passage is to late James: 'Faith thus remains as one of the inalienable birthrights of our mind. Of course it must remain a practical, and not a dogmatical attitude. It must go with toleration of other faiths, with the search for the most probable, and with the full consciousness of responsibilities and risks' (James, 'Faith and the Right to Believe', p. 113). On cognitive risk-taking and personal identity, see Jennifer Welchman's "William James's 'The Will to Believe' and the Ethics of Self-Experimentation," *Transactions of the Charles S. Peirce Society* 42.2 (2006), 229–241.
44. Pappas, 'William James' Virtuous Believer', p. 87.
45. Cited in ibid., p. 87.
46. Ibid., p. 77.
47. Ibid., p. 95.
48. Ibid., p. 95.
49. Ibid., p. 95.
50. James, *Varieties*. p. 272.

51. R. Audi (2008) 'The Ethics of Belief: Doxastic Self-Control and Intellectual Virtue', *Synthese*, 161(3), p. 416.
52. Ibid., p. 404.
53. Ibid., p. 406.
54. For an argument undercutting Feldman's epistemological ground of his ethics of belief, see my "From Internalist Evidentialism to Virtue Responsibilism," in T. Dougherty (ed.) *Evidentialism and its Discontents*, Oxford University Press, 2001, Chapter 4. By contrast with internalist evidentialism, externalist epistemology (including character epistemology) respects the epistemic centrality of diachronic evaluations of agents. The causal history of a belief can matter to its epistemic standing (its doxastic justification); this implies that forward-looking norms are epistemically relevant as well, since they will retrospectively *become* part of the causal history of why a belief is revised, maintained, etc.
55. R. Audi (2011) 'The Ethics of Belief and the Morality of Action: Intellectual Responsibility and Rational Disagreement', *Philosophy*, 86, p. 28.
56. Ibid., pp. 28–9.
57. R. A. Christian (2009) 'Restricting the Scope of the Ethics of Belief: Haack's Alternative to Clifford and James', *Journal of the American Academy of Religion*, 77(3), p. 489.
58. J. Bishop (quoting James, *The Will to Believe*, p. 30). From 'Faith' at http://plato.stanford.edu/entries/faith/ (accessed 25 July 2012).
59. Christian, 'Restricting the Scope of the Ethics of Belief', pp. 468–9.
60. Haack, '"The Ethics of Belief" Reconsidered', p. 129.
61. Mill, *On Liberty*, chapter 1, URL: http://www.utilitarianism.com/ol/one.html (accesed 11 September 2012).
62. J. Rawls (1995) *Political Liberalism* (New York: Columbia University Press), p. 249. We err gravely in trying to reduce 'reasonable' people and reasonable 'disagreement' to the elusive evidentialist's notion of synchronic rationality or evidential 'fit'. If the *Overlap Thesis* is correct, and helps us, as Haack has argued, to conceptualize the sources of normativity that an ethics of belief draws upon, then reasonable habits of inquiry, proper intellectual motivation and a more holistic account of the relationship between 'overbeliefs' and their grounds, is clearly called for.
63. Ibid., p. 248.
64. P. Clayton (1989) *Explanation from Physics to Theology: An Essay in Rationality and Religion* (New Haven: Yale University Press), p. 41.
65. Rawls, *Political Liberalism*, p. 248.
66. James, *The Will to Believe*, p. 234. Mill possessed what James sought to support in 'The Will to Believe', 'that spirit of inner tolerance without which all our outer tolerance is soulless, and which is empiricism's glory'. 'We ought ... delicately and profoundly to respect one another's mental freedom [and] ... live and let live, in speculative as well as in practical things'. Ibid., p. 234.
67. 'To hate that fact is to hate human nature, for it is to hate the many not unreasonable expressions of human nature that develop under free institutions' (Rawls, *Political Liberalism*, p. 249).
68. Haack, '"The Ethics of Belief" Reconsidered', p. 120. 'Inquiry into a belief's epistemic standing will be tied to context, and assessment of epistemic

responsibility will be person-relative and on occasion role specific. Given this orientation and the terms of the overlap thesis, the tasks in any particular case will be to determine whether the belief at issue is unjustified from an epistemic point of view; whether the individual embracing unjustified belief is to be deemed responsible for so holding it; and whether the belief at issue has resulted in, or threatens in a fairly direct way to result in, harm. Only when all three conditions are met will an overlap of epistemic and ethical appraisal obtain' (Christian, 'Restricting the Scope of Ethics of Belief', pp. 474–5).
69. Haack, '"The Ethics of Belief" Reconsidered', p. 138.
70. Christian, 'Restricting the Scope of the Ethics of Belief', pp. 488–9, quoting directly from Haack's paper, p. 138.
71. See Philip Kitcher's (2010) insightful and pragmatist-friendly 'Militant Modern Atheism', *Journal of Applied Philosophy*, 28, pp. 1–13, doi: 10.1111/j.1468-5930.2010.00500.x.
72. Lakatos, *The Methodology of Scientific Research Programs*, p. 359.
73. R. Pouivet (2002) 'Religious Imagination and Virtue Epistemology', *Ars Disputandi*, 2, pp. 3–4.
74. Ibid., pp. 8–9.
75. Mill, *On Liberty*, p. 24. John Bishop is only staying true to this Millian approach of an ethic of belief applying to an agent's holding a belief true for the purposes of their practical reasoning.
76. M. Moffett (2007) 'Reasonable Disagreement and Rational Group Inquiry', *Episteme*, 4, p. 360.
77. N. Murphy (1997) *Reconciling Theology and Science: A Radical Reformation Perspective* (Scottsdale, PA: Pandora Press), p. 18. What James calls 'intellectual operations' related to religion (James, *Varieties*, p. 433) include primarily those of our overbeliefs, those of philosophy, and those of a science of religion.
78. M. Thune (2010) 'Religious Belief and the Epistemology of Disagreement', *Philosophy Compass*, 5(8), p. 713.
79. G. Pappas (1994) 'William James' Virtuous Believer', *Transactions of the Charles S. Peirce Society*, 30(1), p. 86.
80. J. Dewey, *The Middle Works, Vol. 12: 1899–1924* (Carbondale, IL: Southern Illinois University Press, 2008), p. 220. See Pappas, 'William James' Virtuous Believer', for comments. James, of course, also contrasts the evidentialist's universal 'veto' of experiments of living with an alternative personal and social ethic highlighting 'the spirit of inner tolerance, which is empiricism's glory', returning us to the Rawlsian concerns treated above.
81. G. Gutting (1982) *Religious Belief and Religious Skepticism* (West Bend, IN: University of Notre Dame Press), pp. 175–6.
82. Pappas, 'William James' Virtuous Believer', p. 78.
83. Ibid., p. 77.
84. Our approach thus might also provide an answer to Richard M. Gale's (2002) worries about James' inconsistency, in 'A Challenge for Interpreters of Varieties', *Streams of William James*, 4, pp. 32–3.
85. James, *Varieties*, p. 339. In developing a 'Christian Possibilism', Clayton and Knapp show how the boundary between evidential justifiability of Christian belief and what is perceived possibility (Jamesian 'liveness') has substantially shifted over the course of history.

Index

absolute conception of the world, 80
absolute idealism, 89
absolute reality, 35
Absolute, the, 84–6, 89, 91, 94
Adler, J., 190
afterlife, 38
agnosticism, 117, 191
al-Ghazālī, 63
analogy thesis, 111–12
analytic philosophy of religion, 4–5
anti-dogmatism, 30–1, 49
anti-foundationalism, 16
anti-intellectualism, 175
anti-naturalism, 64
anti-realism, 78, 86
Aquinas, T., 190
Aristotle, 24
Armstrong, D. M., 80–1
Arnold, M., 28
atheism, 4, 87, 89–90, 159–62, 163n24
Audi, R., 181–3
Axtell, G., 10

Barbour, I., 166–8, 172, 174, 195n17
Barth, K., 145–6
belief-acquisition, 147–8, 156
Bernstein, R., 97, 104n51
block universe, 19, 89
Bradley, F. H., 85, 96
Brunsveld, N., 9
Bucke, R. M., 62
burdens of reason, 186

Caird, J., 175
Calvinism, 193
Cardinal Newman, 175
chance, 3
Chernobyl, 154, 161
Chisholm, R. M., 112–14, 121–3, 123n2, 126n31
Christ, 63
Christian, Rose Ann, 183–4

classical foundationalism, 190
Clayton, Philip, 186
Clifford, W. K., 9, 15–16, 112, 117–23, 125n14, 129–30, 144n1, 145, 147–8, 152–61, 162n3, 163n16, 170, 179, 181, 183–4, 188, 192
Colapietro, V., 105n68
comprehensive conceptions of the good, 186
conceptual relativity, 86
Conee, E., 158, 190
confirmation holism, 186, 192
conflict model, 166
consciousness, 61, 63–5, 72n4, 74n39
conservativism, 191–2
contextualism, 186, 191
conversion experience, 24
correlation thesis, 111, 114–17, 125n13
correspondence theory of truth, 79–81
credulity, 119, 123
cultural politics, 5

Darwin, C., 20
Dawkins, R., 7, 161, 164n29
death, 44, 51, 106n70
deliberative democracy, 186
democracy, 178, 181
descriptive fideism, 169, 171–2
determinism, 87, 170
Dewey, J., 4, 25–8, 30, 34, 48, 50–1, 54n81, 78, 180–1, 192
dhyâna, 63
dialogue model, 166–70, 174, 178, 191
Diamond, C., 92
disbelief, 133
divided self, 166
dogmatism, 31, 35, 44
doubt, 18, 131, 133–4, 140–1, 144
Duhem, P., 177–8, 191, 196n33

199

electromagnetism, 47
empirical realism, 82
empiricism, 16, 187
epistemic appraisal, 111
epistemic conservativism, 191
epistemic evidentialism, 192
epistemic justification, 112, 118, 121–2, 127n34, 157, 158, 184
epistemic practices, 71
epistemic rationality, 171, 180
epistemic virtue, 183
epistemological evidentialism, 188
epistemological internalism, 180
epistemology, 1, 5, 123n2
ethical appraisal, 111
ethical justification, 112, 118, 120–2
ethics of belief, 1, 9, 111, 165, 167, 179–85, 187–8, 193–4
ethics, 37–8, 78, 88–9, 92, 123n2, 142
evidence, 8–9, 15–16, 20, 31, 39, 42, 46–7, 115, 119–21, 127n33, 128–32, 137, 139, 141, 143, 145, 147, 151–5, 158, 161, 169, 173, 186, 189, 190
evidential justification, 187
evidentialism vs. fideism, 6
evidentialism, 4, 84, 145–6, 181, 183–4, 188, 192
evidentialist atheism, 159, 163n24
evil, 27, 50–1, 78, 92–9, 104n51
experience, 25–6, 33–6, 40–1, 44, 48, 56–7, 67–8, 71, 76n72, 81, 90, 182
experimental method, 30, 49
experimentalism, 9, 31, 35
experimentation, 128, 134–5, 140–1
experiments of living, 170, 185, 189
externalism, 180

fact/value dichotomy, 184
faith-ladder, 166, 171–2, 178
fallibilism, 16
Feldman, Richard, 158, 181, 190, 192
fideism, 4, 84, 166–7, 170, 178, 185, 188, 192
finitude, 98
Firth, R., 112
Flanagan, O., 72n4, 74n39
Fontinell, E., 10
free will, 87, 170
freedom, 3, 19, 176
Freud, S., 44

Gale, R., 125n15
genuine option, 15, 148–9, 151, 152
global warming, 154–5
God, 4, 8, 19, 21–2, 26–8, 36, 39, 46, 50, 62–4, 82, 88–90, 130, 138, 159, 162, 173, 189
God's-Eye View, 80, 86–8
Goodman, N., 82, 101n19
Goodman, R. B., 105n55
Grube, D.-M., 10
Gutting, G., 192–3

Haack, S., 9, 181, 183–4, 187–8, 197n62, 198–9n62
habits (of action), 8, 133, 180, 186
Harris, S., 181, 188
Hegel, G. W. F., 19
Hick, J., 146, 177, 179
hidden unity thesis, 166–7, 172, 174, 178–9
holism, 182, 191
Hollinger, D., 165–6, 168, 169–70, 174–5, 178–9, 193, 194n8
Holocaust, 98–9
Hook, S., 105n56
hope, 151–2
humanism, 52n16, 78, 82, 99, 101n16
humanized pragmatism, 52n31
Hume, D., 42, 87

idealism, 8, 18–19, 51, 79, 99
independence model, 166, 170, 178
independence thesis, 111
ineffability, 59, 64, 70
inquiry, 18, 121–2, 165, 180, 186
integration model, 166
intellectual integrity, 123
intellectualism, 67, 148, 166–7, 175–6
internal realism, 86
internalism, 183
internalist evidentialism, 180
irrationality, 152, 178
irrevocability, 98
Islam, 101n29, 193

Jackman, H., 164n31
Jesus, 190
Judaism, 193
justification, 116, 147

Kant, I., 82–3, 88, 103n38
Kierkegaard, S., 171

Lakatos, I., 176–8, 189
Lamberth, D., 10, 21, 72n4
Lewis, C. I., 123
liberal democracy, 185
liberal Protestantism, 193
liberal theology, 145
limit question, 167, 169, 173–4, 179, 185–9
limit situation, 172
loss, 97
Luther, M., 24

Mach, E., 87
Marx, K., 44
materialism, 18–19, 22, 26–7, 51, 87, 89
McDermott, R., 30
melancholy, 93, 95, 97
meliorism, 2, 93, 143
meta-metaphysical pluralism, 87
metaphysical realism, 79, 80, 87
metaphysics, 1, 5, 32, 36, 48, 78, 88–9, 91, 102n37
methodism, 29n31
Mill, J. S., 20, 166, 169–70, 185, 187, 190, 193
miracles, 42
mis-belief, 117
Moffett, M., 190–2
monism, 84–5, 87, 96
monistic idealism, 102n33
Moody, R., 44
moral beliefs, 136, 139
moral evidentialism, 180, 188, 192
moral holiday, 84, 89, 93–5
moral inquiry, 143
moral luck, 94–5, 98
moral scepticism, 141
moral science, 143
moral seriousness, 97
morality, 17, 83, 106n70
Morse, M., 39, 44–5, 47
mortality, 92, 98
Myers, F., 43
mystical experience, 36, 45–6, 48, 58–9, 60–3, 65–6
mystical states, 75n67
mysticism, 19, 39, 63

Napier, S., 180
naturalism, 26
near-death experience, 47
Neiman, S., 97
neopragmatism, 5, 82
neutral monism, 87
New Atheists, 161
Nietzsche, F., 44
nihilism, 38
noetic quality, 59
nominalism, 22, 29n24
normativity, 189
novelty, 3, 19

O'Connell, R., 10
optimism, 64
otherness, 90
otherworldliness, 64
over-belief, 37, 83, 117, 166, 171, 174–8, 181, 187, 189, 193
overlap thesis, 111–12, 117, 125n13, 184, 187, 197n62

panpsychism, 3
pantheism, 64, 102n35, 176
Pappas, G., 165–6, 168, 170, 180–2, 191–2
parapsychology, 43
Pascal, B., 8
Peirce, C. S., 2–4, 9, 16–19, 21–3, 27, 37, 47, 78, 90–1, 98, 126n28, 128, 134–5, 138, 140, 144n19, 144n26, 169
perception, 71
Perry, R. B., 112
phenomenology, 21
Phillips, D. Z., 7
philosophy of language, 5
physico-teleological argument, 162
Pihlström, S., 9–10, 146
Plantiga, A., 7
pluralism, 2, 6, 9, 27, 40, 78, 83–9, 91, 93, 96, 99–100, 101n29, 102n33, 103n39
positivism, 31, 51
postulates of practical reason, 83
Pouivet, R., 180, 190
pragmatic criterion of meaning, 21
pragmatic method, 2–3, 31, 40–1, 44–6, 79, 84–5, 87, 89–91

pragmatic pluralism, 67–8, 71, 78, 84, 86, 89–90, 97
pragmatic principle, 2
pragmatic realism, 78
pragmatism, 2–3, 9, 15–29, 49, 52n16, 78
pragmatist maxim, 8, 98
problem of evil, 96, 102n35
problem of realism, 78
protective belt, 177
Proudfoot, W., 9–10
psychical research, 2, 30
psychological fideism, 172
psychology, 2, 42
pure experience, 3, 86
Putnam, H., 4, 9, 56–7, 59, 68–9, 72n4, 77n82, 80, 86, 100n7, 104n49
Putnam, R. A., 10

radical empiricism, 21, 32, 40, 45, 86–7, 93
rationalism, 35, 51, 58, 88, 167
rationality, 6, 131
Rawls, J., 186–8
real generals, 98
realism vs. antirealism, 6
realism, 1, 9, 51, 78–9, 82–4, 86, 92, 99, 100n2
realistic spirit, 78, 92–3, 95, 99
reasonable pluralism, 181, 186–8
reflective equilibrium, 183
reflexivity, 91
relational identities, 93
relativism, 6, 8, 89, 91
religious exclusivism, 193
religious experience, 5, 9, 25, 30, 36–7, 46, 48–50, 56–77, 90, 93
religious hypothesis, 7, 17, 20, 129, 139, 173, 175–6, 178
religious pluralism, 177
religious realism, 79, 83
religious studies, 2
(scientific) research program, 177, 189
responsibilism, 180
rigid evidentialism, 121, 126n31
Röntgen rays, 149
Rorty, R., 4–5, 178, 186, 188, 193
Royce, J., 26, 85, 96, 105n68, 175
Russell, B., 7, 87, 146, 159, 163n18
Rydenfelt, H., 9

salvation, 105n68
samâdhi, 63
scepticism, 30, 37–8, 139, 143, 150, 153, 159, 190, 192
Schiller, F. C. S., 101n16, 124n6
science of religions, 20, 49, 161, 176, 178
science vs. religion controversy, 4
science vs. religion dialogue, 6, 101n29
science, 17
scientific community, 121
scientific method, 140, 173
Seigfried, C. H., 9
self-deception, 115, 117
sensationalism, 51
sensitive truths, 132–4, 136–7, 139–40, 141
sick soul, 9, 51, 92, 93–8, 105n55, 105n68
Slater, M. R., 10, 79, 80–4, 87–8, 99–100, 100n3, 101n17
Smith, H., 44–5
social epistemology, 187
special-case thesis, 111–14, 123, 125n13
spiritualism, 22, 26–7, 51
St. John of the Cross, 64
St. Teresa, 64
Stephen, F.-J., 120
strenuous mood, 142
subjective method, 166, 170–1, 176, 189
subjectivity, 171
subliminal experience, 44
substance, 87
suffering, 51, 78, 92–3, 95–9
Swinburne, R., 7

theism, 4, 19, 22, 26–7, 87, 89–90
theodicy (problem), 96
Tolstoy, L., 92
tragedy, 93, 97
tragic sense of life, 93, 105n68
transcendental arguments, 81, 83
transcendental idealism, 26, 82, 86–8, 103n41
transcendental philosophy, 88, 92
transcendental pragmatism, 82–3, 87
transcendental subject, 88

transcendentaiism, 51
truth-indicativeness, 122
truth, 4, 17, 33–5, 56–8, 60, 62, 65, 67–9, 72n4, 75n61, 79–82, 122, 130–3, 135, 140–1, 143, 146, 150, 171, 174, 187
truthmaking, 80–1

under-belief, 117
underdetermination, 191
unseen, 39

Vattimo, G., 5
verification, 137
Viale, C., 105n68

vicious intellectualism, 89
virtue epistemology, 190
virtue, 182, 189
Vivekananda, S., 62

Wernham, J. C. S., 195n14
will to believe argument, 1, 7–10, 15–20, 39, 48, 128, 131, 143
will to believe doctrine/strategy, 126n30, 129, 143
willful ignorance, 117
wishful thinking, 151, 171
Wittgenstein, Ludwig, 5, 92, 104n49
worldmaking, 82
Wright, C., 44

Printed and bound in the United States of America